ASSESSMENT OF INDIVIDUALS WITH SEVERE HANDICAPS

ASSESSMENT OF INDIVIDUALS WITH SEVERE HANDICAPS

AN APPLIED BEHAVIOR APPROACH TO LIFE SKILLS ASSESSMENT

by

DIANE M. BROWDER, PH.D.
Associate Professor
Department of Special Education
Lehigh University
Bethlehem, Pennsylvania

·P·A·U·L·H·
BROOKES
PUBLISHING CO.

Baltimore • London

Paul H. Brookes Publishing Co.
Post Office Box 10624
Baltimore, Maryland 21285-0624

Typeset by Brushwood Graphics Studio, Baltimore, Maryland.
Manufactured in the United States of America by
The Maple Press Company, York, Pennsylvania.

Photographs courtesy of Kenneth Friedman.

Library of Congress Cataloging-in-Publication Data
Browder, Diane M.
    Assessment of individuals with severe handicaps.

    Bibliography: p.
    Includes index.
    1. Handicapped children—Education.   2. Educational
evaluation.   3. Handicapped children—Testing.
4. Handicapped children—Life skills guides.   I. Title.
LC4015.B747   1987   371.9   86-32672
    ISBN 0-933716-72-9 (pbk.)

CONTENTS

FOREWORD

Some educational assessment is an evil necessity. Behavior must be measured in order to determine objectively whether our teaching efforts are associated with desired changes in students' behaviors. Of course, there are other educational reasons to observe and measure the behaviors of our students. These reasons include the identification of disabilities and their extent, the selection of needed services, the identification of needed skills, and the determination of students' baseline or entry behaviors (both their skills and their maladaptive behavior).

On the negative side, assessment has a lot going against it. Those who are being assessed generally do not learn much, if anything, during assessment. In fact, students may dislike being assessed, since little reinforcement or assistance is provided, and difficult tasks often are presented in order to determine the student's baseline performance or "ceiling" of failure. Assessment takes time, not only professional time but the student's time. Many assessments using formal tests yield little information directly beneficial to student learning, and are repeated too often. Intelligence, adaptive behavior, and developmental test results are used to determine and periodically reaffirm which program or classroom a student is assigned. Assessments of student skills may be made to benefit teachers, parents, program administrators, or even researchers or lawyers who use results to show growth or a lack of growth. However, only if assessment results are accurate, meaningful, and used by the teacher or program will assessment actually benefit the student. These tasks constitute the purpose of this book: to describe procedures for collecting accurate and meaningful data relevant to the students we teach and procedures for using these data to determine and improve educational programs.

Assessment is a broad term. For the purposes of this discussion, assessment is meant to imply meaningful evaluation procedures used by teaching staff to obtain data pertinent to the instruction of students with severe handicaps. This category of assessment usually excludes standardized, normative tests, with the possible exception of some tests of adaptive behavior given infrequently to establish initial goals or to evaluate programs in a global and approximate fashion. Assessment procedures that, without question, fall into this essential category include:

1. Assessment of students' current and future environments to target needed skills
2. Selected, direct observations of student behavior (communicative, social, movement, and maladaptive acts) and performance of tasks (vocational, domestic, leisure, and community) as necessary to specify skill needs further so that instructional objectives can be written
3. Ongoing, direct observation of student performance of all targeted skills both during intervention *and* under criterion conditions

If it is true that these assessment procedures are essential to the proper instruction of students, then why do so many educators fail to conduct these assessments? It has been reported that few teachers collect and use data in a manner that benefits students. Some teachers simply do not have the skills to collect reliable or pertinent student data or to use those data. Others may not be convinced of the necessity of data-based programs. Teachers who have not been trained to collect or to use student performance data to evaluate progress rely on their subjective opinion of student gains or losses in performance. While the opinions of experienced teachers are valuable, opinion is not a substitute for accurate data. Even teachers who know the mechanics of data collection may find that data-based instruction is quite tedious, that use of these procedures is not required (or admired) by their supervisors, or that they really do not know how to use the data that were so time-consuming to collect and organize.

No one ever said that operating a state-of-the-art program was easy. When students have severe disabilities, the definition of an "appropriate program" is complex; it involves: (a) teaching functional skills identified through ecological inventory, (b) setting up and maintaining a community-based teaching program, (c) promoting interactions with nonhandicapped peers, (d) implementing systematic teaching methods, (e) making data-based decisions, and (f) working with parents to plan for the student's future in an individualized and sensitive manner. Meaningful assessment is one part, but it influences every aspect of teaching.

Meaningful assessment is essential to good programs, a point not argued by many individuals regarded as experts. Yet, ironically, there is much that is not known about assessment. And it is true that valid measurement of human behavior, we currently believe, is only a sampling of something much more complex. In time, more will be known, for example, about how often teachers should collect student performance data, about the ways that different sets of data (those collected under test or training conditions) best contribute to instructional decisions, and about the assessment conditions that yield an accurate picture of student progress but also are practical for use in the school and community.

It is clear that the small computer will revolutionize data collection and analysis. Not only will data collection by teachers become easier, but its management and display will be faster and neater, and will contain less error. Computers already are used to collect and graph data, in addition to applying decision rules to determine whether progress is sufficient or requires an instructional change.

However, there are many practical logistics of using computers in community settings or even away from a tabletop that still need resolution, as do software problems, costs, and attitudes toward computers. Computerized data collection and analysis will make it possible to measure more behavior at a time, to be more reliable, to measure response latency, and generally to obtain much more information than is possible with paper and pencil observation. Ultimately, however, the success of these advancements in assessment procedure must be evaluated by examining their contribution to student learning and to improvements in students' day-to-day quality of life.

Martha E. Snell, Ph.D.
University of Virginia

PREFACE

This text is a resource for professionals who are involved in developing educational programs for individuals with severe handicaps that focus on their life skill needs and that utilize applied behavior analysis. In the 1980s, many new resources emerged for educating individuals with severe handicaps. For nearly 2 decades, professionals have been developing programs for teaching students with severe handicaps in, and for, community settings. As professionals have found methods that have been validated by their students' new independence, they have been inspired to share them through books, articles, and professional meetings. This book on assessment is possible because of this shared knowledge.

Assessment requires synthesis of many areas of knowledge and experience. In conducting initial assessment, a teacher must have some overview of the possibilities from which to select areas for testing and priorities for instruction. This book focuses primarily on this synthesis, and assumes knowledge of existing resources on educating individuals with severe handicaps. Specifically, it is assumed that the reader understands the rationale for teaching students the skills related to community independence that are appropriate to their chronological ages. It is also assumed that the reader has background in applied behavior analysis. To replicate the wealth of knowledge in these areas in this book would not be feasible. However, these two principles—normalization and applied behavior analysis—do guide the focus of this book. For the reader to fully understand the suggestions given, he or she will need to be familiar with planning instruction for students' current and future environments, developing and using task analyses, principles of differential reinforcement, writing operational definitions of behavior, planning instruction for community settings, and general principles of measurement. References for background reading are given throughout the book.

Assuming this background knowledge, this book offers guidelines for "putting it all together" in order to develop longitudinal educational plans and to use data on an ongoing basis for making instructional decisions. Often, teachers trained in special education have had exposure to academic assessment, and may have received training in progress monitoring. By contrast, assessment of life skills is often embedded in methodology courses, or given minimal attention in general assessment courses. When faced with the need to conduct a comprehensive educational assessment for a student with severe handicaps, the teacher may be lost. What topics should such an assessment cover? How does the teacher "test" the student? How can such an assessment provide meaningful information about educational priorities? The teacher may have more ideas on what *not* to do (e.g., not to use developmental scales, not to try to adapt preschool academic assessments), than ideas on what *to do* to plan such an assessment. This book offers an approach for planning and conducting this assessment.

A teacher may also have been trained during preservice to collect data on student progress. However, as the graphs pile up and no one seems concerned with their existence, it becomes easy to neglect this aspect of instruction. This is often due to the contingencies that were introduced in preservice for data collection (i.e., you have to take data to get an "A" or the intern supervisor's praise). The natural contingency for data collection is student progress, but many teachers do not know how to read their graphs and modify instruction to obtain the accelerating slopes that can be so gratifying. This book offers an approach for using graphs to make instructional decisions. The general philosophy is only to collect as much data as is needed for these decisions.

Not everyone in this discipline uses the same approach to these assessment goals. This book offers one defined approach. This approach has been field-tested extensively by teachers who have taken graduate classes at Lehigh University. It is teachers' feedback that led me to develop this approach and document it in a book for others in the field. I also felt that it was important to obtain feedback from colleagues in higher education to determine whether or not this approach met general standards for our discipline. (Please see acknowledgments.)

While the book does assume that teachers have the background stated above, it offers many examples to guide understanding of the assessment procedures defined. I thought that teachers would find it most helpful to have real-life examples of how suggestions have been applied. So, I recruited a group of teachers to develop and submit comprehensive assessment plans and ongoing assessment examples to use throughout the book. These teachers all had received training in the approaches described in this book and use them in their educational programs. There are five people whose case studies provide the book's examples: two children, one adolescent, and two adults. You may want to read Appendix A first to get an overview of these people and the nature of their disabilities. Then, as you read the rest of the book, you will know the handicap "challenges" that the teacher encountered while planning assessment. Although these are five real people, changes have been made in their personal characteristics and assessment plans to protect confidentiality and better illustrate points.

Additionally, the teachers who contributed these case studies reviewed a draft of the book and offered feedback on the practicality of the book in general and on the changes from their original assessment reports. Their encouraging feedback provided some social validation of this book's applicability.

In summary, this book provides one approach to the challenging goal of identifying priorities for instruction and monitoring instructional success. I hope that you will find it useful in your work to enhance the community integration and family living of individuals with severe handicaps.

ACKNOWLEDGMENTS

The creation of this book evolved through several phases with the support and feedback of people who deserve recognition. I am especially grateful to Marti Snell for her review and feedback on the original outline of the book, and for her contribution of the foreword. Her leadership in our field and supportive collegiality have been an inspiration to this, as well as many other, professional projects.

I also wish to acknowledge colleagues in higher education whose chapter reviews provided valuable feedback on the quality of writing and validity of ideas expressed. My thanks go especially to Wayne Sailor whose review of early drafts of Chapters 3 and 4 helped me target the focus and develop the practical style of the entire book. I also thank Fredda Brown, Kathleen Liberty, Adelle Renzaglia, Paul Wehman, Sherril Moon, Joe Reichle, and Steve Luce for their chapter reviews. I especially thank Kathleen Liberty for inspiring my use of data-based instructional decisions, and for providing feedback on my adaptation of her work as presented in Chapter 4.

Two colleagues at Lehigh provided reviews of the entire book: Meredith Heller, Supervisor of the Life Skills Program at Centennial School, and MaryAnn Demchak, Research Scientist and Managing Director of Lehigh Continuing Education for Adults with Severe Disabilities. Their thoughtful feedback on the professional quality and practicality of the book was especially helpful. They also knew the individuals whose case studies were developed into examples for the book, and were able to provide feedback on the appropriateness of the information used. I also thank MaryAnn Demchak for her contribution to the book in Chapter 9, and for her ongoing informal feedback on many aspects of the book.

The teachers who contributed case studies to the book deserve particular recognition: Tom Albright, Natalie Sadofsky, Debra Kopp, JoAnn Prekel, and Janet McGowan. I thank each of them for their willingness to share their work and to provide their reviews of the entire book. Through their reviews, I received feedback on the way that the people in the case studies were portrayed, and on the general practicality of the book. Other students and teachers also deserve recognition for their contributions. I thank Diane King and Jeffry Friedman for their collaboration on Chapters 2 and 5. I also thank students from my courses on assessment whose feedback helped shape this book. I would especially like to acknowledge Doris Martin, whose work with Tommy inspired many ideas for Dennis, Nancy Montanari, who worked closely with Natalie Sadofsky, and all of those who were the first to use a draft of this book in SpEd 424—Assessment of Individuals with Severe Handicaps, in the spring of 1986, and who inspired revisions for the final draft. I also thank Brian Cooke and Sharon Yaszewski for their editorial assistance in the preparation of the manuscript submitted to Paul H. Brookes Publishing Co., and Kenneth Friedman for providing photographic services.

Finally, I wish to acknowledge the individuals whose pictures are included on the cover and throughout this text, and those whose case studies are used as examples. While they and their guardians or advocates prefer that they remain anonymous, I do wish to acknowledge their contribution to this book.

To my niece,
Marjorie Elizabeth Browder

ASSESSMENT OF INDIVIDUALS WITH SEVERE HANDICAPS

CHAPTER 1

OVERVIEW OF EDUCATIONAL ASSESSMENT FOR INDIVIDUALS WITH SEVERE HANDICAPS

The 1980s have provided expanding opportunities for individuals with severe handicaps. Educators have encouraged and responded to these opportunities by teaching students the skills that they need for further independence. Many programs for students with severe handicaps now include instruction that moves beyond classroom walls. Teachers are providing instructional opportunities in school cafeterias, shopping malls, restaurants, factories, and even on streets and buses. This encouraging trend in instruction in and for community settings has created new challenges for educational assessment.

Both skill selection and ongoing evaluation are complicated by the variety of experiences available in the community. Many teachers have begun to respond to this challenge by adapting assessment procedures formerly utilized in classroom settings. But new questions arise in making this adaptation. For example, how can assessment be conducted given the logistics of riding a bus or making a purchase in public? How can skills be selected that have the most functional use for a student at a given point in his or her life? Can assessment be conducted to plan for longitudinal development of skills such as grocery shopping?

These assessment questions suggest the need to take a new look at the tools and procedures used in educational assessment. They call for an expansion of current methodology to accommodate the new skills and environments that are targeted in community-referenced instruction. This book provides this "new look" by synthesizing and summarizing some of the approaches being used in community-referenced instruction in programs for students with severe handicaps. Thus, the procedures themselves may be familiar, but a new perspective evolves when guidelines for putting them all together in well-planned, comprehensive educational assessment are followed.

Before focusing on the specific procedures in the chapters to follow, this chapter examines the general goals of educational assessment for people with severe handicaps. These goals may be clarified by considering the following questions:

1. What is the purpose of educational assessment?
2. What type of educational assessment will best identify individual student needs?
3. What approaches have been taken to this type of assessment for individuals with severe handicaps?
4. What criteria should be used to evaluate whether specific assessment procedures are appropriate and adequate?
5. How can students' human rights be protected during the assessment process?

DEFINING THE PURPOSE OF ASSESSMENT

Assessment, in general, is the process of gathering information to make a decision. All educators assess students to make decisions about their performance, but this is only one type of decision that teachers must make. Special education teachers in particular must gather information on students' specific learning needs when deciding what to teach. These teachers also need information so they can decide when to change instructional strategies to improve student success. If the view is taken that all students can learn, and that learning is facilitated by good teaching, then teachers will be especially concerned when students are not acquiring target skills.

Educational assessment is usually the responsibility of a teacher or a specialist with a background in teaching. The determination of what students need to learn is often made through an interdisciplinary effort. The information that teachers gather is shared with other professionals such as the school psychologist, physical therapist, and speech-language pathologist who also contribute recommendations for the type and content of educational services. This book focuses on teachers' contributions to this interdisciplinary effort. While most of the book concentrates on teachers' efforts per se, Chapter 5 suggests ways that parents can collaborate with teachers in this process, and Chapter 9 provides guidelines for supervisors to encourage each teacher's success. Chapter 7 also addresses the importance of teachers coordinating assessment with therapists and other specialists.

To clarify the teacher's role in this interdisciplinary assessment, it is important to consider the purpose of the assessment to be conducted, the philosophical ideals for students with severe handicaps, and the teacher's general role in educational settings.

Purposes of Educational Assessment

Educational assessment is conducted to identify students in need of special services, to determine students' eligibility for services, to identify specific skills to be taught, to evaluate students' progress, and to evaluate a program. In addition, some educators follow a medical model by conducting assessment to "diagnose" the cause of learning problems. This latter purpose is discussed first because it sometimes conflicts with other assessment goals.

Identification of Cause   In the medical model, problematic symptoms are attributed to some underlying cause. When educators attempt to identify the cognitive deficits that cause learning problems, they sometimes overlook the specific, functional skills that a student needs to succeed in school and society. The assessment of cognitive deficits that cause learning problems was popular in special education in the 1960s and 1970s. The following examples describe this approach.

The first example is the "process" approach to learning disabilities. In the late 1960s and early 1970s, educators sought to identify the cognitive deficits that impeded academic progress. Assessment was designed to identify these processing deficits that caused delays (e.g., the *Illinois Test of Psycholinguistic Abilities* [ITPA] by Kirk, McCarthy, & Kirk, 1968). The premise of this assessment and related instruction was that academic progress could not be expected until these processing deficits were remediated. Thus, direct academic instruction was sometimes neglected. By the mid-1970s, critics questioned the validity of tests like the ITPA and promoted a return to direct academic assessment and instruction (Hammill & Larsen, 1974). The critics noted that students need direct instruction in academic skills to learn them. Generalization from "process training" to improved reading skills, for example, could not be assumed.

A parallel example can be found in the developmental approach to education for students with severe handicaps. Educational programs for students with severe handicaps experienced tremendous growth in the 1970s. As educators developed curricula for students with severe handicaps, sometimes for the first time, they borrowed from existing literature. One set of literature from which they adapted was early childhood and infant development. The premise in making this adaptation was that students with severe handicaps could be educated according to their "mental age" by following the sequence of normal child development. Learning problems could be attributed to lags in cognitive development. Assessment and instruction were developed, in accordance with this premise, by adapting developmental theories such as Piaget's theory of infant cognitive development. For example, Dunst (1980) adapted Uzgiris and Hunt's (1978) assessment for infants to assessment for students with severe handicaps of all ages. However, evaluation of the applicability of the Piagetian stages of sensorimotor development to older individuals with severe handicaps provided mixed results (Kahn, 1978).

While some educators in the 1960s and 1970s were trying to improve the adaptation of developmental psychology to curriculum planning for students with severe handicaps, other educators began to make a philosophical appeal for teaching chronologically age–appropriate life skills to students with severe handicaps using real, age-appropriate activities and environments (Brown, Nietupski, & Hamre-Nietupski, 1976). Thus, historical efforts to identify and remediate the cause of learning problems (i.e., cognitive deficits) detracted from the primary goal of identifying academic and life skills that students needed most.

What, then, should a teacher conclude regarding assessment to identify the cause of learning problems? One safe conclusion is that students can be taught the life skills that they need to learn without identifying the exact nature of their cognitive deficits. However, other sources of learning problems may be an important assessment question for an interdisciplinary team. For example, teachers and other professionals may identify variables that "cause" or impede learning by focusing on observable events such as consequences of problem behaviors.

Screening and Selection of Service A second purpose of educational assessment is to determine students' eligibility for specific services. First, students may be screened to determine if assessment for eligibility should be conducted. Then, assessment is conducted to see if students' characteristics match the eligibility criteria for a given service. Students with severe handicaps often have skill deficiencies that make the need for some special service obvious. Assessment is conducted to match students to the appropriate services. Screening, which is often a broad assessment of skills to see if students meet age expectations, can also support referrals for related services such as speech, physical, or occupational therapy. The teacher's role in screening and eligibility decisions is to collect information on students' skill needs. If students' primary needs are life skills rather than academics, then a program with a life skills approach is most appropriate. Often, a vocational training program or group home may have specific entry skill requirements. Such requirements, when appropriate to the demands of the setting, clarify the teacher's initial assessments. That is, the teacher will determine whether or not students meet these entry requirements by assessing each criterion.

In Chapter 2, many suggestions are given for initial assessment. This initial assessment provides information to help with placement by identifying educational needs. When initial educational assessment must be abbreviated due to staff and time constraints, teachers can still take the same approach of using ecological inventories, skill checklists, observations, and so on, but limit their use to the time available. This information is contributed to that collected by a multidisciplinary team, parents, and students for use in deciding which services are appropriate.

Psychologists may turn to teachers for assistance in providing the psychological component of the multidisciplinary evaluation for students with severe and multiple handicaps. Because the psychologist's evaluation often has considerable influence in determining student placement, it is worthwhile to consider in detail the problems that complicate this psychological evaluation and potential solutions. A survey of psychologists conducted by Irons, Irons, and Maddux (1984) revealed that most (83.4%) wanted more training in assessing students with severe handicaps. Respondents rated their competence especially low in assessing students with physical and medical handicaps. Several problems complicate psychological assessment, although, ironically, mental trait assessment often carries the most weight in determining educational placement. Simeonsson, Huntington, and Parse (1980) describe four problems in assessing students with severe handicaps: (a) definitional issues, (b) limitations of the child, (c) limitations of the instruments, and (d) limitations of the examiner. Each of these problems complicates traditional psychological assessment.

Definitional Issues To place students in services, state definitions of a handicap often must be met. Geiger and Justen (1983) reviewed state definitions for public school services and found that 35 states had definitions pertaining to students with severe handicaps. Of these 35 states, 19 had *categorical* definitions, while the remainder had *generic* definitions. Categorical definitions made explicit reference to a category such as autism or severe mental retardation. Generic definitions (e.g., for "severe handicaps") referred to commonalities of educational need for a diverse population. When *educational need* is the basis of the definition, psychologists and educators have the pleasant task of identifying educational need, rather than gathering evidence to distinguish between labels. Some states complicate the psychologist's task by defining IQ ranges or psychiatric labels that must be obtained to qualify for services. The problems created by such categorical definitions evolve from the difficulty of testing students with severe handicaps. Another problem with categorical definitions is that they often only focus on students with severe and profound mental retardation. States that only provide life skills services for students classified as severely or profoundly retarded often leave out children with very diverse characteristics, but with similar curriculum needs (e.g., severe multiple handicaps, autism).

Limitations of the Child The second problem facing the psychologist is testing a student who is different from most special students. Students with severe handicaps may be blind and/or deaf, physically handicapped, or prone to frequent seizures. Students may use an alternative form of communication, such as signing or a communication board, and may have limited social skills.

Sometimes, interfering behaviors occur at a high rate (especially with a stranger in a novel setting with unfamiliar tasks). When confronted with the challenge of giving a traditional IQ test to such students, psychologists may conclude that a student is "untestable." More fairly, the test is not suitable to such students because of physical or behavioral differences. In fact, making evaluations based on tests that students cannot complete because of such differences is discriminatory (Duncan, Sbardellati, Maheady, & Sainato, 1981).

Limitations of the Instruments   The testing situation is also complicated by the limitations of the tests. Many IQ tests have too few items to establish a basal level for students with limited skills. Although infant developmental assessments are sometimes used, these tests and checklists fail to provide opportunities for students to demonstrate skills appropriate to their chronological ages, and thus, present a stigmatizing mental age assessment. However, psychologists often face the pressure of needing a normative score to justify the extra expenditure of more intensive special services.

Limitations of the Examiner   In addition to these problems, psychologists face their own personal limitations. Many training programs for school psychologists do not provide specialized training in assessing students with severe handicaps. Psychologists may provide little to no testing rather than risk inappropriate management of the student (e.g., positioning and handling the student with physical handicaps, or preventing behavioral outbursts).

What is the solution to the problems encountered by psychologists when they make contributions to decisions regarding services? By working together, teachers and psychologists can make this one of the most meaningful components of the multidisciplinary evaluation. Psychologists have begun using curriculum-based assessments to make placement decisions and help teachers solve instructional problems (Shapiro & Lentz, 1986). That is, psychologists assess students to determine their placement in school curriculum by using criterion-referenced testing matched to the curriculum. This practice needs only to be extended to the curriculum appropriate for students with severe handicaps. Some of the newer adaptive behavior scales include many items that are relevant to life skills curriculum planning. Adaptive behavior scales are assessment instruments used to evaluate a student's overall skills in meeting the demands of daily living. Because adaptive behavior scales focus on daily living, they provide more relevant information than IQ tests for educational planning. Some of these scales also provide normative scores that may help support recommended placements. (See the review of adaptive behavior scales in Chapter 2.) These adaptive behavior scales are usually completed by interviewing the teacher or parent. Some of the adaptive behavior scales provide data on the correlation between such reports and direct observations derived from field testing (e.g., Cone, 1984). If time permits, psychologists may make some classroom, workshop, or home observations to verify some of the verbal reports for the students evaluated. Guidelines for such observations are given in the next chapter. These observations may be preferable to a test given by the psychologist in a novel environment because they provide evidence of how students typically behave in familiar surroundings and minimize the need for psychologists to learn to manage complicated medical and behavioral problems for each student assessed.

Skill Selection and Evaluation of Progress   The most critical decisions that teachers must make concern which skills to teach and when to change instruction to improve student success. Skill selection requires not only assessing students, but also assessing the environment to determine what skills are most critical for the student to function in these environments. Since many skills may be identified, teachers need a system to prioritize skills for instruction. Chapter 2 provides a detailed look at this skill selection and prioritization process. Teachers also need to decide if instruction is effective, and if not, how to change instruction. In Chapters 3 and 4, guidelines are given for this ongoing assessment of progress and evaluation of progress to make instructional decisions.

Evaluation of Program Quality   The final purpose of assessment to be considered here is evaluation of program quality. Often, decisions regarding students' progress, or even educability (i.e., ability to learn), are made without giving consideration to the quantity and quality of services that students receive. Older people with severe handicaps may have spent years in institutions that provided them limited education or other opportunities to learn about their communities. Such individuals may need time to "learn to learn" in new community-based programs. Slow progress can be due to poor teaching, lack of time invested in teaching (e.g., due to numerous daily interruptions), or poor management of interfering behaviors. Thus, evaluation of service quality is related to assessment of student progress. However, this evaluation is often conducted by a supervisor or program consultant. Guidelines for program evaluation are provided in the last chapter of this book.

Planning Assessment Appropriate to Purpose

Teachers will need to plan assessment that will provide the appropriate information for the educational decision to be made. For eligibility considerations, teachers often must compare students' overall skill performance to their chronological age expectations. For skill selection, more information is needed on students' overall skill performance. Information is also needed on environmental demands. If teachers want to evaluate progress so they can make instructional decisions for improving student success, assessment must be matched to specific objectives. Teachers also need guidelines to decide whether students are progressing toward the goal of mastery of the objective. Supervisors who decide whether teachers use procedures that enhance student progress also need guidelines for the assessment and evaluation of teaching.

Given these varied purposes, the next question to consider is which type of assessment will be appropriate to these purposes.

SELECTING AN ASSESSMENT APPROACH

The previous discussion of the purposes of educational assessment proposed that these purposes are best met when assessment focuses on the student's highest priority needs and when these needs are measured per se rather than trying to conduct indirect assessment of underlying cause. The principles that may best guide this assessment are those of *applied behavior analysis* and *normalization*. Applied behavior analysis focuses on measurable, observable responses of the individual. Target responses are encouraged or discouraged through arrangement of stimuli in the learner's environment that occur immediately before the response (antecedents) and after the response (consequences). The methodology of applied behavior analysis has been described in detail in several resources (e.g., Bijou & Baer, 1961; Repp, 1983; Sulzer-Azaroff & Mayer, 1977). Normalization focuses on making opportunities available to nonhandicapped people also available to people with handicaps. In his book on normalization, Wolfensberger (1972) describes the attitudes of professionals who work with people with handicaps and of society in general that blockade this equality of opportunity. The theories of applied behavior analysis and normalization have directly and indirectly influenced recent writing and practice related to the education of people with severe handicaps (e.g., Falvey, 1986; Gaylord-Ross & Holvoet, 1985; Sailor & Guess, 1983; Snell, 1987; Wehman, Renzaglia, & Bates, 1985; Wilcox & Bellamy, 1982). (Readers are encouraged to study these other resources as a background to this book.) In order to understand how the field became aware of and began to accept these approaches and new trends that are emerging, it is helpful to review briefly the history of assessment to individualize instruction for special people. This history also provides some information on the origin of practices still in existence though now viewed by many as inappropriate for meeting individual needs.

History of Individualization in Education

Assessment has relevance when the educational system is designed to be responsive to individual learners. To be responsive, tools are needed to determine the entry level and progress of each learner. Sometimes, instruction is designed to meet the needs of the majority of the learners in a given classroom with some accommodation made for "slow" or "fast" groups. The first evidence of educational systems responding to the individual learner can be noted in this practice of individualization by homogeneous grouping. White (1981) describes how the educational system was modified for such groupings:

> If a child was blind, he needed "mobility" training. If a child were deaf, certain adaptations were required in the communication curricula. If a child were crip-

pled, various occupational therapy or physical therapy approaches would be advised. If a child were mentally retarded, the curriculum would be watered down, a ceiling on expected development would be imposed, and basic skills would be drilled in endless repetition. Each approach was, in retrospect, still likely to be somewhat inflexible, but at least it represented some attempt to meet the special needs of the pupil. It was a start. (p. 1)

The practice of making educational accommodations based on stereotypes and homogeneous groupings is, unfortunately, still apparent in some programs. For example, some school systems place all students with severe handicaps in separate schools or in one wing of a school. All students may receive instruction in the use of infantile and preschool materials regardless of their chronological age because of the stereotype that their "mental age" requires such instruction. In extreme cases, such programming might include little to no assessment.

The diagnostic/prescriptive approach emerged in the 1960s and represented a further refinement of assessment to identify and meet the needs of individual students. In this approach, teachers or "diagnosticians" assessed individuals using a battery of tests. For students with academic skills, these tests often included diagnostic assessments of reading, math, and language skills. This information was used by teachers to design the individualized plan. Problems of inflexibility and overlooking individual student needs also emerged with this model. Teachers often made this assessment a comprehensive, but episodic event. That is, once the individual plan was written, instruction continued without systematic review of learner progress and adaptations based on this review. If such a review were scheduled, it often occurred only a few times per year, allowing students to waste months in ineffective instructional lessons. Sometimes, assessment was not matched to objectives. For example, an adaptive behavior scale might be used to assess progress, but the scale items would be too global to correspond directly to the student's specific objectives. Another problem that emerged was the attempt to diagnose the cause of the learning problem by observing cognitive deficits as described earlier in this chapter. Diagnostic/prescriptive teaching at its best used *criterion-referenced testing* that was matched directly to learner objectives. Criterion-referenced testing compares student performance to preset criteria (e.g., the criteria for mastery of an instructional objective). The items used on such tests are the same or similar to those used in instruction. Even when criterion-referenced testing has been used, the episodic schedule of assessment in diagnostic/prescriptive teaching often makes it an inefficient approach to making decisions about student progress.

The influence of the diagnostic/prescriptive era is still strong in special education, with current emphasis given to academic remediation. This influence has had positive and negative effects on services for students with severe handicaps. Following the "mental age" logic, tests have been developed to diagnose each student's developmental level. Instruction is then designed to match this level. Applications of the diagnostic/prescriptive approach are not limited to the developmental model. Some teachers who focus on chronologically age–appropriate skills only conduct episodic assessment. The value of this episodic assessment is further weakened if the assessment used does not correspond directly to students' specific objectives (e.g., repeated use of adaptive behavior scales).

A third approach to meeting individual student needs also emerged in the 1960s and 1970s as Lindsley (1964) began suggesting ways that teachers could use applied behavior analysis to improve teaching. Lindsley's work became the basis for the precision teaching model (White & Haring, 1980). In the precision teaching approach, criterion-referenced testing is used to assess students' progress on defined objectives. Assessment is also direct (i.e., the teacher tests or observes the student and counts responses) and frequent (e.g., daily). Through systematic review of these data, teachers make ongoing instructional changes to improve student progress.

The precision teaching approach is still evident in special education programs for students with mild or severe handicaps. The advantage of this approach is that it relates assessment directly to instructional objectives, and encourages using data to make decisions about student progress. The disadvantage is that the model itself does not specify how skills should be selected. Unfortunately, some teachers use precise, ongoing assessment and charting of objectives related to skills that are neither age-appropriate nor relevant to a student's environments. To remedy this problem, the precision teaching approach can be used *after* selecting skills from a life skills assessment. Also, the precision teaching model provides one of the few approaches that gives teachers guidelines to make data-based instructional decisions.

Current Trends in Individualization

Current trends in assessment for the purpose of individualizing instruction follow Lindsley's (1964) direction of frequent, direct assessment matched to specific objectives. For example, texts on educating students with severe handicaps describe ways to design this criterion-referenced assessment and suggest frequent schedules for data collection and review (e.g., Sailor & Guess, 1983; Snell, 1987). In special education in general, educators are being encouraged to use this curriculum-matched assessment for both eligibility decisions and evaluation of student progress (Blankenship, 1985; Deno, 1985; Tucker, 1985). Because ongoing assessment originated from applied behavior analysis, some teachers have used single-subject designs to evaluate data. Voeltz and Evans (1983) note that such designs have limitations that make them particularly unsuitable for instructional decision-making (e.g., prolonged baselines or replications of baseline). In the 1980s, an alternative approach has been made available; the precision teaching model uses empirically derived rules to make instructional decisions based on trend (Haring, Liberty, & White, 1980, 1981). This book offers an assessment approach based on applied behavior analysis in which criterion-referenced assessment is designed to measure specific objectives, and student progress is evaluated based on empirically derived guidelines for data review.

Two other trends that relate more to the principle of normalization than to applied behavior analysis also provide important considerations for individualizing instruction. In response to the "bottom up" approach of developmental models in which students are limited to the sequence of skills of normal infant and child development, Brown, Branston et al. (1979) advocated a "top down" approach to skill selection in which skills are matched to students' chronological age peers. Brown, Branston-McLean et al. (1979) provided guidelines for developing this curriculum based on *ecological inventories* that are assessments of the activities and skills required in given environments (see Chapter 2). Brown and his colleagues have provided an important new component to assessment of students with severe handicaps—assessment of the environment as well as of the student. In applied behavior analysis, a similar concern for ecological assessment arose when behavior analysts began to discuss the need to obtain social validation of behaviors selected for treatment (Kazdin, 1977; Wolf, 1978). The ecological inventory is a way to select socially valid skills for instruction by identifying the need for these skills in the student's own environments.

Brown, Branston-McLean et al. (1979) also advocated that all students be included in curriculum planning based on selecting skills appropriate to a student's chronological age that will be useful in community environments. They suggested that teachers select skills for "partial participation" in community-referenced activities if students could not master independent performance of skills needed in the environment. The idea of partial participation has become especially important for students with severe physical limitations, medical complications, and for older individuals with profound mental retardation who lack basic self-care and communication skills. The ideal that all students can produce some responses necessary for participation in the community with their same-age peers is an important one for normalization.

The influence of these various trends has led to interesting and differing approaches to assessment of and program planning for students with severe handicaps that are based on applications of applied behavior analysis and normalization or a "life skills" approach. The pros and cons of these various approaches are discussed next as an introduction to the approach taken in this text.

DIFFERING APPROACHES
TO BEHAVIORAL ASSESSMENT OF LIFE SKILLS

During the period of rapidly expanding services for people with severe handicaps that took place in the 1980s, several service models emerged that provided data-based instruction of life skills. These models differ in several aspects: (a) the way in which skills are chosen, (b) the selection of discrete versus chained target behaviors, (c) assessment of massed versus interspersed opportunities to respond, (d) the inclusion of noninstructional tests or observations, (e) the use of time-based data, (f) methods of data display, and (g) procedures for systematic data review. This diversity enriches the field with options to achieve the same goal, but teachers often use only the procedures that they acquired in their educational program. Each of these models has its strengths and weaknesses. By becoming more familiar with each, teachers may learn new methods for assessment that can complement current practice.

Behavioral Psychology
and Assessment of Individuals with Severe Handicaps

Special education and applied behavioral psychology have had overlapping roles in providing service and research findings for people with severe handicaps. Often, professionals in these fields have collaborated to develop service models. However, an approach does exist that is more closely aligned with applied behavioral psychology than special education. In the applied behavioral psychology approach, skill selection is viewed as identification of target behaviors. One of the outstanding strengths of this model is that these behaviors are carefully defined to be observable and measurable. Often, emphasis is placed on defining interfering behaviors. Because of the way that a single behavior is selected and defined, assessment is often focused on discrete behaviors rather than chains of behavior. Time sampling is then employed to record accurately the occurrence of one or more behaviors. Data are typically displayed in a grid graph typical of behavioral publications. Data evaluation is based on the utilization of single-subject research designs that provide replications of treatment results across behaviors, settings, or individuals. The application of this behavioral assessment model has been described by Powers and Handleman (1984). The strengths of this model are the exemplary definitions of target behaviors, and precise data collection methods. Its disadvantages are that skill selection does not always take into consideration students' priority life skill needs, and that task analytic assessment is deemphasized. The data collection and evaluation methods are also difficult for teachers to implement. Such designs also do not provide the best empirical orientation for teachers, who must judge the effectiveness of instruction and make changes on an ongoing basis (Voeltz & Evans, 1983).

Task Analytic Model

A second model to consider can be called a "task analytic" model because of its strong reliance on the use of task analyses for assessment and instruction. This model also grew out of applied behavioral psychology and was documented in research that focused on daily living skills (e.g., Cuvo, Leaf, & Borakove,

Following a task analysis to collect data while teaching is an approach utilized by many teachers.

1978; Tucker & Berry, 1980). While the choice of skill in this model may be subjective, the task analysis developed for instruction may be carefully validated through observations of nonhandicapped peers and consultation with experts (Cuvo, 1978). Thus, the defined target behaviors are typically chains of behavior with some demonstrated validity for these chains. Assessment usually involves setting up the task and observing students performing it. Often there are "test" observations that are distinct from teaching observations in that no prompts or reinforcements are given. These test observations are then graphed using a grid graph (e.g., the graph may display the number of steps performed independently on the task analytic assessment). The observation is typically not timed. Evaluation of the data is based on review of the graph after a period of teaching. Single-subject designs may be used to provide further evidence of effectiveness. Snell (1983) and Wehman et al. (1985) describe task analytic assessment in detail. They also present a blending of this approach with other applied behavioral analysis procedures (e.g., time sampling) and with ecological inventories (described in the next section).

The advantages of task analytic assessment are that it can be implemented by classroom teachers for a wide variety of skills, it typically focuses on life skills, and it provides a method to measure performance of a chain of behaviors. A disadvantage is that the different "steps" or behaviors in the chain may have quite different topographies and levels of difficulty. Collapsing such divergent skills into a graph of the "number of steps correct" sometimes masks the source of learning difficulties (e.g., a student has difficulty with steps that require small finger movements). Sailor and Guess (1983) note that students with severe handicaps may need to learn one step of the chain at a time. When such serial chaining is used, a graph of "number of steps correct" will show minimal progress. Task analytic assessment as traditionally used also provides no time-based measure. Often, instruction is terminated when all or most steps are performed correctly. However, a chain of behaviors, such as pulling up pants, that is performed extremely slowly, may have limited functional utility. To evaluate functional performance of a skill like dressing, criteria are needed for the duration of responding as well as for accuracy. Finally, graphs of task analyses are often not evaluated systematically. Instruction may continue for long periods of time before improvements are made.

Ecological Inventories

The ecological inventory was described earlier as a trend that has generally influenced assessment of students with severe handicaps. This work also deserves further discussion as an approach in and of itself because of the detailed guidelines it provides for skill selection. Brown, Branston-McLean et al. (1979) describe this approach in which the characteristics of students' current and future least restrictive environments are identified to determine the skills that are needed for students to achieve community integration. The life domains of community, recreation, vocational, and domestic skills provide a framework for this planning. For example, in identifying domestic needs, a teacher observes or interviews caregivers in a student's current home and next possible home (e.g., group home for adults). By analyzing each sub-environment in these settings (e.g., kitchen, bathroom, bedroom), a list of activities and skills is generated. The advantage of this approach is that it helps teachers generate or adapt curricula that meet every student's individual needs. The disadvantage is that it can lead to an unmanageable list of skill needs. Setting priorities can be the most difficult part of the process. With this approach, some related skills that are useful across domains (e.g., language, motor) may be omitted from the skill selection process because of the domain focus. Obviously, this approach is only relevant to skill selection; other procedures would be needed to assess students' performance of selected skills.

Massed-Trial Assessment

Another approach that grew out of the behavior analysis tradition is massed-trial assessment. It involves the presentation of repeated opportunities to respond in a test or teaching session. In this model, a single skill is chosen. Teachers usually give a verbal cue (e.g., "What is this?"). Students' responses are scored and the teacher immediately presents the next "trial" (e.g., new item and the question "What is this?"). These data are usually graphed using a grid graph (e.g., number correct). Evaluation is similar to that used in the task analytic model. This assessment model is documented in research on language (e.g., Browder, Morris, & Snell, 1981; Striefel, Wetherby, & Karlan, 1976). The advantage of this model is that it provides multiple opportunities for the student to respond correctly. The disadvantage is that these responses may not generalize from the massed-trial format to natural opportunities for their use. This model also has limited evaluation and skill selection.

Individualized Curriculum Sequencing Model

One approach that has the advantage of providing repeated opportunities to respond, but builds in the component of generalization, is the individualized curriculum sequencing model (ICS model). This model, developed by Guess and colleagues (Guess et al., 1978; Holvoet, Guess, Mulligan, & Brown, 1980) provides a series of trials in which one response logically sets the occasion for the next. Skill clusters are selected from traditional areas, such as language, motor, self-care, and socialization skills. In instruction, students are given the opportunity to make a chain of responses. However, this chain is usually unlike those presented in task analyses that typically present only one skill domain. Instead, students might communicate the need for an item, use the item, and pass the item to a peer (language, self-care, socialization). Opportunities to use this chain (e.g., communicate, use, pass) are then presented across people, materials, and tasks throughout the day. Data are recorded and graphed in a manner similar to the task analytic graph. However, teachers can also note the percentage correct for each type of response (e.g., communication of "I want-"). This model typically does not provide "test" observations, but rather bases data evaluation on the data collected during teaching. Data evaluation is similar to that described for task analytic assessment but has the added advantage of easier monitoring of individual responses. The advantages of the ICS model are that acquisition and generalization of skills are assessed concurrently. This model also provides an excellent method for assessing language and motor skills in the context of varied response chains that are typical of daily living. However, the disadvantage of this model is that the response chains selected may not be comprehensive enough to teach students to perform activities independently.

Precision Teaching Model

The precision teaching model improves upon the massed-trial assessment format. However, in this model, students are given the opportunity to perform a response repetitively or to perform a chain of responses without teacher interruption while the teacher counts correct responses and errors, and times responding. Correct responses and errors per minute are then plotted using a standard graph that is a 2½ cycle semilogarithmic graph. Haring, Liberty, and White (1979) describe how this data collection system can be used with students with severe handicaps. They also provide empirically derived rules for reviewing the data obtained to make instructional decisions. This model provides systematic data evaluation procedures, and thus makes optimal use of data obtained. The use of standard graphs simplifies the data evaluation process. The consideration of time-based data can reveal subtle improvements when students become more fluent at a task. The disadvantage of this approach is that it is difficult to use with the varied response chains that are typical of task analytic assessment or the ICS model. The semilogarithmic graph and collection of time-based data also make the system difficult for teachers who have not been trained in this model.

Synthesis of the Models

While these various models take different approaches to data collection and evaluation, they share the common foundations of applied behavior analysis and life skills curriculum planning. By utilizing some features of each, teachers may find options for different students and different skills. This book relies predominantly on the task analytic assessment model. However, the advantageous features of other models are presented to broaden and improve this approach. Ideas are presented for developing task analyses that include related communication and motor skills, thus creating chains that, like the ICS model, provide opportunities for generalization assessment and instruction. Massed-trial assessment is not omitted since this can be a key technique to test quickly for mastery of numerous exemplars. Skill selection is described in detail building on the work of Brown, Branston-McLean et al. (1979) and others who have expanded the idea of ecological inventories. Careful consideration is given to the evaluation of data using an adaptation of the precision teaching model's rules for instructional decisions. Practitioners currently trained in applied behavioral psychology will find that this synthesis offers more specific ideas for deciding which skills to select, and an empirical approach for evaluating data that are not derived from baselines and replications typical of single-subject research.

CRITERIA TO GUIDE
PLANNING OF APPROPRIATE ASSESSMENT

This book provides a model for assessment that follows the traditions of applied behavior analysis and normalization. It offers a blending of behavioral, life skills approaches, emphasizing task analytic assessment. Given this framework, several criteria can be suggested for planning assessment that will be appropriate for the purposes of skill selection and ongoing evaluation of student progress:

1. Skills must be selected that will enhance students' integration in their community environments with nonhandicapped peers, and lead to the opportunities available to nonhandicapped people (e.g., employment).

2. Reliable, valid assessment strategies must be developed for skill selection and ongoing assessment.
3. Ongoing assessment must be frequent (e.g., daily or semiweekly) and direct.
4. Data must be collected during ongoing assessment.
5. The data must be summarized on a graph or chart.
6. The graph must be periodically reviewed to make and record data-based instructional decisions.
7. These instructional decisions must be implemented.
8. Skills selected should be reviewed annually, and comprehensive assessment should be conducted at least every 3–5 years to prioritize skills for instruction.

These critiera are discussed below in the sections on organizing assessment and developing valid and reliable assessment.

Organizing Assessment

To meet the criteria suggested above, teachers will need to take an organized approach to skill selection, ongoing assessment, and evaluation. This book provides an organization guide for the teacher to follow, and offers examples of its use in case studies of people with severe handicaps.

The content areas for this assessment are divided into skills used in the home, and skills used in the community. Related skills such as communication, motor skills, academics, and social skills are given additional consideration to ensure that these critical functions are not underrepresented in the curriculum plan. Since many teachers must develop curriculum-based assessment without a written life skills curriculum, instructions are given for generating an individualized curriculum as part of this comprehensive assessment. Obviously, a comprehensive initial assessment and curriculum chart are not needed every year. Rather, these form the basis for initial educational evaluation during placement and updated evaluation that is conducted every 3–5 years. Each year's IEP can be developed from this longitudinal curriculum chart and review of the past year's progress. Ongoing assessment will be a frequent event (e.g., daily), with systematic evaluation of these data to make instructional decisions (e.g., biweekly). A flowchart for developing a comprehensive assessment plan is shown in Figure 1. The remainder of this book describes specific ways to develop this plan for individual students.

In the final chapter, guidelines are also given for supervisors or teachers to evaluate both adherence to this assessment plan and instruction itself. This evaluation can both provide documentation for program evaluation and help teachers identify areas that need improvement.

Developing Reliable and Valid Assessment

As well as following an organized assessment plan, teachers need to consider the quality of each assessment tool that they use or develop. The quality of

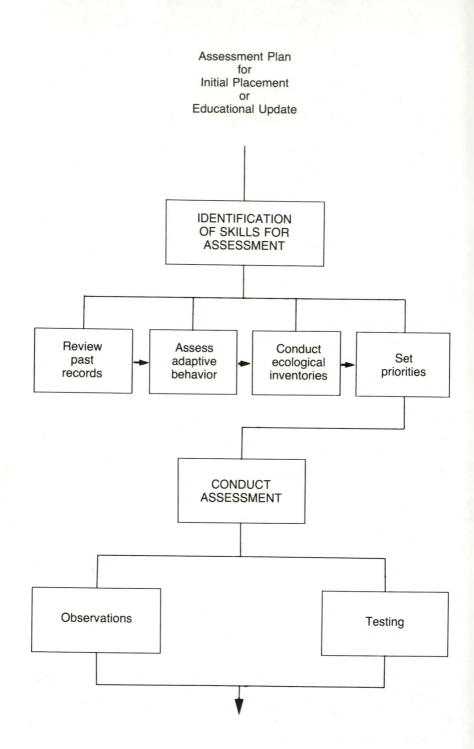

Figure 1.   Flowchart for the development of a comprehensive education plan for students with severe handicaps.

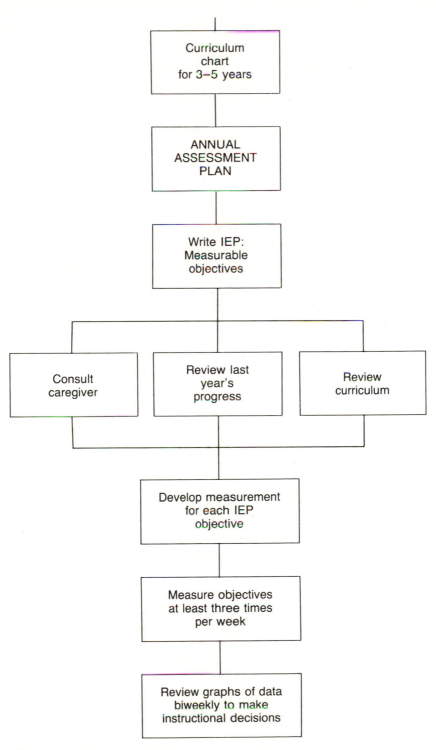

Figure 1. *(continued)*

assessment is usually judged by its reliability and validity. Reliability is the consistency of measurement. When measurement is designed to sample some relatively stable trait (e.g., intellectual functioning), testers are concerned with cross-time reliability. For example, a school psychologist would hope to obtain the same score if an IQ test were repeated in a month, since intellectual functioning is presumed to be a fairly stable trait. Since such retesting seldom reveals the same score, a standard error of measurement is reported. In educational assessment, teachers are not concerned with stable traits, but rather with evolving skills. Fluctuations in performance across days are often typical. However, teachers still hope to obtain a measure of the student's performance at the time of the assessment that would be consistent across observations. With such consistency, teachers can consider fluctuations in performance when making instructional decisions (e.g., Are students motivated to perform the skill consistently?). Without such consistency, fluctuations may be due to inconsistent data collection. In research, consistency of data collection is evaluated by having a second observer collect data concurrently, and comparing results. These reliability checks may be scheduled as frequently as every third observation. Such checks often are not feasible in the classroom. How, then, can classroom teachers be confident of having data that are accurate enough to warrant using them to make instructional decisions? By using one or more of the following suggestions, teachers may improve and maintain data consistency in applied settings:

1. When teachers first learn to collect data, frequent reliability checks should be scheduled (e.g., by a supervisor) until a criterion for agreement has been demonstrated (e.g., 90% agreement across three lessons and settings). This is often an appropriate goal for student teachers.
2. Teachers should use data collection procedures learned with a co-observer. When a new procedure is implemented, someone should be recruited to co-observe for one or more times to check reliability.
3. To maintain reliability, teachers could ask an aide, supervisor, principal, or other professional who sometimes visits the classroom to co-observe a session to check accuracy. Even if infrequent, these co-observations may help maintain consistency.

Measurement must also be valid if it is to be useful. Validity is the degree to which an instrument measures what it purports to measure. For example, a bathroom scale cannot be used to measure height; its only valid measurement is weight. In the construction of standardized tests, validity is often demonstrated by computing correlations with similar tests or between items (Salvia & Ysseldyke, 1981). Content validity also can be evaluated by examining test items to determine how well they sample the skill or concept to be tested. As teachers review adaptive behavior scales, some test items will have questionable "adaptive behavior validity." That is, skills listed will not be needed for daily living. For example, the Fine Motor section of the *Pyramid Scales* (Cone, 1984) contains items related to block stacking and bead stringing. By contrast, this same test has numerous scales related to daily living (e.g., washing and grooming, domestic behavior). Thus, the content validity of this test differs across scales.

When teachers construct their own tests, the issue of validity must again be considered. Teachers need to judge how well an observation or test samples the target behavior. First and foremost, teachers need to write objectives that relate directly to skills of daily living for students' chronological age groups. Then, the assessment procedures developed need to match carefully these objectives. Consider the following objective:

> When Don enters the classroom or work setting, he will put away his belongings and sit in his assigned seat by the time the work bell rings (Mastery criteria: 4 out of 5 days).

This objective is measurable and functional for Don. Now consider the following teacher-made test for this objective that has some validity problems:

Task Analysis for Don's Belongings

1. Walk to teacher.
2. Look at teacher.
3. Say "hello" to teacher.
4. Take off coat.
5. Comply with teacher's request to sit down.

This task analysis measures Don's interaction with his teacher and ability to take off his coat. Review the objective again and note that it implies Don's independent performance of a morning routine. Such independence is most typical of adult settings. Social greetings would also be appropriate, but they are not specified in this objective. To be most appropriate, such social greetings might be targeted for Don's discussion with peers at his workbench prior to the bell or upon first entering the building. Consider the following task analysis, which is a more valid measure of the stated objective:

Task Analysis for Don's Belongings

1. Walk to coatroom.
2. Put lunchbox on shelf.
3. Take off gloves.
4. Put gloves in pockets.
5. Take off hat.
6. Hang hat on hook.
7. Take off coat.
8. Hang coat on hook.
9. Walk to assigned seat.
10. Be seated by the time the bell rings.

For an assessment to be valid, teachers must first write a functional objective and then design an assessment that measures the specific behavior and criteria stated in the objective. When teachers review published instruments to consider validity, thought should be given to the specific skills sampled by each test item.

Protection of the Student's
Human Rights during Assessment

In addition to making sure that educational assessment matches its purpose and meets criteria set for quality, teachers will want to consider students' legal and human rights when planning assessment. Due process (PL 93-380, the Education Amendments of 1974; PL 94-142, the Education for All Handicapped Children Act of 1975) requires that:

1. Consent of both students and the parents or legal guardians must be obtained prior to conducting evaluation to determine if students qualify for special services.
2. Parents or guardians have the right to inspect all related educational evaluations and placement records.
3. PL 94-142 specifies that parents have the right to obtain an independent evaluation for consideration in planning students' educational programs. Professionals in adult programs should also honor clients' or parents' requests to review and consider evaluations by professionals outside the clients' programs.
4. Written notice must be given to parents or guardians prior to an educational placement change. This notice should include descriptions of the evaluation that led to the change and the rationale for the change.
5. Parents or guardians and students have the right to participate in the development of the individualized plan.

Besides these due process considerations, educators should respect students' human rights, including the right to treatment and to confidentiality. PL 93-380 gives parents and students the right to review their records, and forbids the release of identifiable information without written consent. Educators will want to maintain records with assessment information that are confidential and relevant to treatment. The following are professional ethics for assessment:

1. Conduct assessment to plan instruction. Information that does not have relevance to the educational process should not be collected or recorded.
2. Keep in strictest confidence all information obtained in the assessment of students. Do not use personally identifiable information or the students' names when describing one's work to others who do not participate in those students' education. Obtain written parental permission to share any

information about students as part of professional training or for publicity about a program.

3. Share assessment reports with parents, and be careful to state results tactfully.

4. Do not publicly post student data or other information with students' names without parental and student permission. Keep instructional data private. For example, do not share data sheets with names and data of several students with one student's parents. Do not leave clipboards with data and students' names in teachers' lounges. Also, do not post data, even without names, that portray students in a negative manner or violate their rights to confidentiality (e.g., graphs on hitting, recording on the chalkboard number of toilet accidents).

SUMMARY

Assessment of individuals with severe handicaps has as its primary purpose the identification of skills that will increase opportunities for normalized living in community settings. The methodology of applied behavior analysis provides a basis for designing this assessment. By synthesizing the various models of behavioral assessment of students with severe handicaps, a comprehensive assessment plan can be developed that includes initial assessment for skill selection, and ongoing assessment for evaluation of progress. In developing this plan, teachers will want to be careful to develop reliable, valid measurement, and to respect students' due process and human rights.

CHAPTER 2

COMPREHENSIVE ASSESSMENT FOR LONGITUDINAL CURRICULUM DEVELOPMENT

DIANE M. BROWDER AND DIANE KING

One of the most difficult but important steps in assessing a student is to identify priority skills for a longitudinal plan of instruction. When a student's handicaps are severe, and the goal is community integration, it can be especially difficult to select from the many skills that could be included for instruction. This chapter provides guidelines to help the teacher make decisions about skill priorities.

In following the assessment model described in Chapter 1, comprehensive assessment to develop or individualize a curriculum would be conducted when a student first enters a school district, and at regular periods of reevaluation. These periods of reevaluation should be scheduled for times when the student is promoted to new levels of education (e.g., from elementary school to junior high) and can be conducted by the classroom teacher or by an educational or curriculum specialist who has been assigned this responsibility. The time required for both planning and implementation make annual reevaluation not feasible. However, the time investment is both feasible and worthwhile if conducted every 3–5 years. Also, this initial assessment can be abbreviated for use in annual assessment, with periodic comprehensive assessment occurring with each new placement. This comprehensive educational assessment will begin with prior records and, upon completion, yield both a longitudinal, individualized curriculum chart and the first year's plan (e.g., IEP for a school-age student).

Diane King is a doctoral student, Special Education Programs, School of Education, Lehigh University, Bethlehem, Pennsylvania.

To recap, a *comprehensive assessment* is conducted to identify the skills that a student needs for the next several years. This assessment will aid the teacher in writing an *individualized curriculum plan* that is a list of skills targeted for 3–5 years of instruction (e.g., the elementary years). Comprehensive assessment and curriculum planning are most appropriate when a student enters a program or progresses from one level of education to the next (e.g., graduates from elementary to junior high school). By abbreviating the comprehensive assessment approach, the teacher can conduct *annual assessment* that helps verify the 1-year individualized education program (IEP). Comprehensive assessment and the resultant curriculum chart can be viewed as long-range planning that helps link IEPs from year to year.

The need for such long-range planning is especially important when students have many deficiencies and learn slowly. In reviewing qualities needed for services for students with severe handicaps, Certo (1983) noted that such services need to be *longitudinal* and not episodic. If an individual with severe handicaps is to achieve community integration and his or her fullest independence, careful planning must be conducted to ensure that each year's instruction follows the route to these goals.

While teachers typically write the IEP for a student, an individualized curriculum plan based on educational assessment is sometimes the missing link in developing longitudinal service. A school district's life skills curriculum guide can enhance but not replace this individualized planning. While most guides are written with adequate breadth to cover many students' needs, the teacher will need to plan instruction to relate to unique demands and opportunities in students' lives. Picking skills from a guide bypasses the important needs of matching objectives to actual environments in the students' lives, and gathering evidence proving that these objectives are priorities.

To conduct comprehensive educational assessment for developing an individualized and longitudinal curriculum, the teacher will follow several steps: (a) identifying skills to be assessed, (b) selecting priorities for assessment, (c) planning and conducting assessment, (d) making the curriculum chart, and (e) writing the first year's IEP. These steps are described in each of the following sections of this chapter.

IDENTIFICATION OF THE SKILLS TO BE ASSESSED

To identify the skills to be assessed, the teacher needs an organizational framework for the "topics" or skill areas to be assessed, and specific procedures to assess these areas. This section considers how skills can be organized for assessment, and suggests an organization that will be used throughout this book. Following this organizational framework, specific examples of ways to identify skills are described.

Organization of Skills for Assessment

In the academic orientation of special education for students with mild handicaps, educational assessment often focuses on traditional school subjects such as reading, math, and so forth. In a developmental approach to the education of students with severe handicaps, areas of assessment are similar to those selected for preschool evaluations (e.g., motor skills, language, cognitive skills). A life skills approach to the education of students with severe handicaps requires an organization for assessment and instruction that has relevance to the environments of community living. Brown, Branston-McLean et al. (1979) have suggested a curriculum development model for students with severe handicaps that focuses on four life domains: *community, domestic, home,* and *leisure.* Curriculum development that is organized according to these domains has been described in numerous resources on educating students with severe handicaps (e.g., Browder & Stewart, 1982; Falvey, 1986; Sailor & Guess, 1983; Snell, 1983; Wehman et al., 1985). While variations exist across resources, these domains are frequently used as subject areas for life skills planning.

The disadvantage of this domain approach is that it typically leads to the identification of the core skills involved in performing tasks (e.g., washing the dishes). Brown, Evans, and Weed (1985) noted that independent living requires many other kinds of skills, such as communicating about core skills, knowing when to perform skills, and making transitions from one activity to the next. They have begun to classify these other skills in two categories called enrichment and extension skills. Another approach to looking at more than the daily living activities themselves is to consider skills that cross all domains. For example, Sailor and Guess (1983) modify the domain orientation approach by also including motor, self-care, and recreation skills that are needed across domains. Both of these domain modifications might be referred to as *cross-planning.* That is, certain skills that are used across many activities and domains are considered separately for assessment. However, for functional use, these skills would be taught in the context of specific domain activities (e.g., functional use of communication of choice might be taught during a recreation activity). Because these skills are related to many activities of daily living, this book uses the term *related skills* in reference to them. Communication, motor, academic, and social skills are the related skills of focus. These particular "subject" areas are chosen because they are distinct subjects in special education and related literature. However, care is given to emphasize that, to be functional, these skills must be related to some real activity that the student encounters in daily living.

This book proposes that assessment be planned according to the location in which skills will be used—in the home or in community environments outside the home. Community environments outside the home are subdivided using Brown, Branston-McLean et al.'s (1979) approach resulting in vocational, recreation, and other community skills (e.g., travel, shopping). The home environments are subdivided into personal maintenance, housekeeping, recreation and socialization, and preparation for community activities. Cross-planning is then conducted for assessment of related skills that have traditional categories including communication, motor skills, functional academics (if applicable), social skills, and interfering behaviors. Figure 1 shows how the comprehensive curriculum and assessment chart is organized. The chart is used throughout the book to help the teacher plan and summarize assessment.

Once the teacher has selected an organizational framework for curriculum development and assessment, he or she can proceed to identify the specific skills to be assessed. This can be done by reviewing previous records, using ecological inventories, selecting checklists of skills that are related to several environments, and using adaptive behavior scales.

Procedures to Identify Skills for Assessment

Review of Previous Records   The first place to begin planning a comprehensive educational assessment is to review the student's educational progress and information related to it (e.g., medical reports, therapy evaluations, psychological reports). From this previous progress, a list can be made of skills not yet mastered, to be maintained, to be generalized, or to be developed further with related skills. Skills listed will need to be verified and prioritized in the comprehensive assessment that is included in the curriculum plan. The teacher will also note reports from other professionals, and make a list of their recommendations that imply skill needs (e.g., a motor deficiency might be noted for consideration in reviewing and adapting activities that require this motor skill). This information can be summarized on a chart similar to Figure 1 as shown in Figure 2.

If the school psychologist has utilized adaptive behavior scales, as suggested in Chapter 1, this report may provide an important starting point for the teacher's notation of the student's current life skills. The teacher will want to obtain a copy of the actual record form of the adaptive behavior scale to note the specific skills that were assessed.

Use of Ecological Inventories   One of the most useful and important strategies for identifying skills for assessment is the "ecological inventory," which is also called an "environmental analysis." The ecological inventory is a survey, interview, or observation that is used to identify the skills that are needed in specific settings in which the student currently functions and will function in the future.

Identifying the skill needs of each of a student's environments can be difficult. First, the teacher must decide what environments are relevant for a student. Then, the diversity of environments that will be identified will require various methods for conducting the inventories.

Domains and Subdomains

Core skills	Home					Community		
	Personal maintenance	Housekeeping	Recreation/ socialization	Community preparation	Vocational	Recreational	Other	
Related skills Communi- cation								
Motor								
Academics								
Social								
Interfering behavior								

Figure 1. Organization of the comprehensive assessment and curriculum chart.

Teacher: __Ms. P.__   Student: __Ann__

Skill areas	Source Used to Identify Skills Listed				
	Previous records	Caregiver inventory	Other ecological inventory	Teacher-made checklists or adaptive behavior scales	Current testing and observations
Home					
Personal maintenance	Eating skills Toilet-training	Drinking from glass, dressing, toilet-training		Using restroom alone Eating with spoon	Panting up/down Eating finger foods
Housekeeping		Wiping table	Work center: discarding trash		Opening containers
Recreation/socialization		Music	Adult peer: playing piano		Using radio, tape player
Community preparation		Putting on coat Getting lunch	Work center: packing/ carrying bag lunch		

Community				
Vocational			Work center: mailings photocopying		Putting on labels, Sealing envelopes
Recreational		Sports events Buying soda	Senior citizen center: drinking soda	Walking up/down steps	Drinking soda from can Using vending machine
Other (e.g., travel, shop)	No awareness of danger	Eating in restaurant	7-11, restaurant bus station: Selecting choice Grasping/ releasing	Pedestrian skills	Communicating basic needs, using wallet
Related skills					
Communication		Need for help Conversing	Making choices Using I.D. card	Imitating social comments	Yes/no
Motor	Grasp/release Thumb-finger opposition	Walking faster	Walking to rest-room Carrying bag	Opening doors	
Academics					
Social			Imitating social		
Interfering behavior	Decreasing swearing	Choking when eating		Inappropriate comments	

Figure 2. Illustration of skill selection process to plan a comprehensive assessment and curriculum chart.

The application of ecological inventories may be simplified if the parents or caregivers are the first contact. The teacher may want to correspond first by phone and letter or in a school-based meeting. In this first contact, the teacher can solicit parental help in: (a) identifying the relevant community environments to be evaluated with ecological inventories, (b) becoming acquainted with the student and his or her preferences and skills, (c) beginning to consider priorities, and (d) preparing for the home ecological inventory. Figure 3 is an example of a form that could be shared with the parents. This form was

---

Student's name: Dennis   Date: 9/3/85

Teacher: Ms. K   Parents or
                                          Caregivers: Ms. T.

This survey was developed to assist the teacher in developing a comprehensive educational assessment. The information you provide can help make this assessment relevant to this student.

1.   What are Dennis's favorite activities and leisure materials?
2.   What other preferences has Dennis expressed (e.g., preferred and non-preferred food, clothing, temperature)?
3.   Where does your family typically go, or where would your family like to go for each of these activities?

> Shopping:
> Clubs, church:
> Medical appointments:
> Visit friends and relatives:
> Family recreation:
> Other:

For each of the above, circle the places that your family frequently goes. Star the places that Dennis has frequently gone.
4.   What skills were previously taught to Dennis that you would like to see maintained in his future instruction?
5.   What changes need to be made in Dennis's educational program?
6.   Who in the home provides most of Dennis's care? Who would be willing and have time to implement some instruction for Dennis at home that would be designed by the teacher? How much time would be realistic for this home instruction? (e.g., 30 minutes daily)
7.   Attached please find a survey of adaptive behavior. Please follow the instructions to indicate the skills that Dennis currently has.
8.   Please feel free to make any general comments about Dennis's educational needs.

THANK YOU FOR YOUR TIME IN COMPLETING THIS SURVEY.

Figure 3.   Example of a form that can be sent to parents to solicit their input in developing the comprehensive educational plan. (In this example, an adaptive behavior scale has not yet been used, so the parent survey of the Comprehensive Test of Adaptive Behavior will be included with this form.)

introduced with a phone call from the teacher, and then mailed to the parents for their input in developing the assessment plan.

From this parental input, the teacher can organize and develop the inventories. By using the chart shown in Figures 1 and 2, the teacher can list the environments identified by the parents for the home and community. Sometimes, the teacher will have adequate information to plan for one or more of these environments (e.g., the teacher may use the shopping center identified by the parents). Unfamiliar environments (e.g., the student's home) and environments that will be considered for activities unfamiliar to the teacher (e.g., custodial skills for the shopping mall) will require obtaining additional information. For each unfamiliar environment, the teacher then must decide how the information will be obtained. One method is to develop an attitude and information survey to be completed by a significant person in the environment. For example, the teacher might send a survey to a potential employer and ask him or her to rank the importance of specific skills. An example of this type of inventory is provided in Chapter 8 to determine an employer's attitude toward certain social skills. A second method is to go to the environment, and observe and interview significant people. An example of this approach is illustrated in Chapter 5 with an ecological inventory for a home environment. A third method is simply to observe in an environment to obtain information on both the physical layout of the setting and typical activities of nonhandicapped peers. An example of an inventory with a set of questions to be completed while making such an observation is shown in Figure 4. A fourth method is to interview a nonhandicapped peer or the peer's parents to obtain information on typical activities of this age group (e.g., during leisure time). The teacher may think of other approaches to obtain information on specific environments. Regardless of how the information is obtained, consideration of related skills and prioritization will need to be completed before proceeding to develop assessment of the student.

The *rationale* for using ecological inventories to help guide the selection of skills for assessment and instruction is to match the educational program to the expectations of society. The ultimate goal of self-sufficiency can be interpreted to be the ability of an individual to function in a manner similar to his or her peers in society. Ecological inventories enhance the social validity of the assessment to be designed by identifying societal expectations for self-sufficiency.

Social validation was first described as a criterion to evaluate research (Kazdin, 1977; Wolf, 1978). Kazdin described two methods to make behavioral research more socially valid. One is to consult the opinions of "experts" in the environment in which the behavior will be performed. The other is to use normative comparisons (see discussion in next paragraph). Ecological inventories build on this social validation approach to skill selection. For example, Voeltz, Wuerch, and Bockhaut (1982) asked direct care

Life Skills Questionnaire

Site _____ *Date* _____

Interview Contact Person _____

1. Is the facility barrier-free? Are there areas within the facility that are not accessible to a wheelchair?

2. Is there medical treatment available? How close is the nearest hospital?

3. What activities are typical of 12-year-old boys in this facility? How often are these available?

4. What is the average cost of these activities?

5. What accommodations would the staff make for an individual with Tommy's handicaps?

Figure 4.   Example of an ecological inventory. (From Browder, D., & Martin, D. [1986]. A new curriculum for Tommy. *Teaching Exceptional Children,* 18, 261–265; reprinted by permission.)

staff to evaluate the leisure time behavior of adolescents with severe handicaps. Their evaluation provided evidence that improvement in leisure skills would be valued by the people who cared for these individuals during their leisure time. Cuvo, Jacobi, and Sipko (1981) took a slightly different approach to validate the task analysis for laundry skills by consulting an expert in housekeeping (home economist).

The second social validation tactic, to gather information on social acceptability by observing typical performances of nonhandicapped people (normative comparison), has been demonstrated in research by Nutter and Reid (1978), who observed women in public settings to identify popular color combinations to include in a clothing selection program. Sometimes, a normative comparison such as the one used by Nutter and Reid will reveal a range of acceptable behavior that provides more flexibility and efficiency in planning than is suggested by experts (e.g., home economist's recommendation for a schedule for mopping the kitchen floor versus the range of schedules used by adults).

Voeltz and Evans (1983) note the need for empirical validity as well as social validity. Empirical validity requires judgments about whether a behavior will be important to the student's eventual outcome. If the ultimate goal is self-sufficiency, skills will be tested against whether they are efficient means for obtaining the student's greatest potential for self-sufficiency. Thus, ecological inventories address not only skills for current environments, but also skills that will lead to independent performance in future environments (Falvey, Brown, Lyon, Baumgart, & Schroeder, 1980).

Selection and Use of Surveys and Checklists of Related Skills The ecological inventories conducted will suggest many skills for instruction. However, these inventories may not indicate an adequate list of related skills such as motor and communication skills. The teacher may want to supplement the skills identified on the inventories with checklists for communication, motor skills, functional academics, and social skills. Problem behaviors may also require further assessment planning. Examples of these checklists are provided in Chapters 8 and 9.

Use of an Adaptive Behavior Scale To economize assessment, it may also be useful to begin with a global assessment such as that provided by many adaptive behavior scales. This global assessment can be especially helpful in planning for a student whom the teacher does not yet know. Adaptive behavior scales vary in the content and quantity of life skills included. The best scale for use in a comprehensive educational assessment is the one with numerous items in each life skill area. In Figure 5, the content of several adaptive behavior scales is summarized. The teacher may refer to this list as an aid in selecting a scale with the best utility for his or her students.

The most typical method of obtaining assessment information from adaptive behavior scales is for the person most familiar with the student to identify current skills. The Camelot Behavioral Checklist, Comprehensive Test of Adaptive Behavior (CTAB), and Pyramid Scales allow the caregiver to complete the checklist independently. (The CTAB has a form especially developed for parents to use). The American Association on Mental Deficiency Adaptive Behavior Scales, Scales of Independent Behavior (SIBS), Pyramid Scales, and Vineland Adaptive Behavior Scales, can be completed through a parent interview in which the professional asks questions and scores the form. The CTAB provides test situations for any items that are unclear in the survey or interview. While the Balthazar Scales of Adaptive Behavior are designed to be completed by observing the student, most of the adaptive behavior scales could be modified in the same way. Because of the number of skills to be assessed, some use of parent or teacher reports of formerly observed skills is more feasible than observing or testing all skills listed. (For complete addresses of the adaptive behavior scales listed here and in Figure 5, please refer to the appendix at the end of this chapter.)

The information obtained from the adaptive behavior assessment will need to be reorganized by life skills categories such as those shown in Figure 1. For

Scales and number of responses per skill area

Life skills	AAMD ABS	Balthazar[1]	Callier-Azusa[2]	Camelot	CTAB	Pyramid	SIBS	Vineland
Domestic								
Toileting	*	**	***	*	**	***	**	**
Hygiene/grooming	***	N	****	**	**	***	**	***
Dressing	**	****	****	**	****	***	**	***
Eating	**	****	****	**	***	***	**	***
Food preparation	N	N	****	**	****	**	**	**
Housekeeping	N	N	****	***	****	**	**	**
Clothing care	**	N	*	**	**	**	*	*
Lawn/vehicle care	N	N	N	**	**	*	N	N
Health care	*	N	N	*	**	N	*	*
Home leisure	*	N	N	**	**	**	N	***
Community								
Pedestrian	*	N	N	*	**	Z	*	*
Travel/bus	*	N	N	**	**	Z	**	*
Shopping	**	N	N	*	**	Z	*	*
Restaurant use	*	N	N*	N*	*	Z	*	*
Self-identification	**	N	N	**	**	Z	*	**
Telephone use	*	N	N	**	**	Z*	*	**
Banking/money	**	N	N	**	**	***	***	N
Job-specific skills	*	N	N	**	N	*	*	N
Job-related skills	**	N	N	**	**	**	**	*

36

General skills[3]								
Language–vocal	**	N	****	**	***	****	****	****
Language–nonvocal	*	N	**	*	*	*	*	*
Ambulation–walk, sit	*	N	*	*	**	**	*	**
Ambulation–wheelchair	N	N	N	N	N	N	N	N
Social interaction	**	***	****	**	**	***	**	****
Problem behaviors	****	***	N	N	N	****	****	****
Academics	**	N	**	***	****	N	***	****

Key— N   No responses
   *   1–5 responses
   **   6–24 responses
   ***   25–50 responses
   ****   more than 50 responses

[1]Designed for individuals with severe handicaps
[2]Designed for individuals who are deaf/blind
[3]Expressive and receptive communication

Figure 5.   Skills assessed by adaptive behavior scales. Some items had several responses per item. Each response was counted, rather than each item. (Note: AAMD ABS = American Association on Mental Deficiency Adaptive Behavior Scales; Balthazar = Balthazar Scales of Adaptive Behavior; Callier-Azusa = Callier-Azusa Scales, Camelot = Camelot Behavioral Checklist, CTAB = Comprehensive Test of Adaptive Behaviors, Pyramid = The Pyramid Scales, SIBS = Scales of Independent Behavior, Vineland = Vineland Adaptive Behavior Scales.) (From Browder, D., & Snell, M. E. [in press]. Assessment of individuals with severe handicaps. In E. S. Shapiro & T. R. Kratochwill [Eds.], Behavioral assessment in schools: Approaches to classification and intervention. New York: Guilford Press; reprinted by permission.)

educational planning, profiles and total scores will not provide information with adequate specificity. Rather, the teacher should list the student's current skills (or examples of highest-level skills, communication).

SETTING PRIORITIES FOR ASSESSMENT AND INSTRUCTION

Once the teacher has used the strategies to identify skills for assessment, he or she will begin to generate a large list of deficiencies. To conduct further assessment of this large list, or to interpret this list as a curriculum chart, would be difficult and inefficient. Rather, the teacher needs to establish priorities for the student before planning and conducting further assessment to develop the curriculum plan.

Setting priorities must actually occur twice in developing a curriculum plan. First, the teacher must review the skills suggested by previous records, ecological inventories, and an adaptive behavior screening to decide what skill areas warrant further consideration in the assessment of the student. Once assessment has been completed, the teacher must then again set priorities for the curriculum plan itself and the first year's IEP. Setting these priorities can be one of the most difficult tasks in the assessment process. Some of the variables to be considered in setting priorities are: (a) the student's own preferences and the preferences of caregivers, (b) societal values, (c) preferences of significant others in settings targeted for instruction, (d) skill utility and practical issues, and (e) partial participation.

Consideration of the Student's and Caregivers' Preferences

One of the first and most important steps in establishing priorities for assessment and instruction is to consider the student's preferences. Some skills (e.g., leisure) allow a wide range of choice for specific behaviors to be taught. For such areas, the teacher will want to observe the student's preferences. This may be done by offering several materials or activities and noting the student's choice across several opportunities. Another method is to give the student brief exposures to activities and note the student's reaction (e.g., attempts to perform skills, smiles versus tries to terminate activity by pulling away). A chart to assist this assessment of preference is shown in Figure 6. This evaluation requires introducing materials and activities across several days and noting the student's reaction to each.

Two precautions should be considered in this evaluation of preferences. First, the student obviously will need to learn some activities that are not liked but are required by society (e.g., use of a toilet). Such skills would not be appropriate for preference assessment, but rather would be included based on priorities set by other criteria (e.g., parents' preference). Second, as Shevin and Klein (1984) note, students sometimes act out of habit rather than making a choice (e.g., by always selecting same snack). Preference for a novel activity or

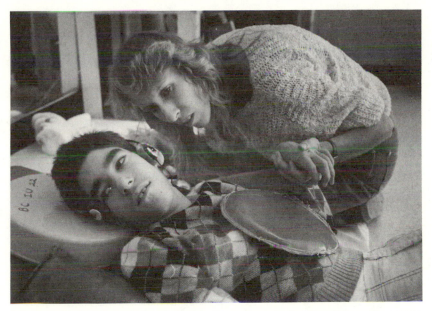

Assessment of preference for students with severe physical handicaps may require adapting switches to their current motor skills. In this photo, the teacher demonstrates how to activate a tape recorder.

material sometimes requires several exposures. Thus, a skill might be included to encourage a student to become familiar with a new experience (e.g., skiing) that has other value (e.g., family preference, health benefits). Obviously, these precautions are not applicable to all of the choices that students with severe handicaps can and should make about their future curriculum.

Parents' preferences are also one of the most important criteria for selecting skills for further assessment. The preliminary form sent to the parents (see Figure 3) helps the teacher decide what environments to use for assessment, and identifies some of the parents' preferences. This home inventory guides choices about domestic skills that vary with family values. The teacher may also contact the parents when all of the ecological inventories and the adaptive behavior assessment are complete to seek their guidance again in including or excluding certain skills in assessment. It will also be important to obtain parental permission for any assessment that involves some risk to the student (e.g., assessment of street crossing or of being alone in public).

Consideration of Societal Values

Besides preferences, there are also some general societal values that can guide prioritization. For example, most people value health, economic self-

Client's name: _____
Week of: _____

Responses

5—Expresses obvious pleasure verbally and/or by nonverbal participation (e.g., smiles, tries task)

4—Some interest as described above (e.g., brief, obvious pleasure, stays near task but doesn't try it)

3—Neutral; complies as directed by teacher

2—Some disinterest; complies with most but not all directions; verbal or non-verbal expressions of displeasure (e.g., frowns, pulls hands away)

1—Strong dislike; crying, tantrums, self-abuse, verbal objection

Times	Activity	Days						Comments

Figure 6. Preference assessment.

sufficiency, and interpersonal relationships. Skills that will enhance any of these general benefits to the student may warrant further consideration.

In considering societal values, the teacher may wish to take into account the principle of normalization. This principle, which was described in Chapter 1, can be stated as the concept that people with handicaps should have the same opportunities as people without handicaps. Thus, the values and opportunities of the general society are considered. Wolfensberger (1972) notes that a true application of normalization also requires society to adapt to differences of individuals so that all people can be accommodated in its opportunities. Thus, the teacher must consider the careful balance between changing a student to conform to societal expectations and changing society to be tolerant of people's differences.

To reflect on the difference between "the norm" and "normal" behavior, consider a man's choice to wear a beard or a woman's choice not to shave her legs. Most men and women in American society are clean-shaven. However, individual choices not to shave are typically viewed as individual preference. Does the teacher help the student learn to be clean-shaven like most men and women, or tolerate individual difference? The teacher might consider that having a clean-shaven appearance, like that of most adults, might enhance the student's acceptance by his or her peer group. However, if the student shows a clear dislike for shaving or preference for a beard, the teacher may wish to respect this choice.

Sometimes, the behavior of "the norm" is not the best to teach individuals because it conflicts with other values such as health or safety. For example, most people do not wear seat belts even though statistics show that they increase the chances of survival in an accident. Thus, the teacher may teach seat belt use because of the consideration for safety, even if it requires providing incentives to overcome the student's dislike for seat belts.

Finally, the characteristics of the person with handicaps may be different from, but preferable to, that of "the norm," or may be unchangeable. In this case, the teacher may advocate for a change in society. Most people do not use wheelchairs, but discrimination against their use is inconsistent with equality of opportunity for people with handicaps. Also, teachers and friends may find that a student smiles or greets others with more enthusiasm than most people do, but that this friendliness might be viewed positively as an example for other people to emulate. A student's stereotypic behavior may be different from that of most people (e.g., hand posturing versus wiggling one's foot or tapping a pencil) but be more difficult to eliminate than to tolerate. Thus, the teacher needs to consider societal values in establishing priorities "with a grain of salt."

Consideration of the Preferences of Significant Others

One of the considerations that can help the teacher decide whether to tolerate a student's differences or teach new alternatives is the preference or requirement of significant people who will make decisions about a student's opportunities. For example, what behaviors will not be tolerated by a potential employer? What skill deficiencies will make a student ineligible for a preferred group home? What behaviors will result in naturally occurring aversive consequences such as being arrested or asked to leave most public facilities?

This information is usually obtained when the teacher conducts the ecological inventories of the settings that are targeted for the curriculum plan. The teacher can review these inventories to identify skills that potential employers, group home directors, store managers, and so on identify as essential, or behaviors that are listed as intolerable by these significant people in the target settings.

Consideration of Skill Utility and Practical Issues

Finally, the teacher may consider the issue of the general utility of the skill. Can the skill be used across activities? Does it have long-term or preferably, lifelong utility? Is it an efficient skill for independent performance in the activity? Does the skill help the student compensate for physical or sensory deficits? White (1980) notes that it is not the specific responses to perform the activity that matter, but the "critical effect" of making a series of responses. There are many behaviors that can achieve the same effect. The teacher will want to find the behaviors that are the most efficient means for the student to obtain the desired end.

Besides skill utility, the teacher may also wish to consider the practical issue of time constraints for assessment and instruction. Time for teachers is like a paycheck. If not budgeted, there may not be enough time for meeting priorities. It sometimes helps a teacher's time management to determine how many skills he or she can feasibly teach per week. By comparing this number of skills to be taught with the amount of available time, the teacher will know how many hours to budget per student and skill. From this planning, the teacher can decide approximately how many skills are feasible for the annual plan and curriculum chart. In setting these necessary limits, the teacher can consider each student's priorities, ways to economize instruction (e.g., selecting skills that can be taught to several students provides opportunities for group instruction), and the balance of assessment across areas (e.g., giving equal emphasis to all life domains versus prioritizing one domain, like vocational training.) The teachers whose case studies inspired this book developed annual plans of from 6 to 14 skills. Most of the teachers found that it was not feasible to teach more than 6 skills per day per student, but that more skills could be included by identifying those that the student could perform with minimal help, and using rotating schedules of instruction. The curriculum charts in Appendix A at the end of this book indicate the number of skills that these teachers selected from their initial assessment.

Consideration of Partial Participation

Along with other guidelines for prioritization, the concept of partial participation deserves consideration. Brown, Branston-McLean et al. (1979) noted that a student who cannot wholly achieve independence in an activity might still accomplish mastery of some skills within the activity. Skills that cannot be performed independently might be adapted for partial participation by: (a) providing adult or peer assistance, (b) simplifying the activity to enhance independent performance, or (c) adapting the environment (e.g., using a bar instead of a doorknob on doors).

In assessment, the teacher will want to find out how much of the activity the student can perform. If sensory and physical deficits do not preclude making the responses required by the activity, full participation should be considered for instruction. If such deficiencies exist, or if the person is an older adult with few or no responses required by the activity, some adaptation may be necessary. Partial participation fits the goal of normalization if one considers that most adults are both independent and *interdependent*. Most adults depend on friends, family, and environmental aids to some extent to perform their daily routines (e.g., a spouse or roommate prepares dinner; a note is taped to the refrigerator as a reminder of an important errand). Expectations for people with severe handicaps should include obtaining the skills to live in harmony with others in their environments rather than doing everything alone. Thus, by considering interdependence, some skills might be selected for the student's companions (e.g., judgment about street-crossing at busy intersections), whereas others will be selected to be taught for independence (e.g., walking and crossing without guidance).

Using Considerations to Rank Skills for Assessment/Instruction

Considering these priorities together can be facilitated by the use of some type of prioritization checklist. Examples of rating priorities have been given by Gaylord-Ross and Holvoet (1985) and by Wuerch and Voeltz (1982). An illustration of this rating is shown in Figure 7.

PLANNING AND CONDUCTING ASSESSMENT OF THE STUDENT

Through the broad skill checklists and surveys, much useful information on the student's current skills and deficiencies can be obtained. However, the comprehensive educational assessment will not be complete without direct observation and testing of the student to develop a relevant and realistic curriculum plan. From the summary of skills to be assessed, the teacher will have identified areas that require further evaluation to pinpoint specific curriculum goals. For example, an adaptive behavior scale might indicate that the student has few

Student's name: _____   Date: _____
Teacher's name: _____

Rate how well each potential skill matches the stated priorities.
Scoring:
  5 All of the time
  4 Most of the time
  3 Frequently
  2 Some of the time
  1 Occasionally
  0 Not applicable

Skills

Priorities								
1. Student preference								
2. Caregiver preference								
3. Societal value								
4. Preference of significant other								
5. Skill utility								
6. Permits partial participation								
Total points								

Figure 7. Sample chart for establishing priorities for assessment and the curriculum.

skills in communication. The teacher will want to gather more information to identify specific communication goals for the curriculum plan. Not every skill area on the curriculum plan need be derived from direct assessment of the student. For some skills, like housekeeping, the parent's survey and ecological inventory may provide adequate information to set curriculum goals. Rather, the direct assessment is used for areas where indirect assessment has been inadequate because: (a) information obtained is not specific enough, (b) conflicting information is obtained, or (c) the student has not had the opportunity to perform the activity, so the skill level is unknown. To obtain this needed information, the teacher might use checklists, task analytic assessment, frequency counts, or repeated-trial assessment.

Many students do not perform well when subjected to prolonged periods of testing and observation. This can be especially true for a student with severe handicaps. The best way to conduct direct, initial assessment of students with severe handicaps is to schedule these tests and observations across several days and weeks. This scheduling can permit the teacher to use the natural opportunities to assess skill performance. The assessment can also be interspersed with instruction to avoid subjecting the student to prolonged sessions in which he or she is asked to make unfamiliar or difficult responses. However, using this approach to assessment requires that this part of the comprehensive educational assessment be conducted after the student has entered the placement, and that the teacher be able to balance a schedule of one student's comprehensive assessment with the entire class's ongoing assessment and instruction. The alternative is for a specialist to conduct this direct assessment in the home and community prior to the student's placement. However, many school districts will not have the resources for this latter option.

Since one of the most difficult aspects of this initial assessment is scheduling the observations and testing, an example of a schedule is shown in Figure 8. As the figure indicates, the teacher plans to include the student in existing instructional groups until that student's curriculum is complete. Individual instructional time for this student is used for testing. Observations are conducted across the day as the opportunities arise. The teacher keeps the checklists that he or she has developed to assess the student close by so that skills can be recorded as they are observed.

Skill Checklists

One of the simplest procedures for direct assessment is to develop a checklist of the skills suggested by the ecological inventories, and observe performance across time. This can be especially useful if the comprehensive educational assessment is being conducted by a teacher who has the student in his or her program and can observe the student on a daily basis. While the format of the checklist may be similar to those found on adaptive behavior scales, the specificity of skills will typically be much more detailed. Throughout this book, examples of skill checklists used in initial assessment are provided (e.g., shopping checklist in Chapter 6; social skills checklist in Chapter 8).

To develop a skill checklist, the teacher first needs to have adequate knowledge of the activity or skill area to be observed. This may be obtained by reviewing the ecological inventories and resources that describe skills in these areas. Chapters 5–8 provide information and references in each domain and

Student: Nat   Teacher: Ms. N.

| Time | Activity | Assignment | | |
		Ms. N.	Ms. M.	Independent
8:00	Greetings; find classroom; belongings	D and Nat*	J, K, A	S
8:30	Restroom	Nat**	D, A	S, J, K
9:00	Picture schedule	S, D, A	J, K, Nat	
9:30	Snack preparation¹	J, K, Nat*	D, A, S	
10:00	Snack	Nat**	J, K, D	A, S
10:30	Dress for PE	S, D, A	J, K, Nat	
11:00	Gymnasium—PE	D, Nat*	A, K, S	J w/Mr. S.
11:30	Restroom	D, A, Nat	(Break)	S, J, K
12:00	Lunch	D, J, Nat*	A, K	S
12:30	Clean up	(Break)	J, A, S, Nat	K, D
1:00	Mainstreaming for recess and recreation	Nat**, D, A	J, K, S	
2:00	Restroom	D, A, Nat	(Group game)	
2:30	Belongings/ good-bye/walk to bus	Nat**, J	D, A, K	S
3:00	Student's day ends			

¹Schedule for 9:30 to 11:30:
   Monday—Classroom and gym as shown
   Tuesday—Purchase snack at convenience store (store varies)
   Wednesday—Classroom and gym as shown
   Thursday—Purchase snack at convenience store
   Friday—Rotate for once per month: visit physician; generalization for classroom activities in a home (e.g., snack prep, chores); shopping mall; fast food restaurant

Figure 8. A schedule for assessing a recently placed student. Assessment is scheduled throughout the day and conducted by the teacher. In this example, Nat is a student being assessed in a young elementary age classroom. (Other students are indicated by the first initials of their names.) Each student is assigned to the teacher (Ms. N.), to the aide (Ms. M.), or to independent work throughout the day. One asterisk indicates when Ms. N. will observe Nat and record his response(s) on a checklist. Two asterisks indicate when Ms. N. will directly test Nat on a scheduled activity. The schedule below the chart provides different activities for the 9:30–11:30 period each day.

related skill area to help the teacher develop these checklists. Second, the teacher must decide the format for the checklist. The simplest format is to list the skills. A more involved organization is to list skills in order of difficulty. This latter approach requires obtaining information on difficulty levels, which often is not possible without extensive research. Finally, the teacher must decide how responses will be scored. The teacher may simply note whether the skill is or is not performed. On other checklists, further distinctions might be made for coding responses by: (a) level of assistance needed to perform the response, (b) frequency of the response, or (c) consistency of performance (e.g., some of the time, all of the time).

Other Observational Assessments Throughout this book, skill checklists are recommended to guide observations of skills. These checklists are especially helpful to organize observations of rarely performed skills (e.g., social response to meeting a new person). The teacher can keep the checklist nearby and note performance whenever this infrequent opportunity arises in the weeks in which the assessment is conducted.

For other behaviors to be observed, occurrence is more frequent. The teacher may also be interested in the situations in which these frequent behaviors occur. To organize observations of frequent behaviors, the teacher can use several procedures. Sometimes, the teacher will use verbatim recording of every response (e.g., language samples; see Chapter 7), or the teacher may make anecdotal notes on the behavior and the situation in which it occurs (e.g., the ABC analysis described in Chapter 8). Or, the teacher may choose instead to make anecdotal notes while observing a student perform a routine (e.g., preparing materials to go home) that later will be reviewed to develop more specific assessment (e.g., task analytic). If the teacher is able to define a specific behavior to be observed, a frequency count of its occurrence across the day or periods of the day may also be used.

Testing the Student

When the target skills to be assessed are not observed in daily use, the teacher may want to test the student to see if these skills can be elicited in a highly structured situation. For example, if a student does not use a communication board in daily use, the teacher cannot tell if the student is unable to use the board or does not know when to use the board. By giving repeated opportunities to use the board in a highly structured testing situation, the teacher can identify whether the student needs instruction in generalization across situations, or instruction in use of the board itself, as well as generalization. To test the student, the teacher can use: (a) repeated opportunities to perform a discrete response that are given together or distributed across the day (repeated trials), or (b) task analytic assessment of a chain of responses. These two test procedures are described in detail in Chapter 3 since they are often used for ongoing assessment. When adapted to initial assessment, a broader list of responses may be targeted for either the repeated opportunities or the task analytic assessment, since at this stage of student assessment the teacher seeks to pinpoint the student's current repertoire of skills. In ongoing assessment, these tests will be made specific to the objectives of instruction (i.e., the specific skill the student is to learn).

DEVELOPING THE CURRICULUM CHART: A CASE STUDY

The organization of this comprehensive educational assessment and the preparation of the curriculum chart can be illustrated by Al's case study. Mr. A. had taught Al for a year when he conducted this assessment. Mr. A. thought that this reevaluation was critical at this time because Al only had 3 more years of school before he turned 21. Therefore, the purpose of Al's assessment was to identify skills needed for his future adult environments. Mr. A. reviewed Al's prior records. Al's previous IEPs had been organized to include life skills, but had underemphasized vocational training. A specialist's review of Al's ongoing progress that had been written the year prior to Mr. A.'s assessment recommended that vocational training and social skills be targeted as Al's highest priorities for his last years of school. Other relevant reports indicated the parents' satisfaction with Al's program. When Al's IEP first reflected a life skills approach, his parents noted their pleasure that this new focus had been taken. Al also had a recent physical examination that indicated the need for further evaluation of Al's potential need for glasses.

After reviewing Al's records, Mr. A. contacted the parents to discuss the need to plan for Al's future. The parents were especially concerned about Al's job options. They had not considered Al living anywhere except with them, but were interested in knowing more about area group homes. Mr. A. also completed the classroom version of the Vineland Adaptive Behavior Scales by using his knowledge of Al (i.e., he didn't test Al). Al had most of the skills in the motor and daily living skills domains of the Vineland. His poorest performance was in the area of communication and socialization. This information, along with the specialist's observation, led Mr. A. to make special note of the need for social skills assessment of Al. Mr. A. did not find the Vineland adequate for pinpointing Al's vocational needs.

Mr. A. talked with Al about his interests and preferences, especially as they related to his future vocation. Al stated a strong preference to work in a bowling alley. Mr. A. decided that this preference should be pursued in this comprehensive assessment.

Mr. A. identified the following environments for Al's current and future activities: (a) his family's home, (b) a group home, (c) the streets in his neighborhood and town (walking), (d) the local public bus, (e) fast food restaurants, (f) the bowling alley, (g) a discount department store that was in the shopping center popular with his family and the area group homes, (h) a video arcade, (i) a park with a fishing stream, (j) the family's church, and (k) the sites cleaned by a supportive mobile work crew (in case he lost or did not get the bowling alley job). He then conducted ecological inventories to identify skills for these sites through interviews and observations in Al's home and the group home. Mr. A. had worked with Al in the shopping center, fast food restaurant, and video arcade and thought he had adequate information on the requirements of those sites. He also reviewed a published inventory of skills expected by employers (Rusch, 1983) to identify potential skills. From this published inventory, he designed a specific interview for the bowling alley manager. This interview included both job and job-related skills and a checklist of social behaviors (since social skills were a particular deficiency for Al).

From these inventories and the adaptive behavior assessment, Mr. A. was prepared to plan Al's direct assessment. Mr. A. had generated a list of direct assessments that would require several weeks to complete (see Table 1). However, he felt that this list would help him identify Al's curriculum for adult living. His next step was to schedule times in his day across the next month to test or observe Al in each activity listed. Since Mr. A. already gave each student some one-to-one instruction, as well as group instruction, he assigned these times for testing and other times for observations. He then developed a data sheet and instructions for each of the informal tests to be used. These tests would be included with Al's case study to clarify how the information on his current performance was obtained. Over the next month, Mr. A. conducted the specified assessments. Once he had completed them, he again reviewed the guidelines for priorities to set specific goals for the next 3 years. He then wrote the curriculum chart and distinguished items for the first year. This chart and the case study were shared with the parents. With their recommended revisions, Mr. A. then finalized the chart and wrote Al's IEP. (Al's curriculum chart is shown in Appendix A on page 257. For each case study, a similar procedure was followed. Examples of assessment for each case can be found throughout this book. The curriculum chart that was designed for each student is included in Appendix A.)

WRITING OBJECTIVES FOR THE FIRST YEAR PLAN

Once the curriculum chart has been developed, the teacher is ready to write the objectives for the first year's plan. The quality of these written objectives can influence both ongoing assessment and instructional decisions about mastery. In writing the objectives, the teacher has two primary goals. First, the objective must be stated in observable and measurable terms if ongoing assessment is to be matched to it. Second, the objective must specify conditions and criteria for performance that reflect the normalized, independent performance expected. Currently, many IEPS include objectives that are too vague to meet either of these criteria. In a statewide review of IEPs, Browder, Lentz, Knoster, and Wilansky (1984) discovered that most objectives contained on IEPs for students with severe handicaps were so vague that it was difficult to tell what functional skill was being targeted or how assessment would be designed.

To write the objective so that it clearly relates to functional activities of daily living, the teacher will want to specify the conditions of these settings. If the typical conditions are setting cues (e.g., entering a restaurant), the teacher would not want the objective to be a response to artificial teacher cues (e.g.,

Table 1. Planning for direct assessment of Al

More information needed for	How to assess

Skills for the home

Housekeeping
  Meal preparation — Skill checklist
  Dishwashing — Task analysis
  Laundry skills — Task analysis

Personal maintenance
  Shaving — Task analysis
  Laundry skills — Task analysis
  Grooming (hair) — Task analysis
  Emergencies — Repeated trials ("What if . . .")

Recreation/socialization
(information adequate from parent interview)

Skills for the community

Vocational
  Duration on task — Time duration
  Social skills — Observe–checklist (some simulation needed)
  Time management — Observe–checklist
  Break time behavior — Observe–checklist
  Custodial skills — Task analyses

Other community
  Being alone in public — Observe–checklist
  City bus, varied routes — Task analysis
  Purchase groceries, clothes, and so on from list — Task analysis

Recreational
(information adequate from parent interview)

Related skills for cross-planning

Communication
  Social conversation — Observe–language sample

Motor
  Fitness — Fitness test

Academics
  (information adequate from previous instruction)

Social
  (included with vocational)

Interfering behavior
  (information adequate from ongoing assessment)

"When the teacher says 'Buy a hamburger' "). Criteria also should match normal expectations. The criteria of "90%" has become popular for objectives because it suggests excellent, but not perfect, performance. However, a criterion of 90% may not be comparable to social norms for life skills. Some skills (e.g., use of the toilet) must be correctly performed every time to meet age expectations. Other skills (e.g., social responses) can have much lower criteria and fall within normalized performance. Thus, when the teacher gathers information on the need for a skill in a target setting, information also should be obtained on the criteria. For example, how frequently do 8-year-olds greet other children and adults? How often do adults forget to take their lunch to work? How long do employees pause between assignments?

Writing the objective so that assessment can be matched to it requires careful wording. Cole and Cole (1981) recommend using the letters A, B, C, and D to remember the components of the objective to be included:

> A—represents the *audience* that is to perform the objective. More specifically, who will be doing the learning?
> B—represents the desired *behavior* that will be exhibited by the child. The behavior should be stated in clear, observable terms.
> C—represents the *conditions* under which the audience will perform the desired behavior. This segment is sometimes called the "given," and represents the setting in which the child will perform the learning task. The resources needed are also commonly stated as a condition.
> D—represents the *degree of mastery* required to meet an acceptable level of performance on the objective. Mastery statements are frequently stated with one or both of the following components: the number or percentage correct and the specific time limitations required for the completion of the objective by the child. (p. 83)

Here is an example of an objective written in this manner for Al:

> Al (Audience) will clean the sink (Behavior) of the school or bowling alley when cued by his picture schedule (Condition) within 5 minutes of the time shown on the schedule to begin and end the task, and no dirt or cleanser residue can be seen on the sink (Degree of Mastery).

Here are some poor examples adapted from actual IEPs:

1. John will improve balance. (While doing what? Where? What degree of performance will be accepted as improvement?)
2. Jerry will point to his toothbrush. (Under what conditions? For what purpose? Does he only need to point to it, or pick it up to use it?)
3. Cary will tie her shoes—90% correct. (What is 90% of shoetying? Sometimes tied or partially tied? Under what conditions does she need to be able to perform this skill?)
4. Sally will develop her dressing skills. (What specific behavior is Sally to perform? Under what conditions and to what degree?)

SUMMARY

A comprehensive educational assessment can help the teacher chart the course for several years of instruction. Through such assessment, longitudinal services can be developed that lead to the goal of community integration. The approach suggested for the comprehensive plan is most appropriate for initial assessment and reevaluation every 3–5 years. The teacher is the person most likely to have access to the student and the knowledge required to conduct this assessment. This evaluation will not be conducted in prolonged testing sessions, but rather over the course of several days or weeks as natural opportunities to perform skills arise. Specific skills to be assessed are identified through ecological inventories and prioritization. At the end of this process, the teacher has a curriculum chart and an IEP for the first year of this longitudinal plan.

APPENDIX
Adaptive Behavior Scales

Balthazar Scales of Adaptive Behavior
Earl E. Balthazar (1976)
Consulting Psychologist Press, Inc.
577 College Avenue
Palo Alto, California 94306

AAMD Adaptive Behavior Scale
Nadine Lambert, Myra Windmiller, Deborah Tharinger, Linda Cole (1981)
Publishers Test Service
CTB/McGraw-Hill
Del Monte Research Park
Monterey, California 93940

The Callier-Azusa Scale
Robert Stillman (Editor) (1978)
The University of Texas at Dallas
Callier Center for Communication Disorders
1966 Inwood Road
Dallas, Texas 75235

Camelot Behavioral Checklist
Ray W. Foster (1974)
Camelot Behavioral Systems
P.O. Box 3447
Lawrence, Kansas 66044

Comprehensive Test of Adaptive Behavior and *NABC*
Gary L. Adams (1984)
Charles E. Merrill
Columbus, Ohio 43216

The Pyramid Scales
John D. Cove (1984)
PRO-ED
5341 Industrial Oaks Boulevard
Austin, Texas 78735

Scales of Independent Behavior Woodcock-Johnson Psychoeducational Battery: Part Four
Robert H. Bruininks, Richard W. Woodcock, Richard F. Weatherman, Bradley K. Hill (1984)
Developmental Learning Materials
Allen, Texas 75002

Vineland Adaptive Behavior Scales
Sara S. Sparrow, David A. Balls, Domenic V. Cicchetti (1985)
American Guidance Service
Circle Pines, Minnesota 55014-1796

CHAPTER 3

ONGOING ASSESSMENT

Once the initial assessment has been conducted to develop a 3–5 year curriculum chart and the first year's plan, the teacher needs to design procedures to measure each objective on the annual plan. If this measurement is conducted frequently (e.g., daily or several times per week), the teacher can quickly identify areas of progress or lack of progress. Collecting data has little utility if it is not used to make decisions to improve instruction. Thus, ongoing assessment is conducted for *formative* evaluation. That is, objectives are measured throughout the year to evaluate progress and make necessary changes to achieve the desired outcome. Formative evaluation can be contrasted to *summative* evaluation that is conducted after a program has been implemented to judge the final results. When a teacher measures progress, but does not use this information to modify instruction, he or she is implementing summative evaluation. A teacher who only judges results (as opposed to progress) may become discouraged and abandon ongoing data collection because he or she receives no reinforcement from the data to maintain the effort required by data collection. The key to making ongoing data collection worthwhile is learning to "read" the data to improve instructional success. Thus, this chapter and the next (titled "Evaluation of Ongoing Assessment") are critically interrelated. To implement formative evaluation, accurate, valid measurement is needed. This chapter provides guidelines for ongoing assessment. The next chapter suggests ways to reap the investment of ongoing assessment by using the obtained data in instructional planning.

While published instruments are sometimes useful in initial assessment, they are rarely useful for ongoing assessment. Ongoing assessment must correspond to the specific skill to be taught and the specific characteristics of the learner (Deno & Mirkin, 1977). Given these requirements, even published task analyses have limited utility unless modified to match the learner. Thus, ongoing assessment is teacher-made to match the objectives of the individualized plan.

The first chapter of this book describes several assessment models that are used in programs for learners with severe handicaps. The difference between these models becomes especially evident when organizing ongoing assessment. In some classrooms, responses during instruction are recorded and graphed. In others, teachers use "probes," which are observations or tests of performance without instruction. Some teachers measure chains of responding (e.g., task analytic assessment). Others focus on one or a few specific distinct responses. As mentioned above, assessment must be matched to the learner and his or her objectives. The teacher is wise to avoid data collection "fads," and use the best measurement to answer the instructional question. For example, is the teacher concerned with performance of a chain of responses, or with early performance of a new and complex response (e.g., the first symbolic communication)? These two different questions require different types of measurement.

Whichever data collection techniques are utilized, the teacher needs to consider the principles of applied behavior analysis and normalization. The methodology of applied behavior analysis will help the teacher develop accurate and replicable measurement. Normalization will guide the teacher in measuring skills that are needed for the student to participate more fully in the mainstream of society. For example, the instructional objective is written in behavioral terms so that it can be observed and measured. Typically, the frequency of responding is counted. Sometimes, the latency, duration, or rate is also noted. Assessment procedures are then designed to measure functional and generalized use of the skill so that the goal of community integration can be realized.

In this chapter, several methods of measurement of objectives related to community living are described. The first is *task analytic assessment* that measures performance of each response in a chain of responses. Consideration is given to noncritical responses to be taught and assessed in the chain to encourage their functional use (e.g., language during performance of a leisure skill). The second is *repeated trials* or repeated opportunities to make one or more target responses. These opportunities may be presented together or distributed across time. The trials may present the stimuli to make one response (e.g., I want juice), similar responses (e.g., I want juice, I want cookies), or dissimilar but functionally related responses (e.g., asking for juice, grasping cup, throwing paper cup in trash). The third is *time-based assessment* that may build on either of the above procedures by measuring rate, latency, or duration of responding. The fourth is *qualitative assessment* that also builds on the first two by including judgments regarding qualitative aspects of performance (e.g., meets employer's satisfaction).

TASK ANALYTIC ASSESSMENT

One of the most useful procedures for assessing life skills is task analytic assessment. Most daily routines are performed as chains of behavior. For example, preparing for work is a response chain of getting out of bed, showering, dressing, and so on. Even when individual responses are targeted for instruction, the ultimate goal is that these responses occur in chains of behavior in the natural environment. For example, consider the basic motor skills of grasping and releasing objects. These responses would typically be embedded in a chain such as removing clothes from a dryer, washing dishes, brushing teeth, or dressing. The question that a teacher may pose is whether to measure reaching and grasping as one step of a task analysis for brushing teeth, or to measure these responses across different tasks (e.g., brushing teeth, washing dishes), or to measure these responses in isolation of activities but with real materials. While the last option provides the opportunity to observe repeated attempts to reach and grasp, the first two task analytic options help the teacher know if the student can perform these skills in the context of real activities, and thus, may offer better appraisal of functional use of these skills.

Before considering the construction and use of task analyses, it may be helpful to review the conceptualization of this methodology and research in its use. The term "task analysis" has been used to refer to two different sequences of responses. In one conceptualization, a task analysis is a sequence of skills learned en route to mastery of a competence. For example, addition of single digits, of two digits, and so on constitute a sequence of skills that leads to mastery of computation. The second conceptualization of a task analysis is the chain of responses involved in performing some activity (e.g., tying shoes). All the responses in the chained task analysis are performed in a relatively short period of time. Rarely are all the responses in a skill sequence performed together. In this book, the term "task analysis" is used to refer to a chain of responses. The term "skill sequence" is used to refer to responses that are arranged in sequence for mastery of a specific competence.

Often, checklists are used for initial assessment. A *checklist* does not necessarily reflect a skill sequence, but rather may be a list of related skills with no specification of hierarchy. A checklist of skills without a hierarchy is not typically called a task analysis and is simply referred to as a checklist throughout this book.

Daily routines are a set of skills typically performed together in time and may be viewed as "big step" task analyses. The beginning and end of a task analysis are rather arbitrary. For example, a task analysis could be developed for tying a bow, tying shoes, putting shoes on, dressing, or preparing for school in the morning. The last example, preparing for school in the morning, obviously includes many definable subchains of behavior (e.g., toothbrushing, toileting, dressing). For learners with few self-care skills, teaching the entire routine concurrently would not be feasible because of the more than 100 individual responses that would have to be prompted. However, defining the routine may help the teacher organize longitudinal instruction. For ongoing assessment, the task analysis will often need to be highly specific, with steps reflecting one or two motoric responses for measurement to be sensitive to subtle progress.

Task analytic assessment and instruction has often been a component of successful instructional packages to teach life skills (Browder, Hines, McCarthy, & Fees, 1984; Cuvo et al., 1978; Spears, Rusch, York, & Lilly,

1981; Tucker & Berry, 1980). However, there has been little research on the construction of task analyses. Several authors have suggested guidelines for their construction based on extensive experience in their use (e.g., Bellamy, Horner, & Inman, 1979; Sailor & Guess, 1983; Snell, 1983). The little research that does exist provides tenuous conclusions on the importance of using specific responses as steps of the analysis, and defining stimulus control within the chain of behavior (Crist, Walls, & Haught, 1984; Thvedt, Zane, & Walls, 1984). Until further research clarifies ways to design task analyses to achieve better skill acquisition, the process remains a subjective one. The following guidelines are offered to help the teacher design an efficient and effective task analysis based on logic and experience.

Constructing the Task Analysis

An outline for the steps to develop a task analysis and use it for assessment is shown in Table 1.

In constructing the task analysis, the teacher can consider the following points:

1. How effectively and efficiently does the learner currently perform the skill?
2. What is the best way to perform the skill (e.g., safest, most nutritious, hygienic, socially normative, fastest)?
3. What are the most simple motoric responses that can be used to perform the skill effectively?
4. Can these motoric responses be further simplified by the use of adaptations (e.g., jigs, caregiver's arrangement of materials)?
5. How can responses be arranged or modified so that the discriminative stimuli for each response in the chain are clear?
6. Finally, is the end analysis effective? By following the steps, is the activity achieved?

Observing Current Performance   Before writing the task analysis, the teacher may first want to observe the student attempting to perform the task. If the student is told to brush his or her teeth, what happens? This open-ended, initial observation can help the teacher define and build on existing responses. Once the teacher has defined the analysis, it may be difficult to step back and observe the student's way of performing the skills since the analysis supposedly represents the "correct" way. These few minutes of time to observe current performance may provide a beginning list of responses, or an indication that the student has no skill in this area when given the materials and instructions to perform the skill.

Identifying Best Practices   Teachers of students with severe handicaps often find themselves planning instruction for skills for which their own training has been minimal. Life skills instruction requires knowledge of home

Table 1. Steps to task analytic assessment

Step 1. Plan the task analysis.
—Consider the student's current performance.
—Consult resources on the best way to perform the task.
—Identify simple motoric responses.
—Simplify the task further with adaptations.
—Enhance stimulus control.

Step 2. Write the task analysis.
—Write the sequence of steps using action verbs.
—Clarify steps as necessary.
—Try the task following the written steps.
—Write the steps on a data collection sheet.

Step 3. Plan the assessment.
To plan probes:
—Decide how to secure attention, enhance motivation.
—Identify the discriminative stimulus to begin the task.
—Decide the latency for responding.
—Plan how to handle errors.
—Plan how to end the assessment.
—Write these plans and scoring key on data sheet or the instructional plan.

To plan instructional data collection:
—Decide what will be scored.
—Plan when to record data during instruction.
—Write these plans on the data sheet or plan.

Step 4. Conduct the assessment.
—Follow the assessment plan.
—Schedule reliability observations when possible.

economics, industrial trades, nursing, and so forth. Relying on one's own practices may not lead to identifying the safest, most hygienic, or nutritious practice. Consider the example of food preparation. Teachers may choose recipes based on their own preferences and teach them according to their own cooking styles. When these plans are reviewed, it may become evident that: (a) foods selected are not best for the student's dietary needs, (b) the student does not like the menu, (c) the preparation style may not be efficient or safe, and (d) the teacher may omit critical hygienic steps (e.g., food handling and handwashing). The work of Cuvo and his colleagues illustrates well the methods that teachers may use in developing task analyses for skills for which their own training is minimal. For example, Cronin and Cuvo (1979), Cuvo et al. (1981), and Johnson and Cuvo (1981) consulted with a professor of home economics to develop task analyses for cooking, laundry, and mending. To develop an emergency telephone use analysis, Risley and Cuvo (1980) consulted with the telephone company and emergency stations. They also observed nonhandicapped people performing these skills to validate further their task analyses. While the teacher may not have the time for such extensive validation of each task analysis, other sources of information that are readily available might be consulted. For example, the teacher might check a public library for a book on the subject, call the high school teacher with expertise on this subject (e.g., home economics teacher), or keep a file of popular magazine articles and government booklets on various life skills that can be consulted quickly when writing task analyses. The student's caregivers may also have expertise, ideas, and preferences for how certain skills should be performed.

Defining Simple Motoric Responses Bellamy et al. (1979) have described methods to minimize the response difficulties of vocational tasks. Their recommendations have utility across life skills task analyses. They suggest that responses can be simplified by changing the sequence of responding and using response classes. For example, consider the steps required to put on a bra. If the sequence is arranged so that the bra is hooked in front first and then pulled around and up, the hooking response is much simpler than when performed behind the back. As an example of response class training, consider the various ways to assemble a ballpoint pen (vocational task). The simplest might be to hold the base and pick up and put on each piece. This "pick up and put on" response could be taught across the stimuli of the spring, barrel, and so forth. Research by Browder, Shapiro, and Ambrogio (1986) provides an additional clue for defining efficient responses. They observed that performance of a vocational bagging task was slowed by extraneous and inefficient movements. Productivity was improved by teaching the most efficient movements to bag the materials (e.g., moving the hand horizontally from piece to piece rather than returning the hand to the lap after bagging each piece). To apply these ideas for simplifying the motoric response, the teacher might first consider the following:

1. Can an early response be made that stabilizes materials or puts the learner in position for easier execution of the task (e.g., laying clothes on the bed in order to be able to perform dressing while sitting)?
2. Can the requirements for balance be minimized (e.g., put pants on over feet and calves while sitting)?
3. Can some responses that are not critical to the outcome be eliminated (e.g., use presifted flour rather than sifting)?
4. Can responses be sequenced so that the learner moves across a plane in space rather than shifting from area to area (e.g., materials required for the task arranged so that the learner moves his hands from left to right across the table or counter; or the learner dresses from feet to upper torso)?

A second consideration in defining the motoric movements that will be the steps of the task analysis is the degree of specificity for each step. For example, in the task of watering houseplants, the first step might be "Fill the watering can." This "big" step actually includes many motoric responses. By contrast, the first steps could be "Grasp the watering can., Walk to the sink., Grasp cold water knob., Turn knob on., Move can under faucet., Turn knob off." The specificity of each response defined will obviously influence the number of steps in a task analysis. Crist et al. (1984) found some support for using longer task analyses with learners with more severe mental retardation. It would be an overgeneralization to assume that people with severe handicaps need long task analyses for every task. Rather, the teacher will want to match the specificity of the analysis to the learner's current ability to perform the task. The teacher will not want to make steps so specific that they create responses "frozen" in midair while teaching. For example, in putting on a sweater, a step may be pushing the arm through the sleeve. The teacher would not want to define an analysis with "1 inch into sleeve, second inch into sleeve" and so on because this is typically one fluid motion.

Simplifying Responses with Adaptations   Some students will have difficulty with the task because certain motoric responses are not in their repertoire due to physical handicaps or delay in motor development. The teacher may be able to overcome these barriers to independent performance of the task analysis by building in the use of adaptations. For example, an occupational therapist may be able to provide a dressing hook for a learner who cannot reach down to put on his or her pants. The new toothpaste pumps can eliminate the need to screw on and off caps. Velcro tennis shoes eliminate difficult shoetying. Some students' physical impairments are so extensive that the teacher cannot identify or design the technology to overcome the barriers to independent performance of the skill. Brown, Branston-McLean et al. (1979) have advocated that when such handicaps exist, the teacher should target partial participation as a goal for the activity. When the goal is partial participation, the teacher can define the task analysis to enable the student to perform as many of the responses in the chain as is feasible and practical in daily living. An example of a task analysis based on partial participation is shown later in this chapter (see Figure 4).

Enhancing Stimulus Control   In performing a chain of responses, some stimuli set the occasion for the chain to be performed. Then, each response in the chain sets the occasion for the next response to be performed. It is unclear whether the response itself becomes the discriminative stimulus to perform the next response, or whether changes in the environment created by a response set the occasion for the next response (Sulzer-Azaroff & Mayer, 1977; Thvedt et al., 1984). Defining how each response cues the next response may minimize the teacher-delivered prompts in instruction. To do this, the teacher needs to define what the discriminative stimulus is for each response in the chain. This is well illustrated and described by Bellamy et al. (1979). An example of a task analysis with defined stimuli for each step is shown in Figure 1. Defining responses to enhance stimulus control can be a challenging procedure. However, some of the ideas that teachers may consider in trying to enhance stimulus control are:

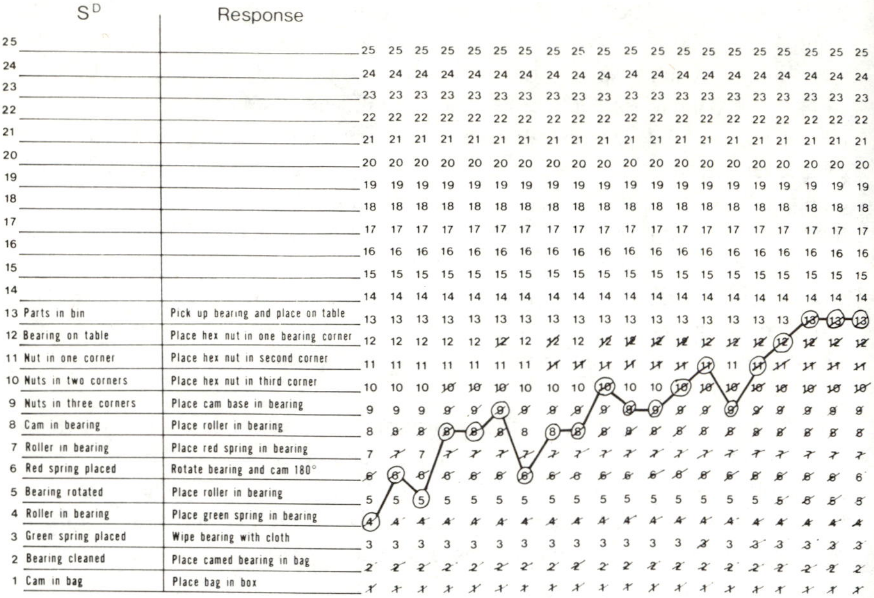

Figure 1. A task analysis data sheet indicating task acquisitions across 20 training probes. Slashes indicate correct responses on a step. Circles show total number correct. (From Bellamy, G. T., Horner, R. H., & Inman, D. P. [1979]. *Vocational habilitation of severely retarded adults*. Baltimore: University Park Press; used with permission.)

1. Can a response be introduced early in the chain that sets up materials to serve as cues for what comes next (e.g., when clearing the table, lining up the dishes by glasses, silverware, plates, and pots to cue the order for washing or loading the dishwasher)?

2. Can the responses be sequenced so that a distinctive visual or auditory effect is created that cues the next response (e.g., loading glasses in the dishwasher from back to front by rows so that one glass is a cue for where the next glass belongs)?

3. Can the movement of the chain of responses be defined so that the learner moves toward the next response (e.g., One way to bathe is to soap a sponge or wash cloth well, to scrub from face to toes, rinse the cloth, and rinse from face to toes. Contrast this to soaping the cloth, washing the face, rinsing the face, soaping the cloth, and needing to remember to move to the neck after soaping again)?

Writing the Task Analysis Based on This Planning The ideas for planning task analyses serve as a resource to improve, as well as develop, task analyses. The teacher need not try to develop the perfect task analysis, but rather should keep in mind the guidelines suggested to make each task analysis the best possible, given time and logistic constraints. When this planning has been done, the teacher is ready to define the responses in the chain that will be the task analysis. To do so, the teacher will:

1. State each response as an observable behavior
2. Write the stated behavior beginning with an action verb stated in the second person (e.g., "Grasp the waistband." "Turn on the water.")
3. Write the responses in the order that they are to be performed.
4. Review the list of responses to clarify any that are ambiguous or that have special criteria for performance (e.g., "Grasp the waistband with both hands.")
5. Watch someone perform the task following the steps written to see if doing so results in performance of the activity.
6. Record the steps on a data sheet.

Example of Development of a Task Analysis   The planning and writing of a task analysis can be illustrated by an example from John's case study. The teacher developed a task analysis for John to pour his drink from a thermos during lunch. If not assisted, John would open and pour the drink on the table and on himself. When Ms. M. observed John before writing a task analysis, she noted that he could open the thermos alone but then poured the entire contents downward without aiming toward the cup or judging when the cup was full. She decided to include the response he had mastered of opening the thermos to help define the correct response that should follow. Since John's pouring skills were complicated by his lack of vision and hearing (i.e., he could not see or hear the spill), Ms. M. asked a vision specialist for ideas about the best way to teach John to pour. The vision specialist showed Ms. M. how to place a finger on the inside of the rim of the cup to feel when the liquid filled the cup. Ms. M. next considered how to define the specific motor responses to make them as efficient as possible. By practicing with her eyes closed, she came up with these responses:

Unscrew cup and put on table.
Unscrew lid and put on table.
Put finger inside rim of cup.
Pick up thermos and tilt against rim beside finger.
Pour until liquid touches finger.
Set thermos down.

Ms. M. considered adaptations to simplify these responses. She considered a thermos with a spout that would minimize spilling. However, she decided to try to teach the skill without this adaptation for two reasons. First, John's current thermos looked more typical of the type of thermos used by male adults. Second, John showed a strong preference for his thermos and became concerned on occasions when he did not find it in his lunchbox.

When Ms. M. reviewed the task analysis to consider stimulus control, she noted these natural cues to perform each response:

The open lunchbox already cued the pouring activity for John. No verbal direction to pour would be needed.

John typically unscrewed the cup and lid once he got his thermos out of the box.

Putting the lid down would need to serve as a cue to put his finger in the cup. This seemed like a weak cue.

The finger on the rim also could be used for tactile feedback on when the thermos was on the edge of the cup so he could pour into the cup (i.e., tilt thermos to touch finger).

The feel of the liquid on his finger would be a distinct cue. It could be more distinct if the liquid were very cold or hot (not scalding).

Ms. M. was generally pleased that the responses had clear stimuli except for putting his finger in the cup. She decided to have him move his hand immediately from holding the thermos while unscrewing the lid to the cup without placing his hand on the table or his lap. Now, she was satisfied that she had planned a good task analysis to begin instruction. This is how she wrote the steps.

Stimulus to begin: John wants a drink and takes his thermos out of the lunchbox and sets it on the table.

1. Hold thermos with left hand.
2. Take off the cup.
3. Take off the lid (left hand holding thermos).
4. Move left hand to rim of cup.
5. Put finger of left hand in rim of cup.
6. Tilt thermos (right hand) to touch rim beside finger (correct if no spill).
7. Pour drink until liquid touches finger.
8. Put thermos down before liquid spills over cup.

Ms. M. tried pouring a drink with her eyes closed while a friend read the steps, and was satisfied that the defined chain of behavior worked well for pouring.

Conducting Task Analytic Assessment

Once a well-defined task analysis has been constructed, the teacher can develop the task analytic assessment procedure. To plan this procedure, the teacher can consider several questions:

1. How will attention to the task be secured and maintained? How will the student be motivated to do his or her best?
2. What stimulus should set the occasion to begin the chain of responses?
3. How much time should the student have to begin the task, and how much time should elapse between steps (response latency)?

4. What will the teacher do if the student does not perform a step correctly (incorrect or no response)?
5. How will the assessment end?

Attention and Motivation   One of the challenges of assessment is motivating students to perform to the best of their abilities. Ideally, assessment approximates naturally occurring environmental events. A person who performs a routine like cleaning the house can do so with few to no prompts to attend to the task, or praise for performing well. Sometimes, a teacher may be able to conduct task analytic assessment by watching the student perform the task without interacting with the student. This would obviously be ideal for tasks typically performed without social interaction. However, if the student does not perform the task, the teacher may not know if the student *cannot* do the task or *will not* do the task. Additional motivation may be provided to try to assess performance of the skill in this case. For example, the teacher might praise the student for "working hard." Or, some preferred activity might be scheduled to follow performance of the skill to be tested. In rare instances, every response in the chain might receive reinforcement (e.g., praise) if the teacher wants to determine exactly what the student can do if highly motivated. In research on motivation during testing with students with severe behavior disorders, Handleman, Powers, and Harris (1981) found that providing reinforcement for every response on the test, regardless of whether the response was correct, enabled the tester to evaluate the performance of students who previously would not respond. Some students have serious and high rates of interfering behaviors that make up most of their responding throughout the day. For example, a teacher may be using differential reinforcement of other behavior to decelerate self-injurious behavior. Such reinforcement would typically also be used during testing to obtain the student's best performance (e.g., praising student every minute that she does not bang her head). The use of these contingencies should be exceptions in ongoing assessment if the goal of instruction is for the student to respond given the naturally occurring contingencies available in the environment.

Discriminative Stimulus to Begin Responding   Similar to the goal of assessing students under conditions of natural contingencies, assessment preferably also is conducted with natural cues to begin and continue responding. Often, teachers get into the habit of giving verbal directions for all tasks because students respond to these directives. However, the functional use of many daily living skills requires responding to environmental cues that are not a stated direction. For example, entering the classroom is the natural cue to walk to the closet and take off a coat, not someone saying, "Take off your coat." If a student is still dependent on the teacher's directions to get through daily routines, the teacher may wait for the student to respond to natural cues and then give one verbal prompt to see if the student can perform the task if told to do so even if environmental stimulus control has not yet been achieved.

Response Latency   The teacher must decide how long to wait to determine if the student will begin the task, and how long to wait between steps before providing assistance or ending the assessment. For example, Browder, Hines, et al. (1984) allowed 3–5 seconds to begin responding and to begin each response in the chain.

Incorrect or No Response   A special problem that arises in assessing a chain of responses is that if one response is not made, the rest of the responses in the chain cannot be assessed. The teacher may use several methods to handle the failure to respond correctly prior to the end of the chain of responding. These include the *single opportunity method, the multiple opportunity method,* or a *variation* (Snell, 1983). In the single opportunity method, the teacher ends the assessment as soon as the student fails to respond or to respond correctly in the given latency period (e.g., 5 seconds). Credit is only given for steps performed up to the failure to respond correctly. The rationale for this approach is that often in the natural environment, continuation of the activity is unsafe or impossible if failure to respond correctly occurs (e.g., street crossing, cooking, telephone use). This method requires no teacher intervention, so it has the advantage of allowing the teacher to step back and observe performance under natural conditions. The disadvantage is that the teacher has no idea whether responses that occur later in the chain can be performed correctly.

In a multiple opportunity probe, this teacher waits for the student to perform a step. If the student does not respond, then the teacher performs the step and waits for the next response.

In the multiple opportunity method, the teacher intervenes to perform the step when the student fails to respond. The student is not prompted to respond, but rather the teacher gets materials to the point that the student can continue the chain of responding. This intervention is repeated as necessary until the entire chain has been performed.

In the variation method, certain steps may be omitted if a critical response is not performed; then the teacher skips to a later point in the chain, at which the student can perform a sequence of steps, to continue assessment. Figure 2 illustrates each method of handling the failure to respond correctly during task analytic assessment. The data show how results may differ depending on the teacher's reaction to errors. In the single opportunity method shown in Figure 2, the assessment is ended when the student does not select the correct coins. Obviously, in daily living, failure to select the correct coins precludes using a vending machine. In the multiple opportunity method, the teacher selects the coins and waits for the next response. The student inserts the coins in the wrong place on the machine, so the teacher inserts them. The student does not take the change, so the teacher collects it. Then, the student does not push a selection, so the teacher pushes a selection. The student can reach to the bin and pick up the soda. This multiple opportunity gives the teacher useful information about the

This example shows hypothetical performance of the same student when tested with the three methods for handling errors. In the single opportunity method, the test is stopped after the first error. In the multiple opportunity method, the teacher correctly performs erroneous responses for the student. In the variation method, the teacher does not test steps 4 and 5 if 3 is wrong because these steps are interdependent, but continues testing on step 6.

Response	Single opportunity		Multiple opportunity		Variation	
	S	T	S	T	S	T
1. Approach machine.	+		+		+	
2. Take out wallet.	+		+		+	
3. Select coins.	−	End test	−	Puts coins in S's hand	−	Goes to step 6
4. Insert coins.	−	Not tested	−	Inserts coins	−	Not tested
5. Collect change.	−	Not tested	−	Takes change	−	Not tested
6. Push choice.	−	Not tested	−	Pushes choice	−	Pushes choice
7. Reach to bin.	−	Not tested	+		+	
8. Take out soda.	−	Not tested	+		+	
Total correct	2		4		4	

Figure 2. Examples of methods to handle errors during task analytic assessment. (S = student's responses; T = teacher's responses; + = correct response; − = response not correct)

student's ability to perform the end of the chain. If one step at a time will be trained, the teacher might instruct this student first on step 6, since he can then finish the chain alone. The variation method is shown in the last column of Figure 2. In this variation, a single opportunity is given to perform the money-related steps 3–5, and then the teacher begins assessment again for selecting a choice and getting the soda.

Ending the Assessment   The termination of assessment depends on the teacher's plan for the student's failure to respond. That is, the teacher may end the assessment at the first failure, or at the end of an opportunity to perform each and every step. An alternative that has been used by Cuvo et al. (1981) is to end the assessment after a defined duration for performing the entire task, or after the student communicates that he or she has finished. Some teachers like to acknowledge performance since the student is often aware that he or she has been observed (e.g., by saying "Thank you for trying that alone.").

Example of Task Analytic Assessment   The example of the pouring task can be reviewed to illustrate how task analytic assessment is planned. Figure 3 shows the data sheet with the task analysis and the assessment instructions. Note that no special provisions are needed for motivation. The cue to begin is initiated by John whenever he takes out his thermos during lunch. The teacher allows John only 3 seconds to begin each correct response because John typically will pour the liquid quickly and erroneously. Ms. M. has chosen a single opportunity method for failure to respond correctly for two reasons. First, the natural consequence for an error creates unpleasant lunch conditions for the teacher and John (spilled liquid). Second, Ms. M. will use this natural time to teach the skill also. As soon as John makes an error or fails to respond, she tells him to try it again with her nearby to help.

Variations of Task Analytic Assessment

Probe Data versus Instructional Data   Teachers typically follow one of three patterns of data collection. The first is to collect data only during noninstructional "probes" or tests. The assessment procedure described previously was for noninstructional probes. Some teachers do not use noninstructional probes and only collect data while teaching. This is the second approach. The third option is to use some combination of probes and instructional data as shown in Figure 3. The teacher in Figure 3 probed the first trial and also recorded data on performance on the first and last trials of instruction. Intervening instructional trials were not recorded.

When data are collected on performance during instruction, the teacher may wish to note the level of assistance that the student required to make the response. For example, Figure 3 shows scoring for a prompt hierarchy (e.g., correct without help, correct after gesture, correct other verbal prompt, correct with physical guidance). This type of data can help a teacher note if the student is using less assistance across time to perform the task.

Behavior: __Pour a thermos__   Name: __John__   Mastery: __100%/2 days__

8. Put thermos down.	−	P	V	−	G	G	
7. Pour drink to finger.	−	P	P	−	V	V	
6. Tilt thermos.	−	+	+	−	+	+	
5. Put finger in cup's rim.	−	V	V	−	G	G	
4. Move left hand to cup.	−	P	P	−	P	P	
3. Take off lid.	+	+	+	+	+	+	
2. Take off cup.	+	+	+	+	+	+	
1. Hold thermos left hand.	+	+	+	+	+	+	

Dates: October   4* 4   4 5* 5   5

Probe data

Schedule: First attempt to pour at lunch on Monday
Attention/motivation: No special procedures
Discriminative stimulus to begin task: John picks up thermos.
Response latency: 3 seconds to begin each step
Error treatment: Single opportunity method
Ending the test: Stop at first error and begin task again with instruction
Scoring: + = correct, − = incorrect

Instructional data

Schedule: First instructional trial each day
Coordination with instruction: Score entire TA after last step
Scoring: + = correct without help, G = correct after gesture (touch or tap),
        V = correct after verbal prompt, P = correct with physical guidance

Figure 3.   Example of task analytic assessment. (* = probes)

There are advantages to collecting instructional data just as there are advantages to collecting probe data. Probes obviously provide an opportunity to observe the student perform the task with natural cues and consequences and minimal teacher interaction. The first advantage of collecting data during instruction is that it may help the teacher self-monitor the accuracy of his or her own performance (e.g., was a prompt given when not required?). A second advantage is that instructional data can help teachers make decisions about prompt fading. Such data are especially important in using a procedure such as time delay, when specific fading criteria are used (Snell & Gast, 1981). For example, if the level of delay will be increased with three prompted correct responses, data are needed as a record of when these responses have occurred. Third, instructional data provide documentation of the investment of teaching that has been made for a given skill.

Despite these advantages, some teachers find data collection during teaching to have several disadvantages. A major disadvantage is that data collection can disrupt instruction by requiring the teacher to have his or her hands in two places at once. The teacher may minimize this problem by waiting until the end of the task analysis to record data. However, the teacher then may have difficulty remembering performance of early responses in the chain. Rarely does a teacher need to collect data on every trial of instruction for every student to make instructional decisions. Also, task analytic assessment of instructional prompts while teaching in community settings may be difficult or impossible.

Given these advantages and disadvantages, the teacher needs to decide how much "teach" versus "test" data are needed. The guidelines for evaluation of data given in the next chapter may help the teacher decide how much data are enough.

Partial Participation   For some students, performance of an entire activity chain is impossible given their physical handicaps and our current limitations in technology. For such students, caregiver assistance is often an ongoing reality. Given this reality, the teacher may design the task analysis to be interactive with a caregiver. Responses are defined for the student to participate in the task to the fullest extent possible so that he or she is an active, rather than passive, participant (Brown, Branston-McLean, et al., 1979). An example of an interactive chain of responding is shown in Figure 4. Both the teacher's and student's responses are defined and sequenced for the task analysis.

Community-Based Assessment   When task analytic assessment is conducted in the community, the teacher must be concerned with managing students in the uncertainties and confusion of public settings, and with public reaction to data collection. Obviously, the teacher will need simple data collection procedures for public settings. Ideas for collecting data in public are described in detail in Chapter 6. For task analytic assessment, one simple

If partial participation is the goal, the teacher performs some steps and the student performs others.

adaptation is to assess only one or a few target responses in the chain during each outing. Figure 5 shows a potential order for assessment of the responses in street crossing. The teacher might use a notepad or clicker to count each street on which the target responses are made correctly by the student.

Inclusion of Related Skills Task analytic assessment has traditionally included the responses that are critical to the performance of the activity. However, related skills such as communication or academics are often performed by nonhandicapped people in combination with other activities in daily routines. Some teachers define and include noncritical steps in the task analysis because they enrich a student's development of communication, social, motor, or academic skills. By including them in the context of a chain of behavior, the teacher may help the student discriminate the appropriate context for the use of the skill. For example, a teacher may include communication and social skills in a task analysis for playing a game with a peer. Even though the game could be played without making these noncritical responses, most nonhandicapped people do communicate and socialize while playing games. Figure 6 provides an example of a task analysis that has been expanded to include related skills.

Chaining Teachers will sometimes choose to teach one or a cluster of steps in the task analysis at a time, rather than the entire chain of behavior. When the target step or steps have been mastered, the teacher targets the next step or cluster of steps for instruction. (For a further description of chaining, the

Task:	Tape recorder use with flipper switch and Yes/No tape choice		Week of:	4/8–4/12			
Teacher	S^D	Response	4/8	4/9	4/10	4/11	4/12
Asks choice	"Want tape?"	Yes or no signal	+	+	+	+	+
	"Want Grandma's tape?"	Yes or no signal	+	+	+	+	+
	"Want Uncle's tape?"	Yes or no signal	NA	+	+	NA	+
	"Want the music tape?"	Yes or no signal	NA	NA	+	NA	+
Opens tape player	—	—					
Gives student tape	Tape in hand	Place tape in.	–	–	–	–	–
Snaps tape in	—	—					
Shuts cover	Cover clicks.	Push switch on.	+	+	+	+	+
	Tape plays to end.	Push switch off.	–	–	–	–	–
Rewinds tape (repeat sequence)	—	—					

Figure 4.   Example of task analytic assessment designed for partial participation. (+ = correct response; − = incorrect response; NA = not applicable, makes prior choice.) (Adapted from a task analysis designed by Doris Martin for use in her classroom in the Bucks County Intermediate Unit, Pennsylvania, with a student who is blind and has severe spastic quadriplegia.)

reader is referred to Sailor & Guess, 1983; and Snell, 1987.) When using chaining, the teacher may still use task analytic assessment as described to evaluate how much of the chain has been mastered. Or, the teacher may choose only to assess the single response that has been targeted for instruction. When a single response is chosen, the teacher may use repeated-trial assessment or a time-based assessment to note progress across time. These are described next.

REPEATED TRIALS OR OPPORTUNITIES TO RESPOND

In task analytic assessment, the teacher typically assesses performance of the chain of behavior no more than once per session per student. The data collected as a measure of progress in this case are the number of steps performed correctly

Task:	Street crossing—Stop sign only		
S^D		Response	Order for data collection
Stop sign	1.	Stop at curb.	Fourth
Standing	2.	Look both ways.	First
Moving vehicle	3a.	Say "cars."	Second
Says "cars"	4a.	Wait and repeat 2, 3.	Third
No vehicles	3b.	Say "no cars."	Second
Says "No cars"	4b.	Cross the street.	Third

Figure 5. Example of task analytic assessment adapted for use in the community. (This analysis is adapted from the street crossing programs developed at Centennial School. The use of the verbal response "cars" or "no cars" is included to assess if the student has made the discrimination of vehicles approaching the intersection prior to stepping off the curb.)

and independently on the task analysis. Sometimes, the teacher targets a specific response to be acquired alone and later introduced into a chain of behavior. Assessment of this target response is usually based on repeated opportunities to make the response. Evaluation of progress is then based on the number of correct responses per day or session. These opportunities may occur together or across time (massed or space). The opportunities to respond may be given for one specific response or for several responses that are conceptually or functionally related (distributed trials). Sometimes, the opportunities to respond will not be teacher-controlled "trials" but naturally occurring opportunities that are observed. These naturally occurring opportunities may be episodic or nearly continuous (free responding). To help the teacher develop each of these types of repeated trials or opportunities to respond, each will be described with examples.

Before considering each, it is important to review again the necessity of assessing student performance in the naturally occurring events of daily activities. If a student is able to make a response 9 times out of 10 opportunities, but cannot make it once when required to do so in daily living, the skill has not been mastered. It is also significant that comparative research suggests that distributed trials and task analytic instruction may be more effective ways to schedule instruction than massed-trial instruction (Kayser, Billingsley, & Neel, 1986; Mulligan, Lacy, & Guess, 1982). Repeated-trial assessment can be a convenient way to assess whether or not a response is emerging, but cannot substitute for assessment of the student's ability to make the response in a functional context.

Developing and Implementing Repeated-Opportunity Assessment

The teacher may follow several guidelines in developing repeated-opportunity assessment. These are:

1. The teacher selects either a single response, response class, stimulus class, or skill cluster to assess.

Behavior: __Play "Cross 4"__   Name: __Nat__   Mastery: 100%/2 days

	100																							
	90																							
	80																							
	70																							
14. Close box.		−	−	−	−	−																		
13. Put board away.	60	−	−	−	−	−																		
12. Put chips away.		−	−	−	−	−																		
*11. Clap when winner.	50	−	−	−	−	−																		
10. Wait turn.		−	−	−	−	−																		
**9. Insert chip.	40	−	−	−	−	−																		
8. Wait turn.		−	−	−	−	−																		
**7. Insert chip.	30	−	−	−	+	+																		
*6. Tell peer to go first.		−	−	−	−	−																		
5. Give self chips.	20	−	+	+	+	+																		
*4. Give peer chips.		−	−	+	+	+																		
3. Take out stand.	10	−	+	+	+	+																		
2. Open box.		−	−	−	−	−																		
*1. Ask peer to play.	0 %	−	−	−	−																			

Dates: October   4 5 6 7 8

Probe data

Schedule: Wednesday with classroom peer, Friday with nonhandicapped peer
Attention/motivation: Praise for sitting
Discriminative stimulus to begin: Teacher gives game to Nat and peer.
Response latency: 3 seconds to begin each step
Error treatment: Multiple opportunity method
Ending the test: After the last step, put game away.
Scoring: + = correct, − = incorrect or no response

Instructional data

(will not be taken)

Figure 6.   Task analytic assessment that includes related skills. (Asterisks identify the skills that are not essential to this leisure skill but help to enrich the individual's experience.) (*Note:* Data has been summarized as percent correct, not the total number. The total number of steps performed correctly on each day must first be calculated, then converted to a percentage, and then the graph line is drawn. The reader is referred to Chapter 4.)

2.   The teacher defines the response(s) in observable, measurable terms. The criteria for correct responding are made explicit (e.g., does the student have to point with the index finger or just extend the hand toward the desired object?).

3.   The teacher defines the stimuli that set the occasion for the response

(preferably, cues that occur in the natural environment). This step may not be possible for problem behaviors.

4. The teacher decides how opportunities to respond will be scheduled (e.g., massed or spaced trials, teacher initiated or student initiated).
5. The teacher designs a method to record each response.
6. The teacher follows the schedule to assess the response(s).

Alternative Ways to Schedule Repeated Opportunities to Respond

Scheduling Opportunities for One Specific Response Sometimes, in initial instruction of a new and difficult response, the teacher decides to measure that response alone. For example, for a student who does not yet use symbolic communication, the teacher targets a requesting response (e.g., pointing to object desired). The teacher's initial goal is for the student to use the pointing response across materials. One method to assess this response would be to schedule repetitions of presentations of objects in a session and to ask the student, "What do you want?" This repeated-trial assessment provides *massed trials* of opportunities to make the same response. A second method would be for the teacher to present opportunities across the day and ask "What do you want?" This repeated-trial assessment would use *spaced trials* (not occurring together in time) that would also be *distributed* (i.e., many other responses would be made between pointing to objects.)

The teacher might wonder which is the best way to assess a single response like pointing. Massed trials present rapid, repeated opportunities for the teacher to assess, and the student to practice, the response. Trials that are presented throughout the day provide a better picture of functional use of this response and will be preferable for assessing many single responses. Massed trials are never adequate alone since they do not provide information on functional use in other contexts. But, the teacher might note acquisition of a response like pointing earlier in these massed opportunities and thus may consider it worthwhile to use both a quick, massed-trial assessment and generalization assessment across the day. Figure 7 provides an example of a massed-trial assessment and instruction that supplements the functional use of this skill.

Scheduling a Response Class Assessment Sometimes, the goal of instruction is the acquisition of a response class. A response class is a set of differing responses that are made to the same discriminative stimulus. For example, for the discriminative stimulus of the teacher asking "What do you want?" the student's response might be any one of a class of responses that he or she has learned (e.g., apple, sweater, juice, crackers, game, to go outside). Similar to a single response, the teacher may give the opportunities for responding together in time or may schedule them throughout the day. In either case, the opportunities are for the student to make varied responses and thus, each response is distributed across trials (e.g., for a response class assessment, the teacher would not give repeated opportunities to respond "apple"). To

Behavior: <u>Select quarter</u>   Name: <u>John</u>   Mastery: <u>90%/2 days</u>

		1	2	3	4
	10	+	+	+	+
	9	(+)	(+)	+	+
	8	(+)	(+)	(+)	(+)
	7	(+)	(+)	(+)	(+)
	6	(+)	(+)	(+)	(+)
	5	(+)	(+)	(+)	(+)
	4	(+)	(+)	(+)	(+)
	3	(+)	(+)	(+)	(+)
Teach trials	2	(−)	(+)	(+)	(+)
Probe	1	−	−	−	−

Dates: Dec.   1 2 3 4

Probe data

Schedule: Just prior to vending machine use; 10 trials
Probe first trial; teach nine trials.
Attention/motivation: No special procedures on probe; praise during instruction.
Discriminative stimulus: Change purse plus teacher request to "Find two quarters."
Response latency: 10 seconds to find each quarter
Error treatment: Single opportunity method for probe
Present quarter as a model with time delay fading during instruction.
Ending the test: Only probe first trial, then teach.
Scoring: + = correct without help, − = incorrect without help, (+) = correct with model, (−) = incorrect after model

Figure 7. Data collection for repeated-opportunity assessment: An example of assessment of a single response. (*Note:* This assessment and instruction is a supplement to John's instruction in vending machine use that includes coin identification in context of machine use.)

evaluate progress, the teacher would note the number of correct responses. If some specific response or responses did not yet occur, these might be targeted for single response assessment and then reintroduced in the response class assessment. Consider, for example, a student who responds to some opportunities to communicate for juice, crackers, sweater, and so on, but never uses the picture or sign for "game." The student indicates interest in performing the game by reaching for it and whining. The teacher may target repeated opportunities to sign "game" so that the student can master this specific vocabulary item, and evaluate this separately from the student's emerging response to "What want?". Figure 8 provides an example of assessment of a response class in the use of a picture communication wallet.

Scheduling Assessment of a Functionally Related Response Cluster
The Individualized Curriculum Sequencing (ICS) model provides a method for sequencing assessment and instruction by using skill clusters (Guess et al., 1978; Holvoet et al., 1980). Individual target responses are linked together and taught across activities. Responses from traditional skill areas such as motor, language, and self-care that can be functionally related and taught across activities are selected. For example, the skill cluster might be to request an item, use the item, and pass a material to a peer. This cluster might be taught across eating, grooming, and leisure activities. Assessment would also be conducted across these activities during the day. The teacher might describe progress in several ways: (a) number of correct responses across the day, (b) number of correct performances of the cluster across the day, and (c) number of correct performances of each response within the clusters across the day (e.g., number of correct responses for requesting, using items, and passing materials). Figure 9 shows an example of assessment of a response cluster used across activities.

Scheduling Assessment of Student-Initiated Responding: Episodic or Continuous   One of the important, but difficult types of responses to assess is the student-initiated response. For example, the student approaches the teacher and points to an object desired. This may occur while the class is in the grocery store, walking down the sidewalk, preparing to go home, and other occasions when the teacher may not or cannot have the student's data sheet for "pointing." Yet, this may be an important student accomplishment. If the initiation is very infrequent (less than daily), the teacher might note it on the graph of teacher-initiated opportunities with an asterisk under that day's date. If the responses occur throughout the day, the teacher may want to count the number of responses. Keeping a tally might be done by using a simple method such as transferring pennies from pocket to pocket for each occurrence, switching masking tape from sleeve to sleeve, or using a hand-held clicker. There is an obvious limit as to how many such responses a teacher can count across the students in his or her classroom. One or two of the highest priorities in the classroom may be all that are feasible for such counts across the day. Some

Behavior: Use picture wallet to request _____ Name: __Nat__ Mastery: __81%/2 days__

	100																						
	90																						
	80																						
	70																						
	60																						
2:30 Restroom	50 (+) (+) (+)																						
2:00 Drink	(+) (+) (+)																						
1:00 Music	40 (−) (+) (+)																						
12:30 Walk	(+) (+) (+)																						
12:00 Restroom	30 (+) (+) (+)																						
11:30 Food	(+) + +*																						
10:45 Games	20 −* (−) (+)																						
Restroom	(+) (+) (+)																						
10:00 Food	10 (+) (+) (+)																						
9:30 Drink	(+) (+) +																						
8:45 Games	(+) −* +																						

%

Dates: Nov.   6 7 8

Probe data

Schedule: During each break that follows lesson (10 per day)
            Probe one break per day—different break for probe each day.
Attention/motivation: Natural consequence—give item requested
Discriminative stimulus: Display objects and ask "What do you want?"
Response latency: 5 seconds
Error treatment: On probe, if no selection indicated, say "I'm sorry. I'm not sure what you want." Delay presentation of item. In instruction, model use of wallet with time delay fading and give item if imitates model.
Scoring: + = Correct without help, − = incorrect without help, (+) = correct after model, (−) = incorrect after model

Figure 8.   Data collection for repeated-opportunity assessment: An example of a response class assessment. (* = probes)

Behavior: Store/carry belongings Name: Ann Mastery: 100%/2 days

	%	Oct 4*	4	5*	5														
DEPARTURE	100																		
3. Walk to van.	90	−	P	−	M														
2. Carry bag.		−	P	−	P														
1. Grasp bag.	80		M	−	V														
CLEAN-UP	70																		
4. Release bag.		−	V	−	M														
3. Walk to trash can.		−	P	−	V														
2. Carry bag.	60	−	P	+	P														
1. Grasp trashbag.	50	−	M	+	M														
WORK PREP.																			
4. Release box.	40	−	M	−	M														
3. Walk to table.		−	P	−	M														
2. Carry box.	30	−	P	−	P														
1. Grasp box.		+	V	−	+														
ARRIVAL	20																		
4. Release bag.		−	M	−	P														
3. Walk to shelf.	10	−	P	−	P														
2. Carry bag.		−	P	−	P														
1. Grasp bag.		−	P	−	P														

Dates: October 4* 4 5* 5

Conditions

Probe data

Schedule: Four times per day
Attention/motivation: No special procedures
Discriminative stimulus: Allow 2 minutes for Ann to follow others. Then say, "Ann, get (or put away) your things for lunch (or from home)."
Response latency: 30 seconds to begin, 5 minutes to finish
Error treatment: Single opportunity method
Ending the test: End the test when Ann does not begin in 30 seconds, stops responding for one full minute, or after 5 minutes. Then, begin instruction.
Scoring: + = correct, − = incorrect

Instructional data

Schedule: Each instructional trial
Coordination with instruction: Score after teaching each response.
Scoring: + = Correct without help, G = gesture, V = verbal prompt, M = model, P = physical guidance

Figure 9. Data collection for repeated opportunity assessment: An example of assessment of functionally related skills. (* = probes)

opportunities such as a break or independent play might allow more counts for that one period (e.g., of social initiations). Noting that at least one initiation occurred during the day by starring a graph of teacher-initiated opportunities could be feasible for several responses and students. An especially difficult type of response to record is a high-rate problem behavior that occurs throughout the day. An all-day frequency count is sometimes feasible by using a portable method of tallying as previously mentioned. An alternative is to count the frequency within one or more sample time periods during the day. Or, the teacher might use a less precise but practical assessment of occurrence or nonoccurrence in each 15- or 30-minute period. These periods might correspond to instructional sessions, and the tally might be kept on the data sheet for instructed skills. The data to be summarized might be, for example, percent lessons in which self-abuse occurred. This latter approach has the advantage of not only being simple to utilize, but also provides information on the occurrence of problem behavior by specific lesson, which can help the teacher evaluate the relationship between skill acquisition and deceleration of behavior by lesson. Problem behaviors are also amenable to time-based assessment, which is discussed later in this chapter. Figure 10 provides an example of assessment of a student-initiated response.

TIME-BASED ASSESSMENT

When a student is first learning to perform a skill, the teacher will typically use the task analytic or repeated-opportunity assessments previously described. This initial phase of learning is called *acquisition*. After a student acquires the skill, the teacher will write objectives for *extended performance* of the skill to meet normalized criteria for performance (e.g., improved fluency). For example, when a student is learning to prepare a lunch for school or work, the teacher will probably use task analytic assessment of the student's acquisition of this skill. Once the student can perform all the steps of the task analysis, his or her performance may still be too slow for the time constraints of a family's routine. Thus, the teacher would set an objective for extended performance of this skill to meet a normalized time criteria to make is useable in the family setting. Assessment of this extended performance often requires time-based assessment.

This time-based assessment might include measurement of *rate, duration,* or *latency* of responding. For example, in the example given above for lunch preparation, the family's concern is the duration of the task. To measure duration, the teacher can note the time when the student starts and stops the task to determine the total time to complete the task. A stopwatch is a useful tool for time-based assessment. The teacher can simply start the watch when the student begins the task, and stop it when the student completes the task. Rate, which is the number of responses per some unit of time (e.g., number per minute), is

Skill: Initiate conversation by touching arm	Student: Nat

Schedule: Student initiated

Attention/motivation: Natural consequence–social exchange

Discriminative stimulus: Others greet Nat

Response latency: 5 seconds

Error treatment: If whines or grabs, prompt touching

Scoring: Tally number of touches to initiate by transferring penny from right to left pocket

Figure 10. Data collection for repeated-opportunity assessment: An example of assessment of student-initiated responding.

often the concern in vocational assembly work in which placement and pay may be based on rate. To calculate rate, the teacher can set a predetermined time period for the time-based assessment (e.g., 30 minutes) and provide the student with adequate materials to work throughout the time period. At the end of the time, the total number of pieces completed are counted. Then, the number of pieces completed are divided by the number of minutes to calculate rate (i.e., responses per minute). Latency, or time to initiate a response, may also be a concern when the teacher assesses extended performance of an acquired skill. For example, the teacher might provide a picture schedule for the student to perform custodial tasks. The teacher may then measure the number of minutes or seconds from the time the schedule is assigned until the student begins the first task. Figures 11, 12, and 13 show examples of data collected for each of these time-based assessments.

In conducting time-based assessments of extended performance, the teacher is usually observing performance only. To assist the student in meeting the criteria set for the rate, duration, or latency of performance, the teacher might be using instructional procedures such as teaching the student to self-monitor the response or providing consequences based on meeting the time criteria (e.g., if the student cleans the table after lunch in 5 minutes, he or she has 5 minutes of leisure time). However, the teacher typically will not interact with the student during the time-based assessment itself.

Extended performance objectives may also target criteria other than improved fluency. The teacher may set objectives for generalization across materials or settings, or for maintenance of performance as artificial reinforcement and teacher presence is faded. Such objectives can be measured using the time-based, task analytic, or repeated-opportunity methods described. Further discussion of evaluation of these extended performance objectives is provided in the next chapter.

The time-based assessment suggested here relies on the simple use of a clock, watch, or stopwatch, and can be conducted while teaching or assessing other

Student:	John		Behavior:	Stuff envelopes

Student: __John__   Behavior: __Stuff envelopes__

Assessment: Record the time that session begins and ends, and count the
                        number of envelopes stuffed (letter and inserts collated and
                        inserted into envelope).

Date	Session	Time started	Time ended	Number	Rate
2–7	1	9:00	9:30	60	2/min.
	2	9:35	10:00	45	1.8/min.
	3	10:15	10:43	52	1.9/min.
	4	10:45	11:30	67	1.5/min.
	5	12:15	1:05	37	1.4/min.
	6	1:10	1:45	42	1.2/min.

Daily summary:
  Sessions worked: all 6
  Average rate: 1.6
  Average session length: 35 minutes

Comment: Teacher graphs average rate for the day.

Figure 11.   Data collection for time-based assessment—rate.

students in the group. A time-based assessment method that is frequently used
in applied behavior analysis research is interval recording (Sulzer-Azaroff &
Mayer, 1977). In interval recording, a cue tape or other device is used to signal
observers to record occurrence or nonoccurrence of defined target behaviors
within given intervals. These intervals may be as short as 10 seconds, but are
rarely longer than a minute. Two advantages can be derived from using interval
recording. First, agreement between two observers to check the reliability of
assessment can be more easily and accurately determined by comparing
intervals. Second, the interval recording lends itself to time sampling, that is,
recording some estimation of the occurrence of the behavior. For example, the
observer may only record whether the behavior occurs during the time interval
(partial interval), throughout the time interval (whole interval) or at a certain
moment in time (momentary time sampling). Unfortunately, interval recording
is difficult to implement during instruction, and rarely portable for instruction
in community settings. While momentary time sampling is the interval recording procedure that does not require constant observation, it also may not be
adaptable to teaching situations because of the short intervals required to get a
representative sample of the behavior. In research to compare interval lengths,
Lentz (1982) found that 30-second intervals were required to get a momentary
time sample comparable to the actual rate or duration of the response. Obviously, a teacher cannot instruct a group of students and conduct 30-second
interval momentary time sampling. Because of these logistics, this book does
not cover interval recording except for use by supervisors who typically
observe without interaction with students (see Chapter 9).

Behavior: Raise hand for "hello"   Name: __Nat__   Mastery: 2 sec./2 days

Number of seconds latency to raise hand after "Hello"

20	20	20	20	20	20	20	20	20	20	20	20	20	20	20	20	20	20	20	20
19	19	19	19	19	19	19	19	19	19	19	19	19	19	19	19	19	19	19	19
18	18	18	18	18	18	18	18	18	18	18	18	18	18	18	18	18	18	18	18
17	17	17	17	17	17	17	17	17	17	17	17	17	17	17	17	17	17	17	17
16	16	16	16	16	16	16	16	16	16	16	16	16	16	16	16	16	16	16	16
15	15	15	15	15	15	15	15	15	15	15	15	15	15	15	15	15	15	15	15
14	14	14	14	14	14	14	14	14	14	14	14	14	14	14	14	14	14	14	14
13	13	13	13	13	13	13	13	13	13	13	13	13	13	13	13	13	13	13	13
12	12	12	12	12	12	12	12	12	12	12	12	12	12	12	12	12	12	12	12
11	11	11	11	11	11	11	11	11	11	11	11	11	11	11	11	11	11	11	11
10	10	10	10	10	10	10	10	10	10	10	10	10	10	10	10	10	10	10	10
9	9	9	9	9	9	9	9	9	9	9	9	9	9	9	9	9	9	9	9
8	8	8	8	8	8	8	8	8	8	8	8	8	8	8	8	8	8	8	8
7	7	7	7	7	7	7	7	7	7	7	7	7	7	7	7	7	7	7	7
6	6	6	6	6	6	6	6	6	6	6	6	6	6	6	6	6	6	6	6
5	5	5	5	5	5	5	5	5	5	5	5	5	5	5	5	5	5	5	5
4	4	4	4	4	4	4	4	4	4	4	4	4	4	4	4	4	4	4	4
3	3	3	3	3	3	3	3	3	3	3	3	3	3	3	3	3	3	3	3
2	2	2	2	2	2	2	2	2	2	2	2	2	2	2	2	2	2	2	2
1	1	1	1	1	1	1	1	1	1	1	1	1	1	1	1	1	1	1	1
0	0	0	0	0	0	0	0	0	0	0	0	0	0	0	0	0	0	0	0

Dates: Nov.   12 13 14 15 16 19 20 21 22 23 26 27 28 29

Assessment: Time latency with stopwatch; round to nearest second; begin timing from moment someone says "Hi, Nat."

Figure 12.   Example of data collection for time-based assessment—latency.

FURTHER SUPPORT FOR ASSESSMENT: QUALITY AND RELIABILITY

The traditional approach to measurement in applied behavior analysis is to count observable responses. This approach will be the foundation for most ongoing assessment of objectives. However, the teacher may sometimes wish to evaluate the quality of responding to judge criteria for normalized use of a skill. Often, this judgment will be recruited from experts or significant others in the student's life. This qualitative assessment is often in the form of social validation. Social validation was described in detail in Chapter 2 as it relates to skill selection. The same procedures (e.g., peer comparison, expert judgments) are also applicable to the validation of treatment outcomes. For example, the teacher may send the parents a questionnaire to determine if the student's

Behavior: <u>Walk to seat</u>   Student: <u>Ann</u>   Mastery: <u>1'/3 days</u>

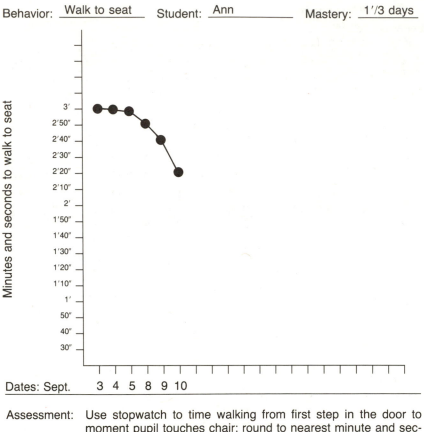

Dates: Sept.   3 4 5 8 9 10

Assessment: Use stopwatch to time walking from first step in the door to moment pupil touches chair; round to nearest minute and seconds; end assessment after 3 minutes if not at chair.

Figure 13.   Example of data collection for time-based assessment—duration.

emerging skills are useable in the home environment. Or, an employer may be asked to rate an employee's performance. These qualitative assessments alone are rarely adequate to evaluate progress. However, they can help the teacher determine if the criteria of performance will be encouraged and/or tolerated by the significant people in the student's environments.

While the social validity of performance is important in evaluating progress, the reliability of the direct assessment of target objectives is also important. When a teacher hopes to see improvement, data may be biased toward change rather than accurately reflecting responses made. Such fluctuations in measurement have been demonstrated in research (Fixsen, Phillips, & Wolf, 1972; Romanczyk, Kent, Diament, & O'Leary, 1973). Reliability checks by a second observer can influence observers to be more consistent in recording (Craighead, Mercatoris, & Bellack, 1974). Unfortunately, scheduling a second observer for assessment in teaching settings can be extremely difficult. The teacher is faced with the dilemma of needing reliable data to make instructional decisions, but not having the means to obtain data on reliability. The compromise in teaching settings is that reliability data will be taken much less frequently than is typical of research. However, even if infrequent, demonstrations of reliability can help teachers make instructional decisions with more confidence that the data evaluated are reliable. In this book, reliability observations are suggested as a role for the supervisor and are described in further detail in Chapter 9. Methods to schedule reliability observations and to calculate coefficients of agreement have been described in detail in other resources (e.g., Kazdin, 1980; Sulzer-Azaroff & Mayer, 1977).

SUMMARY

This chapter has provided guidelines for developing procedures for ongoing assessment. Ongoing assessment enables the teacher to engage in formative evaluation of progress and to make changes in instruction, if necessary, to improve the student's success. Assessment of a student's acquisition of new tasks will typically be conducted as either task analytic or repeated-opportunity assessments.

Task analytic assessment requires planning and writing steps in the chain of responses to perform a task in the most effective and efficient way. Once a well-developed task analysis has been planned, the teacher can follow the steps to assess the student's performance of this chain of responses. During noninstructional probes, the teacher might give the student one opportunity to perform this chain and then end assessment, or several opportunities to begin the chain again after errors. The teacher might also assess performance during instruction by noting the level of assistance needed to perform each step.

Repeated-opportunity assessments may include the teacher's initiation of these opportunities or "trials" in close succession, or distributed across the day. For other behaviors, the teacher may note the frequency of student-initiated responding (e.g., for problem behaviors).

When skills have been acquired, time-based assessment of rate, duration, or latency can help the teacher assess extended performance of skills to meet normalized criteria. While interval recording may be used by supervisors, it rarely will be feasible for implementation by teachers. Reliability checks also are difficult to schedule in teaching settings, but may be provided occasionally by supervisors to evaluate the consistency of measurement.

Sometimes, the teacher may solicit evaluation of the student's quality of performance by asking significant others in the student's environments to rate this performance. Once these ongoing procedures have been developed and implemented, the teacher is ready for the next step of assessment—evaluation to make instructional decisions.

CHAPTER 4

EVALUATION OF ONGOING ASSESSMENT

Comprehensive educational assessment to develop a longitudinal curriculum plan, and ongoing assessment of progress in meeting objectives for 1 year of the plan (e.g., for the IEP) are important phases of assessment (described in Chapters 2 and 3). A third critical phase is the evaluation of the data obtained through ongoing assessment. This phase makes ongoing assessment purposeful by using the data obtained to guide decisions about instruction. For example, if a student's objective is to learn to make a snack, the teacher might conduct task analytic assessment of snack preparation to measure the student's progress across time. However, what if the student does not progress? Will task analytic assessment and instruction be continued indefinitely? Will the teacher conclude that the student cannot learn to make snacks, and terminate instruction? What if progress is unclear because daily performance is highly variable? Should the teacher continue instruction to obtain stable performance? These questions exemplify the need to make decisions about the continuation or revision of instruction, given certain data patterns. This chapter provides guidelines to assist the teacher in this decision-making.

To make these instructional decisions, the teacher needs to collect data on a regular schedule, to summarize the data with a graph, and to consider the data pattern. While the need for planning instructional changes may be obvious when progress does not occur, mastery of an objective also requires changes in instruction. Such changes may involve the introduction of a new skill, or extending performance of the mastered skill to meet the standards for normalized use. In the following sections, suggestions are given for these steps to data-based instructional decisions.

PREPARATION FOR EVALUATION

How Often to Collect Data

The first requirement for making instructional decisions is to collect data on a regular and frequent schedule. This schedule might include assessment of objectives daily, or at least a few times per week. Since data collection must be managed across several students and objectives, teachers may want to set up a schedule for ongoing assessment. Some teachers' data collection will be "probes" or tests of the student's performance without instructional assistance. The summary graph will then be prepared for these conservative measures of unassisted performance. Other teachers who do not use probes will collect data during instruction. Often, the graph will then be prepared based on the number of correct, unprompted responses during instruction. A third alternative is to collect data on some combination of assessment during instruction and during probes indicating unprompted responses during each on a graph. These alternatives were discussed in detail in Chapter 3. It is not necessary to record every student's every response during instruction. The voluminous data created would be difficult to summarize and evaluate systematically. Thus, the teacher will need to plan a schedule for data collection that may include probe and/or instructional data. Figure 1 shows a teacher's data collection sheet for a combination of instructional and probe data. This teacher collects instructional data daily and probe data weekly. Figure 2 shows a teacher's data collection sheet for collecting only instructional data, with teaching trials scheduled throughout the day. Figure 3 provides an example of probe data only. Figure 4 shows how one teacher scheduled data collection for all objectives for all students in a classroom.

How to Summarize Data

Before data can be reviewed, they must be summarized by means of a graph. The type of graph most typically seen in applied behavior analysis research is the equal interval linear graph (see graph in Figure 3). Many teachers find this type of graph easy to construct and review. Resources on applied behavior analysis provide descriptions for the construction of equal interval graphs (e.g., Sanders, 1978; Sulzer-Azaroff & Mayer, 1977). These graphs can be constructed using plain paper, and drawing the ordinate and abscissa (i.e., vertical and horizontal axes) with a pen and ruler, or by using graph paper.

Figure 3 illustrates the use of the equal interval graph to summarize task analytic assessment (probes). In all graphs, the vertical axis (the ordinate) reflects the unit of measurement of the target skill. In Figure 3, the unit of measurement is the "number of steps correct on the task analysis." The horizontal axis, or abscissa, reflects the frequency of measurement. In Figure 3, the frequency is the semi-weekly probe (probes scheduled two times per week). It also is important to give the dates on the horizontal axis for graphs used in making instructional decisions, since the data pattern may be influenced by interruptions in the program (e.g., due to school vacations).

A variation of the equal interval graph that can simplify graphing is to use a "self-graphing" data collection sheet. That is, the graph is made on the data collection sheet itself. This self-graphing approach is shown in Figures 1 and 2. In Figure 1, independent correct responses during instruction are summarized with closed circles on the graph. Probes of performance without assistance are

Behavior: __Open bar-press door__   Name: __Ann__   Mastery: __100% / 2/3 days__

10.	Step clear of door.	V	+	+	V	+	V	+	+	+	+	+	+	+	+	+	+	+
9.	Release door.	M	M	−	M	V	M	M	−	V	+	V	+	+	+	+	+	+
8.	Step forward.	P	P	−	P	M	P	P	−	M	M	M	V	+	+	+	+	+
7.	Release lft. hand	P	V	−	M	M	M	M	−	V	V	V	V	−	V	+	V	V	+
6.	Hold door w/rt. hand.	P	P	−	M	M	M	M	−	M	M	M	V	−	V	V	M	V	−
5.	Release rt. hand.	+	+	−	+	+	+	+	+	+	+	+	+	+	+	+	+	+
4.	Step forward again.	V	M	−	+	+	+	+	+	+	+	+	+	+	+	+	+	+
3.	Step forward.	V	V	−	V	V	V	V	−	+	+	+	+	+	+	+	+	+
2.	Push bar down.	V	V	−	V	V	V	V	−	V	V	V	V	−	+	V	V	+	+
1.	Grasp bar.	P	P	−	P	P	P	P	−	M	P	P	M	−	M	M	M	V	−

%

Dates: September   7 8 9* 10 11 14 15 16* 17 18 21 22 23* 24 25 28 29 30*

Date	Trend	Decision

Figure 1.   An example of instructional and probe data on a combination data collection and graph form. Probes are shown as open circles. (* = probes)

shown with open circles. In Figure 2, the numbers listed are used for both data collection and graphing. The teacher slashes each trial on which the student responded correctly without help. The number of slashes is counted and this number is indicated with a closed circle. The closed circles are connected to form a graph.

Behavior: __Point to choice.__ Name: ___Nat___ Mastery: ___80%/2 days___

100	20 20 20 20 20 20 20 20 20 20 20 20 20 20 20 20 20 20 20 20
90	19 19 19 19 19 19 19 19 19 19 19 19 19 19 19 19 19 19 19 19
	18 18 18 18 18 18 18 18 18 18 18 18 18 18 18 18 18 18 18 18
80	17 17 17 17 17 17 17 17 17 17 17 17 17 17 17 17 17 17 17 17
	16 16 16 16 16 16 16 16 16 16 16 16 16 16 16 16 16 16 16 16
70	15 15 15 15 15 15 15 15 15 15 15 15 15 15 15 15 15 15 15 15
	14 14 14 14 14 14 14 14 14 14 14 14 14 14 14 14 14 14 14 14
60	13 13 13 13 13 13 13 13 13 13 13 13 13 13 13 13 13 13 13 13
	12 12 12 12 12 12 12 12 12 12 12 12 12 12 12 12 12 12 12 12
50	11 11 11 11 11 11 11 11 11 11 11 11 11 11 11 11 11 11 11 11
	10 10 10 10 10 10 10 10 10 10 10 10 10 10 10 10 10 10 10 10
40	9 9 9 9 9 9 9 9 9 9 9 9 9 9 9 9 9 9 9 9
	8 8 8 8 8 8 8 8 8 8 8 8 8 8 8 8 8 8 8 8
30	7 7 7 7 7 7 7 7 7 7 7 7 7 7 7 7 7 7 7 7
	6 6 6 6 6 6 6 6 6 6 6 6 6 6 6 6 6 6 6 6
20	5 5 5 5 5 5 5 5 5 5 5 5 5 5 5 5 5 5 5 5
	4 4 4 4 4 4 4 4 4 4 4 4 4 4 4 4 4 4 4 4
10	3 3 3 3 3 3 3 3 3 3 3 3 3 3 3 3 3 3 3 3
	2 2 2 2 2 2 2 2 2 2 2 2 2 2 2 2 2 2 2 2
	1 1 1 1 1 1 1 1 1 1 1 1 1 1 1 1 1 1 1 1
0 *******	0 0 0 0 0 0 0 0 0 0 0 0 0 0 0 0 0 0 0 0

(Y-axis label: Points within 5 seconds without help (10 trials distributed across day))

Dates:
October   7 8 9 10 11 14 15 16 17 18 21 22 23 24 25 28 29 30 31 *

Reviews

Date	Trend/mean	Decision
October 18	Acceleration, $\bar{x}$ = 21%	Continue—no change
November 1	Acceleration, $\bar{x}$ = 56%	Continue—no change

Note: Standard quarter intersect line has been drawn to show trend for each period of review.

Figure 2.   An example of self-graphing data collection sheet for instructional data. (The asterisk indicates that the student was absent on November 1.)

Equal interval graphs are not the only types of graphs that teachers can use to summarize progress. Two other graphs that have been used are the 6-cycle semilogarithmic graph and the columnar-numerical semilog paper. These are shown in Figures 5 and 6. The 6-cycle semilogarithmic graph has been a trademark of the precision teaching model that began with the work of Lindsley

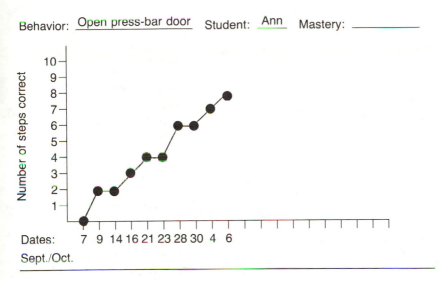

Figure 3. An example of an equal interval graph used to summarize data that are collected on a separate form. This graph summarizes probe data only, not instructional data.

(1964) and has been applied to data for learners with severe handicaps by Haring et al. (1980). Typically in the precision teaching model, time-based data are collected (e.g., rate data) and summarized on a standard precision teaching graph (see Figure 5). The advantage of the precision teaching graph is its standardization that simplifies data review across objectives and students. Haring et al. (1980) also have developed a set of decision rules based on pupil performance summarized on semilog graphs. One of the advantages of the logarithmic vertical axis is that it "straightens" the typical S-shaped learning curve. Most human behavior changes slowly at first and then accelerates rapidly to acquisition. This slow initial progress looks like the bottom curve of the "S" when plotted on equal interval graph paper (see Figure 7).

Another method of graphing that also adjusts to the learning curve is recommended by Sailor and Guess (1983). In this method, 2½-cycle semilog, columnar numerical paper is used. Figure 6 provides an example of task analytic assessment graphed on columnar numerical paper. In this example, the teacher is also using serial chaining (i.e., instruction on one step at a time). Contrast the summary of serial chaining in Figure 6 to the equal interval graph of whole chain instruction shown in Figures 1 and 3.

In this chapter, and throughout this book, equal interval graphs are recommended because of two distinct advantages. First, most figures in research articles are presented as equal interval graphs. Therefore, the model that teachers have to guide their ongoing professional development in data management is the equal interval graph. Second, equal interval graphs can be

Time	Activity	Objectives assessed
8:30	Arrival	—Greetings —Open door. —Walk to seat. —Put belongings away.
9:00	Clerical training Paid jobs or Job simulation between contracts	—Affix labels. —Use photocopier. —Seal envelopes.
10:00	Break (All adults need assistance to use restroom.)	—Communicate choice. —Toileting* —Pants up/down —Handwashing —Drink from soda can
10:30	Clerical training	(Same as 9:00)
11:15	Lunch (All adults need assistance in eating.)	—Communicate choice. —Eat sandwich. —Drink from glass. —Wash table. —Restroom skills (see 10:00)
12:30	Recreation (Sometimes cancelled if toilet accidents or seizures create schedule delays.)	—Communicate choice. —Self-playing piano —"Simon" —Operate radio.
1:00	Purchasing a snack in a snack bar. (Future goal: As skills are acquired and purchasing ac- tivity can be completed more quickly, include social inter- action with nonhandicapped adults in snack bar.)	—Gather belongings. —Open door. —Get in/out belt. —Walk to vending machine or cashier. —Grasp/release money. —Take food item. —Greeting (good-bye)
2:30	Day ends	

*Record toilet accidents at the time they occur.

Figure 4.   Schedule for Ms. P.'s group showing assessment times. Ms. P. works with six adults who have few self-care skills and no communication system. The adults are enrolled in continuing education and job training. None received formal education as children.

constructed easily and can be adapted to the same form as that used for data collection. However, the suggestions given for data evaluation can be adapted to whichever method of graphing is preferred.

Some precautions should be noted in the use of equal interval graphs. First, if graphs are drawn by hand in a nonstandard manner, it is easy to get distorted data simply because of using different proportions for the horizontal and vertical axes across graphs. Teachers are encouraged to make one graph

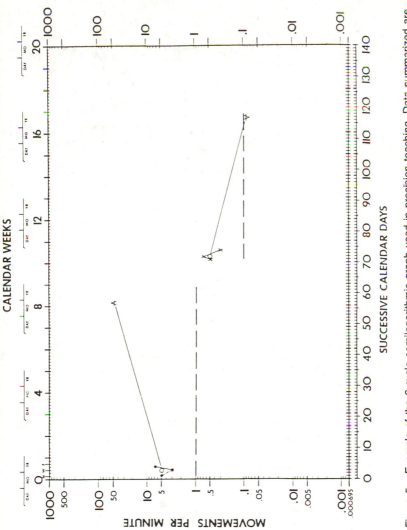

Figure 5. Example of the 6-cycle semilogarithmic graph used in precision teaching. Data summarized are time-based data (e.g., rate). (From White, O. R., & Haring, N. G. [1980]. *Exceptional teaching*. Columbus, OH: Charles E. Merrill; used with permission of author.)

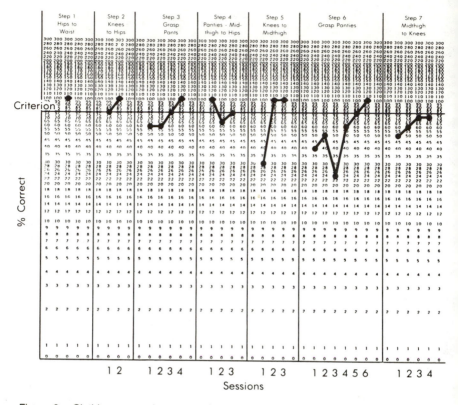

Criterion

% Correct

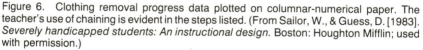

Sessions

Figure 6. Clothing removal progress data plotted on columnar-numerical paper. The teacher's use of chaining is evident in the steps listed. (From Sailor, W., & Guess, D. [1983]. *Severely handicapped students: An instructional design.* Boston: Houghton Mifflin; used with permission.)

form that will be standard across data evaluation to avoid misjudgments created by differing forms. For example, the forms shown in Figures 1 and 2 lend themselves to a wide range of data collection and summary and could be adopted as standard forms. (Figures 4 and 16 show variations of these standard forms.)

Throughout this book, three standard forms have been used for the graphs presented. These forms are shown in Appendix C. These graphs have been set up for a scale of 20 on both the vertical and horizontal axes. Data are converted to percentages to conform to the 20-interval scale on the vertical axis. The horizontal axis represents days. These graphs can hold 20 school days (4 weeks) of data. Again, the advantage of this standardization is that it may facilitate data review and improve its accuracy.

Even when a standard graph is used, the scale of measurement must represent enough of a range of response opportunities to show change over

Student: __John__   Behavior: __Stuff envelopes__

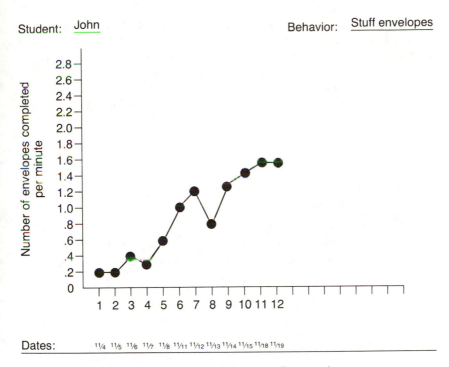

Dates: 11/4 11/5 11/6 11/7 11/8 11/11 11/12 11/13 11/14 11/15 11/18 11/19

Figure 7. An example of rate data summarized on a linear gaph.

time. For example, if the scale is from 0 to 2, the student's progress may be masked by this limited range for the data display. By contrast, if the range is absurdly large (e.g., a 40-step task analysis), it may also be difficult to pinpoint instructional problems. The teacher might use as a goal a scale of measurement with a range of 10. This goal of 10 works well for task analytic assessment since many task analyses have from about 8 to 20 steps. Throughout this text, examples of equal interval graphs are shown that have a scale of measurement of at least 8, but no more than 20. This scale will usually be converted to percentages to use the standard 20-interval scale of the graphs utilized.

Obviously, the horizontal axis (i.e., frequency of data collection) also requires standardization to prevent data distortions. Once the teacher selects this pattern, it should be shown on the horizontal axis. If days are missed in a pattern of daily data collection, for example, these omissions can be shown clearly as missing data points. Distortions will be most evident in a fluctuating schedule for data collection (e.g., the scale of the horizontal axis reflects weekly, daily, and monthly data). The standard graphs used throughout this book are based on daily data collection, with data omissions shown (e.g., absence).

In addition to these data summary considerations that can influence evaluation of ongoing assessment, the teacher also needs to consider whether instruction has been implemented as planned. It would be unfair to judge a student's progress as poor if he or she has not had the opportunity to learn. Opportunities may have been limited by the student's illnesses or disruptions in the program (e.g., teacher absence or snow days). Thus, one of the first considerations that the teacher will make in reviewing the graph is whether there are sufficient data in the period of evaluation to make a decision about progress.

EVALUATION OF DATA

Once the data have been collected on a regular schedule, and the graph for each objective has been prepared, the teacher is ready to begin evaluation of the data to make instructional decisions. This evaluation should occur on some regular schedule. For example, Haring et al. (1980) have recommended scheduling data evaluation on a 6-day cycle. Sailor and Guess (1983) have recommended a similar six–data point cycle but suggest that evaluation be conducted when six nonzero data points have been collected. Since data points usually reflect independent responses, evaluation may be postponed until a few weeks of prompting and fading have been in effect. The guidelines given in this chapter for making instructional decisions require having six data points for the decision. If data are collected on each objective at least three times per week, this review can be conducted every 2 weeks. For example, some teachers schedule data collection daily with a goal of obtaining at least six data points in 10 days. This allows for data omissions due to absence, seizures, schedule changes, and so forth. If only two data points can be obtained per week, then the review would be conducted every 3 weeks. If more than six data points are available in the 2- or 3-week period of review, the teacher would evaluate the data pattern using the first three and the last three data points in the period of evaluation. It is important to note that this "rule of thumb" is based on having no more than 10 data points total in the period of review.

During this regular schedule for reviewing a student's progress on each objective, the teacher might consider three types of objectives: (a) objectives related to the acquisition of new skills, (b) objectives related to deceleration of problem behaviors, and (c) objectives related to extended performance after the initial criteria for acquisition have been achieved. For each of these types of objectives, teachers need guidelines to determine *when* to change instruction, and *what* to change to make instruction more effective. The first decision requires recognition of the data pattern. The second requires using some rules or guidelines for matching instructional changes to specific data patterns.

Evaluation of the Acquisition of New Skills

In the Lehigh University programs at Centennial School and Lehigh Continuing Education for Adults with Severe Disabilities, field testing has begun to evaluate the use of a defined procedure for data review for skill acquisition. The first phase of this field testing provided encouraging results regarding the benefits of standard data review of student progress (Browder, Liberty, Heller, & D'Huyvetters, 1986). The entire data review is summarized as a task analysis below:

1. **Prerequisite Review**
    1.1. Was data collected six times in 2 weeks?
    1.2. Was the student given at least eight opportunities to respond for each of the six data points? (The eight opportunities are the number of steps in the task analysis.)
    1.3. Is the period of review continuous, without program breaks due to illness or vacation of 4 or more consecutive school days?
    1.4. If the answers to 1.1.–1.3. are "yes," proceed to consider data pattern.
2. **Simple Data Patterns (Visual Analysis Adequate)**
    2.1. Has the student met the criteria for mastery during this period of review (can cross to last period of review to note mastery)? If so, note "Mastery—extend performance."
    2.2. Has the student failed to progress at all in this program? If so, note "No progress—simplify." List how you will simplify.
3. **Data Patterns that Require Standard Estimation of Trend**
    3.1. Draw the line of progress using the first and last three data points. Note intersections with a plus sign (+). Decide if the slope is accelerating, decelerating, or flat.
    3.2. Calculate the mean for *all* data points in the period of review. If you have not already done so, calculate the mean for the last period of review. Decide if the mean is higher, lower, or the same as the last period of review.
    3.3. Make a decision about the variability of the data: highly variable or not highly variable.
    3.4. Before proceeding to make a decision, note slope, mean, and bounce under trend on graph review spaces on standard graph.
4. **Making the Instructional Decision to Match the Trend**
    4.1. Use the abbreviated trend/decision page to match the appropriate decision to the trend. Write this in the space.
    4.2. If you decide not to follow the decision rules, write out the rationale.
    4.3. If the decision requires an instructional change, mark a phase change line on the graph and label the specific change you make (e.g., "Use time delay to fade verbal prompt.").
    4.4. If the decision requires new measurement and graphing, note this on the graph (e.g., "Graph discontinued—new task analysis").
    4.5. If changes are required, be sure to write or modify the program format to describe these in adequate detail for future replication by other teachers.

The following paragraphs describe these steps in further detail, giving reference to alternative practices that teachers may consider.

When to Change Instruction Using a Standard Method to Evaluate the Data Pattern   The prerequisite to data pattern review is to determine if there are sufficient data to conduct evaluation (i.e., at least six data points). If not, the teacher should continue instruction and reschedule evaluation. The second consideration for data pattern review is whether mastery has occurred during the period of review. If mastery has occurred (as defined by the criteria in the objective for the lesson), the teacher will plan extended performance instruction as described next in *what* to change. A third consideration is whether any change has occurred. If all data points are at the same level as when instruction began (e.g., at zero), an instructional change is clearly needed. If enough data are present, and some learning has occurred, but mastery has not occurred, then the teacher must determine whether the data pattern shows adequate acceleration, inadequate acceleration, a plateau, deceleration, or extreme variability. This discrimination may require using some standard method for data inspection as described next.

In single-subject research, visual analysis of graphed data has been considered an appropriate alternative to statistical analysis (Herson & Barlow, 1976; Kazdin, 1982). Unfortunately, visual analysis alone can lead to inac-

Data collected during instruction can provide important information concerning when to make changes to improve student performance.

curate conclusions about the data pattern. For example, research has shown inaccuracy in visual analyses conducted by teachers (Liberty, 1972), graduate students (Wampold & Furlong, 1981), and experts (DeProspero & Cohen, 1979). By contrast, using a standard method of data inspection has been shown to improve this accuracy (Bailey, 1984; White, 1972).

One method to evaluate the trend of the data is called the standard quarter intersect method (White, 1972). This method is used to draw a "learning picture" or line of progress. To draw this line of progress, the teacher follows these steps:

1. Identify the first three data points of the series. Find the second highest data point. Find the second day's data point. Mark a + at the intersection of the second highest point and the second day's point.
2. Identify the last three data points of the series (e.g., the last 3 days). Repeat the procedure in #1 to find the intersection. That is, find the second highest data point and the midday of these three points and mark a + at the intersection.
3. Connect the two +s with a straight line. The slope of the line will be shown by this straight line and will be either accelerating (going up), decelerating (going down), or flat. (See Figure 8.)

This method for evaluating the data trend is recommended for application of the instructional decision rules to follow. However, two other methods of data review merit consideration. The first is to compare the student's rate of progress to an expected rate of progress. Haring et al. (1981) describe how to draw the "minimum celeration (acceleration) line" on the graph. To draw this line, the teacher marks an "A" or aimstar on the intersection of the date and level of performance to show when mastery should be achieved. A line is then drawn from the midpoint of the student's current performance to this aimstar. This is the minimum celeration line. Progress is compared to this minimum acceptable rate of progress (see Figure 9). One advantage of the minimum celeration line is that the teacher need not wait to collect six data points to see when progress is not adequate. This may be especially useful for programs that are implemented infrequently (e.g., weekly community instruction). The difficulty in applying the minimum celeration line is that teachers may not be able to set a date for mastery unless there is some naturally occurring deadline such as the end of the student's last year of school.

A third method for evaluating the data is described by Sailor and Guess (1983) and is a variation of both the standard quarter intersect and minimum celeration line approach. In this evaluation, the teacher first draws a line of progress as shown in Figure 8 (standard quarter intersect). Then the teacher extends this line to predict when mastery will be achieved at the current rate of progress. This method can be helpful in making the decision of whether current

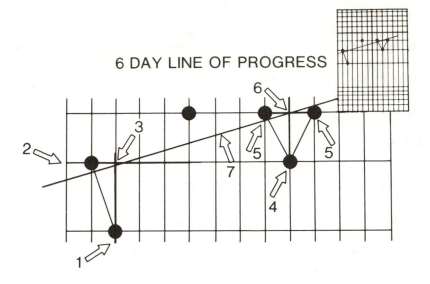

6 DAY LINE OF PROGRESS

1 mid-day of first 3 days	5 mid-level of last 3 days
2 mid-level of first 3 days	when 2 are the same, that will be the middle
3 intersection	6 intersection
4 mid-day of last 3 days	7 connect intersections

Figure 8.   The standard quarter intersect method of trend estimation. (From Haring, N., Liberty, K., & White, O. [1980]. Rules for data-based strategy decisions in instructional programs: Current research and instructional implications. In W. Sailor, B. Wilcox, & L. Brown [Eds.], *Methods of instruction for severely handicapped students,* p. 170. Baltimore: Paul H. Brookes Publishing Co., used with permission.)

acceleration is too slow (e.g., mastery will take several years). This prediction line is shown in Figure 10.

Again, the method of data inspection that is used throughout this book is the standard quarter intersect method shown in Figure 8. This method helps the teacher determine the *slope* of the data pattern by observing whether the line is going up (accelerating), going down (decelerating), or remains flat. In addition to the slope of the data, teachers will also want to compare the *magnitude* of change and the data *variability*. To compare the magnitude of change, the teacher will want to calculate the *mean* performance for the previous data period (e.g., the previous 2 weeks) and the current period of review. In comparing these means, the teacher will note whether the average performance is better (higher mean), worse (lower mean), or the same (same mean). To consider data variability, the teacher will want to note the range of the data points compared to the trend line that was drawn with the standard quarter

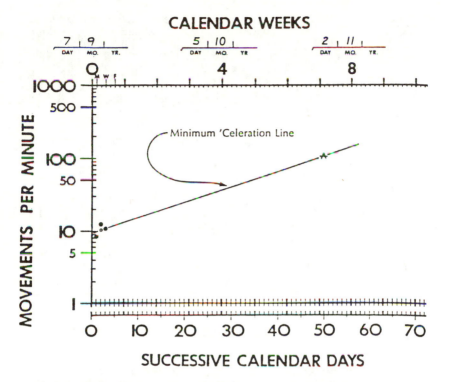

Figure 9. Example of a minimum celeration line. The line is drawn by connecting the midpoint of current performance to the "aimstar"—A. The aimstar is estimated by selecting the criterion and date for mastery (e.g., 100 movements per minute in 50 days is the aimstar selected below). (From White, O., & Haring, N. [1980]. *Exceptional teaching*. Columbus, OH: Charles E. Merrill; used with permission of author.)

intersect method. Do these data points fall at a wide range above and below the trend line (e.g., 40% range)? If so, the data are *variable*. If not, the data are not variable. Thus, the teacher makes three discriminations in reviewing the data pattern:

1. What is the slope of the data trend (accelerating, decelerating, or flat)?
2. What is the mean of the current period versus the previous period of review (higher, lower, the same)?
3. Are the data variable (yes or no)?

What to Change When the Pattern Suggests the Need for Change— Applying "Rules" to Improve the Success of Instructional Decisions
Unless the data pattern shows an acceptable rate of acceleration, an instructional change is necessary. The choice of change need not be made randomly or from "hunches," but can be based on the data pattern itself. Research by Haring et al. (1981) has produced a set of rules that can help teachers match instruc-

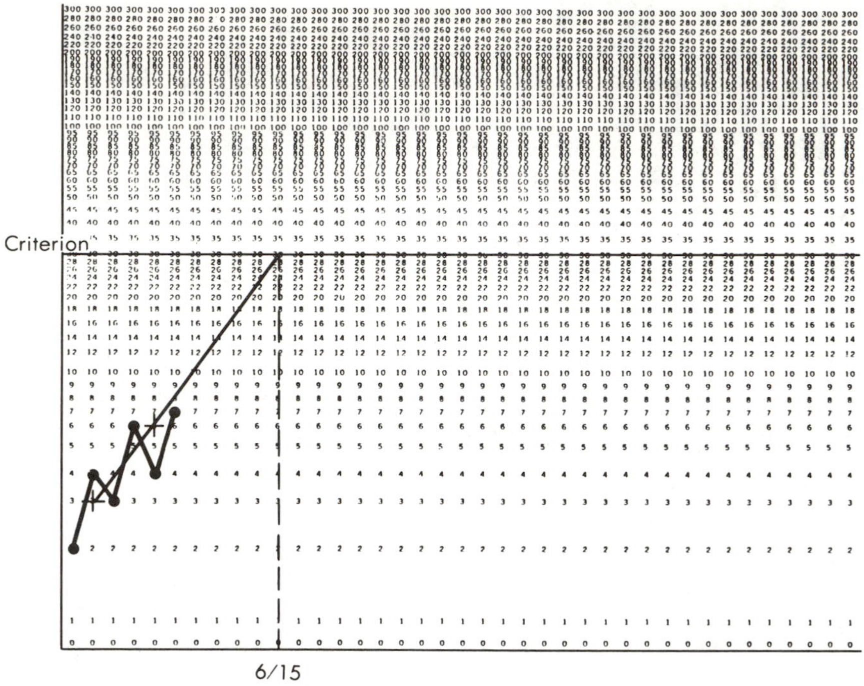

Figure 10. A hypothetical data set illustrating a prediction line, a criterion line, and resultant intersect with ordinate to show projected date of criterial performance. (From Sailor, W., & Guess, D. [1983]. *Severely handicapped students: An instructional design.* Boston: Houghton Mifflin; used with permission.)

tional decisions to data patterns, and improve the success of their decisions. Haring et al. (1981) found that when teachers' instructional decisions adhered to the suggested rules, substantially more instances of student improvement resulted than when teachers chose not to follow the rules. While the Haring et al. (1981) research utilized semilog graphing, a subsequent study by Browder, Liberty, et al. (1986) applied an adaptation of the rules to non-standard equal interval graphs. They found that teachers' self-monitoring improved teacher's accuracy in evaluating the data pattern and rule-based decisions, and that rule-based decisions resulted in substantially more cases of student improvement than non–rule based decisions. Table 1 provides a comparison of the rules as developed by Haring et al. (1981) and adapted by Browder (1986).

Browder, Liberty, et al.'s (1986) research on standard data review focused primarily on the *slope* of the data pattern. In current field testing at Lehigh University, teachers are also using the comparison of means for the previous and current periods of review. Instructional decision rules that best correspond to each data pattern are summarized in Figure 11. General guidelines for

Table 1. Comparison of rules adapted by Browder (1986) and rules derived by Haring, Liberty, and White (1980).

Browder (1986)		Haring, Liberty, and White (1980)	
Pattern	Decision	Pattern	Decision
1. Mastery—met criteria	1. Extend performance.	Decision #1— program was successful (met performance aim).	Move to the next step or another skill.
2. No progress since program initiated (trend is flat; no change in mean since instruction began)	2. Simplify program (e.g., task analyze).	Decision #3— Incorrect instructional step (zero correct responses for last 5 days).	Step back to a simple or less complex skill level.
3. Adequate progress 3a. Slope is accelerating. Mean is higher. 3b. Slope is flat. Mean is higher (data are not highly variable).	3. No change.	Decision #2— Program is working. (Correct rates are accelerating; no more than two consecutive corrects below minimum celeration line.)	Do not make any changes in the program at this time.
4. Acquisition problem—Slope is accelerating. Mean is same or lower. Data are not highly variable.	4. Improve antecedents (e.g., prompts).	Decision #6— Basic acquisition problem (Trend in corrects is up or flat. Data are not highly variable. Data are less than 83%. Three consecutive corrects are below minimum celeration line.)	Provide better information or cues on how to perform skill.

(continued)

Table 1. *(continued)*

Browder (1986)		Haring, Liberty, and White (1980)	
Pattern	Decision	Pattern	Decision
5. Motivation problems 5a. Slope is accelerating. Mean is lower. Data are highly variable. 5b. Slope is decelerating (regardless of mean). 5c. Slope is flat. Mean is lower. 5d. Slope is flat. Mean is lower. Data are highly variable.	5. Improve motivation (e.g., change reinforcement, vary materials, make task more difficult).	Decision #4— Basic compliance problem (Correct rate is highly variable or decelerating sharply.)	Go to more difficult skill or give better consequences.
6. Plateau in progress—Slope is flat (same mean).	6. Remediate difficult steps or provide better consequences for continued progress (e.g., SR for unprompted correct steps only).	Decision #5— Fluency building problem (Pupil reached 83% accuracy. Correct rate is flat or going down. Correct responses are below minimum celeration line and not at performance aim.)	Provide better consequences for continued work and progress.
No parallel decision is available since rules are based on errorless instruction. See #3, #4, or #6 for flat or decelerating slope.		Decision #7— Basic format problem (Trend rate is flat or going down. Data are *not* highly variable. Correct rate exceeded errors.)	Provide better feedback on difference between corrects and incorrects.

instructional changes have been suggested for each rule. Specific instructional changes to be made are beyond the scope of this book, but can be found in resources on teaching individuals with severe handicaps (e.g., Gaylord-Ross & Holvoet, 1985; Sailor & Guess, 1983; Snell, 1987).

Evaluation of Deceleration of Problem Behavior

The guidelines suggested in the previous section are only applicable to behavior to be accelerated (e.g., new skills). Often, in managing problem behaviors, an educative approach will be taken, and the acceleration of alternative adaptive behaviors that replace the function of the problem behaviors will be the data to be evaluated. However, in some cases, direct assessment of the deceleration of the problem behavior may also be important. For example, the problem behavior may be serious enough to warrant documenting deceleration per se. Or, the teacher may want to demonstrate that instruction in alternative skills decelerates a problem behavior without applying contingencies for the problem behavior. (See Chapter 8 for further discussion of the assessment of problem behaviors.)

Although research by Haring et al. (1981) produced decision rules for acceleration projects, no research has produced decision rules for the deceleration of behavior. Research on deceleration of behavior has often utilized single-subject designs for evaluation. However, such designs may not be useful to the teacher who cannot justify extended baselines or replications of baseline conditions for a serious problem behavior.

When to Change Treatment to Decelerate Behavior—Guidelines for Data Pattern Review In the absence of a set of empirically validated decision rules, the teacher may wish to take into account some logical considerations in conducting this review. First, it may be helpful to collect data prior to intervention. This is suggested in Chapter 8 as a first step in verifying the need for intervention. These baseline data can be used for comparison once intervention is begun. Second, the teacher should set criteria for deceleration (deceleration objectives should be written as complete behavioral objectives). These criteria should not arbitrarily be set at zero, but rather should be based on social tolerance for the behavior and its potential danger (e.g., it might be tolerated or not dangerous at low rates).

In reviewing the data pattern on the graph, the teacher might use two methods to standardize review. The first method is to draw two mean lines: a horizontal line for the mean level of the occurrence of the behavior across the baseline period or last period of review, and a mean line across the current period of review. These mean levels can help the teacher decide if the behavior has decreased. A second method is to draw a line of progress using the standard quarter intersect method to judge whether the trend of the current period is deceleration. The teacher may wish to extend this line to determine when the

Directions: Complete this checklist for each graph once every 2 weeks. First, review the prerequisites. Then, use the standard quarter intersect method to estimate trend. Finally, check the instructional decision. Instructional success may be enhanced if the decision rule corresponds to the same number as the trend.

Prerequisite

Data availability	Decision rule
____ 1. Graph has six data points since last review.	____ 1. Proceed to review graph.
____ 2. Data are insufficient due to program break.	____ 2. Complete program break review form for all graphs.
____ 3. Data are insufficient due to problems in scheduling or other problems.	____ 3. Revise schedule to allow more times to collect data.

Data review

Trend estimation	Decision rule
____ 1. Criteria for *mastery* has been demonstrated.	____ 1. Revise instruction and graph for *extended performance* (e.g., fluency, generalization).
____ 2. *No progress* has been made since instruction began.	____ 2. *Skill is too difficult* Simplify (e.g., teach simpler response, conduct further task analysis, or use chaining).
____ 3. Patterns of adequate progress 3a. Acceleration of slope, higher mean 3b. Flat slope; higher mean	____ 3. No change
____ 4. Acquisition problem Acceleration of slope; same or lower mean; no variability	____ 4. Improve antecedents.
____ 5. Motivation problems 5a. Acceleration of slope, lower mean, highly variable 5b. Deceleration of slope 5c. Flat slope, mean is lower 5d. Flat slope, mean is same, higher; highly variable	____ 5. Improve motivation.
____ 6. Plateau in progress—Flat slope, same mean	____ 6. Remediate difficult steps or improve motivation.

Figure 11. Guidelines for data-based instructional decisions. (Adapted from Browder, D., Liberty, K., Heller, M., & D'Huyvetters, K. [1986]. Self-management by teachers: Improving instructional decision-making. *Professional School Psychology, 1,* 165–175.)

behavior is predicted to reach the criterion level. An example of this analysis is shown in Figure 12. The guidelines for this data analysis are given in Figure 13.

To make a decision about the continuation of intervention, the teacher can consider the typical effects of the procedure on behavior change. For example, punishment should have an immediate and clear effect, whereas extinction (withholding reinforcement of the undesirable behavior) may have a delayed effect, with acceleration occurring prior to deceleration (Sulzer-Azaroff & Mayer, 1977). Another consideration in extending intervention is the concurrent acceleration of alternative skills. Figure 13 lists guidelines for the teacher to make data-based decisions about intervention to decelerate unwanted behavior.

Without empirically derived rules such as those presented earlier for acceleration programs, it is difficult to decide what to change when the data pattern shows the need for change. Chapter 8 provides an assessment procedure to help teachers make decisions about what to change to discourage problem behavior and encourage alternative adaptive behavior.

Evaluation of Extended Use of Skills

In writing an objective, the teacher typically sets criteria for initial acquisition (e.g., "puts on shirt alone two out of two observations"). When these criteria have been reached, the objective has been "mastered." But achievement of "mastery" is a critical point for teacher decisions about subsequent instruction. This mastery may not yet approximate the criteria necessary for normalized use of the skill. Typically, the criterion for mastery in initial acquisition is accuracy of responding. For normalized use, the response must also be fluent and generalized across time (maintenance), materials, settings, people, and so forth. This section suggests ways for the teacher to set extended use criteria after initial mastery, and then measure achievement of this extended use. Therefore, this section provides the guidelines for what to change when the data pattern is mastery of an acquisition objective.

Fluency Liberty (1985) notes that there are two phases of learning: acquisition and fluency. While acquisition is measured by accuracy, fluency is usually evaluated using a time-based measure. If an acquired skill is not fluent, it probably will not be used by the student or encouraged by caregivers. Consider again the example given above for putting on a shirt. A student might perform all of the steps in the task analysis to put on the shirt. However, this might take 10 minutes. The caregiver probably will not be able to allow 10 minutes in a busy morning routine for the student to put on his or her shirt. Also, the student may engage in an alternative response (e.g., whining until helped) that results in faster access to reinforcement (having the shirt on) even though he or she has "learned" to put on the shirt alone. Thus, teachers need to consider fluency objectives after acquisition of a response has occurred.

Directions: The teacher evaluates the data by comparing the mean for the baseline and intervention phases and draws a prediction line to estimate when the problem behavior would decelerate to zero.

Student: <u>Nat</u>   Behavior: <u>Tantrums—crying or loud screaming</u>

Assessment: <u>Time each tantrum with a stopwatch. Add total minutes for the day.</u>

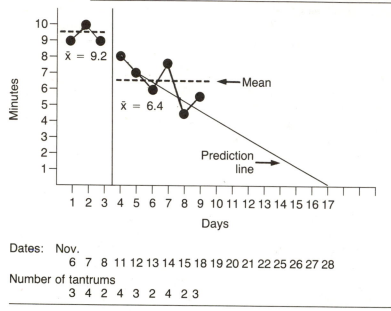

Dates: Nov.
      6 7 8 11 12 13 14 15 18 19 20 21 22 25 26 27 28

Number of tantrums
      3 4 2 4 3 2 4 2 3

Figure 12.   Example of data evaluation for a graph of problem behavior to be decelerated.

Fluency assessment may measure one or more dimensions of time: latency, duration, or rate. The choice of dimension depends on the skill to be evaluated. For example, in the dressing example given above, the important time dimension is the duration of dressing (i.e., the total time to put on the shirt). In a communication response, latency can be critical. For example, if a student does not locate an appropriate response in a picture communication wallet within a socially comparable time period, the listener may lose interest in the conversation (especially if the listener is another child). Rate is important for vocational assembly tasks, especially if pay is based on rate. Other skills may require more than one time dimension assessment to meet normalized criteria for fluency. For example, to master crossing streets with a light, the student needs to respond in a short latency to the green light, and cross in the duration of time before the light turns red.

To set the time-based criteria for fluency, the teacher can use social validation procedures (see Chapter 2). For example, the teacher might measure

Trend	Other considerations	Decision
— 1. Clear, rapid deceleration		— 1. Continue intervention.
— 2. Evidence of deceleration — Intervention mean lower than baseline mean OR — Standard quarter intersect method shows decelerating trend	2a. Considerations to continue intervention — Acceleration in alternative behavior — First period of evaluation — Prediction line shows acceptable rate of deceleration	— 2a. Continue intervention.
	2b. Consideration to change intervention — None of 2a considerations present — Behavior presents physical danger — Behavior or intervention has created major disruption in instruction	— 2b. Change intervention.
— 3. No evidence of deceleration (e.g., flat or accelerating or mean same as baseline)	3a. Consideration to continue intervention — Acceleration in alternative behavior — First period of evaluation — "Extinction burst" apparent	— 3a. Continue intervention.
	3b. Considerations to change intervention — None of 3a considerations present — Behavior presents a physical danger. — Behavior or intervention has created major disruption in overall intervention.	— 3b. Change intervention.

Figure 13. Checklist to guide evaluation of graph for intervention to decelerate problem behavior.

the latency of communicative responses for several nonhandicapped peers. Or, the criteria for rate of vocational assembly can be identified through an interview with the employer. Naturally occurring consequences (e.g., the street light example above) also may dictate the time dimension for normalized use of the skill.

Once the teacher has made the transition from acquisition instruction to fluency instruction, he or she may still need to decide when to change instruction if the fluency objective is not being achieved. To evaluate acquisition of fluency once a criteria has been set, the teacher will want to use a time-based measure (e.g., stopwatch) and graph performance accordingly. Figure 14 is a graph indicating deceleration of duration of loading a dishwasher. To evaluate progress during the regularly scheduled review for each objective, the teacher can draw a line of progress as described earlier to see if progress is occurring in the desired direction. The teacher may also want to extend this as a prediction line to see if this rate of progress is acceptable. That is, will the student reach the criteria in a reasonable period of time (see prediction line in Figure 14). If not, the instructional decision most pertinent for fluency building (i.e, *what to change*) is to improve consequences for fluent performance (e.g., set a timer and allow the student access to a preferred activity if he or she can "beat the clock"), or to teach more efficient ways to perform a task.

Maintenance   Another extended performance objective that should be set is maintenance of the skill when teacher assistance and artificial consequences have been withdrawn. The teacher may want to set fluency objectives first, then, once these criteria are met, measure maintenance. As stated previously, performance that does not meet normalized time criteria probably will not be maintained by naturally occurring consequences. To measure maintenance, the teacher can periodically probe performance once instruction has ended. If performance regresses below the established criteria for fluent performance, an instructional decision is needed for maintenance training. Maintenance training might involve reintroducing and fading more gradually the artificial consequences used to teach the skill. Or, the student might be taught to self-manage the skill. This data collection and evaluation should be continued until the student meets a preset criteria for maintenance (e.g., across a month without instruction, or across a summer).

Sometimes, maintenance is naturally required by breaks in school programs. When a student has not yet achieved a level of performance that will maintain without teacher assistance, such breaks can have a devastating effect on progress across years of schooling. The courts have tended to support extended school years (i.e., summer programs) for students who demonstrate skill regression during program breaks (*Armstrong v. Kline,* 1979; *Battle v. Commonwealth,* 1980; *Georgia Association of Retarded Citizens v. McDaniel,* 1979; *Mahoney v. Administrative School District No. 1,* 1979). Unfortunately, few guidelines exist for the evaluation of skill regression to determine extended school year eligibility (Browder & Lentz, 1985).

Behavior: Unload dishwasher   Name: ___Al___   Mastery: 5 min./2 days

"Beat the clock"

Total number of minutes to load dishwasher (full load)

	20 20 20 20 20 20 20 20	20 20 20 20 20 20 20 20 20 20 20 20
	19 19 19 19 19 19 19 19	19 19 19 19 19 19 19 19 19 19 19 19
	18 18 18 18 18 18 18 18	18 18 18 18 18 18 18 18 18 18 18 18
	17 17 17 17 17 17 17 17	17 17 17 17 17 17 17 17 17 17 17 17
standard	16 16 16 16 16 16 16 16	16 16 16 16 16 16 16 16 16 16 16 16
quarter	15 15 ● 15 15 ● 15 15	15 15 15 15 15 15 15 15 15 15 15 15
intersect ●	■ ●-14-4 14 14-4-●-●-●	14 14 14 14 14 14 14 14 14 14 14 14
line of progress	13 ● 13 ● 13/13 13 13	13 ● 13 13 13 13 13 13 13 13 13 13
	12 12 12 12 ● 12 12 12	12 12 ● ● 12 ● 12 12 12 12 12 12
	11 11 11 11 11 11 11 11	11 11 11 11 ● 11\11 11 11 11 11 11
	10 10 10 10 10 10 10 10	10 10 10 10 10 10 10 10 10 10 10 10
	9 9 9 9 9 9 9 9	9 9 9 9 9 9 ● 9 9 9 9 9
	8 8 8 8 8 8 8 8	8 8 8 8 8 8 8 ● 8 8 8 8
	7 7 7 7 7 7 7 7	7 7 7 7 7 7 7 7 ● 7 7 7
	6 6 6 6 6 6 6 6	6 6 6 6 6 6 6 6 6 ● 6 6
	5 5 5 5 5 5 5 5	5 5 5 5 5 5 5 5 5 5 ● 5
	4 4 4 4 4 4 4 4	4 4 4 4 4 4 4 4 4 4 4 4
	3 3 3 3 3 3 3 3	3 3 3 3 3 3 3 3 3 3 3 3
	2 2 2 2 2 2 2 2	2 2 2 2 2 2 2 2 2 2 2 2
	1 1 1 1 1 1 1 1	1 1 1 1 1 1 1 1 1 1 1 1
**********	0 0 0 0 0 0 0 0	0 0 0 0 0 0 0 0 0 0 0 0

● Pre-
diction
line

Dates:
Oct./Nov.   7 8 9 10 11 14 15 16 17 18 21 22 23 24 25 28 29 30 31 1

Reviews

Date	Trend	Decision
10/16/85	Flat	Change consequences. "Beat the clock"
10/26/85	Deceleration	Predict mastery 11/1.
		No change in instruction.

Figure 14.   Example of trend estimation for a fluency graph.

Evaluation of skill regression is feasible if the teacher is maintaining graphs of ongoing assessment. Shorter breaks, such as winter vacation, may indicate regression. If the break had continued for 3 months (i.e., summer break duration), and a prediction line is drawn for the anticipated regression, then a case can be made for the substantial regression that would be predicted to occur. When evidence to justify an extended school year is inadequate, maintenance data can be compared and evaluated for all objectives from the spring to fall if the same graphs are used in September as were used in June. The time required by the student to recoup the skill after the summer can also show the impact of the summer break on the student's long-term progress. Figure 15 provides an evaluation checklist to use in considering extended school year eligibility.

Generalization   Another type of extended performance that is necessary to achieve normalized use of a skill is generalization, which may be taught during acquisition. For example, in teaching the manual sign for "more," the teacher may introduce use of this sign across activities and materials from the beginning of instruction. However, further generalization might be targeted for extended performance evaluation (e.g., across people, across settings). In other cases, generalization may not have been addressed in acquisition training, and multiple generalization goals may be targeted for extended performance.

One of the simplest ways to assess generalization is to observe performance with untrained examples. For example, consider the goal of learning to cross streets with lights. The teacher could select four streets for assessment. The teacher could then train two of the streets and assess the two untrained streets to evaluate generalization. Or, consider the example of use of the sign for "more." The teacher could target for training four activities in two settings. Two additional activities and a third setting might be used to evaluate generalization to untrained examples. (For information on the concept of sufficient exemplars, see Stokes & Baer, 1977. For more information on assessing generalization, see Horner, Sprague, & Wilcox, 1982; Liberty, 1985.)

The evaluation of generalization might be scheduled at several phases: (a) during acquisition, (b) before fluency, (c) concurrently with instruction in fluency, (d) after fluency training, or (e) concurrently with maintenance evaluation. The example shown in Figure 16 included a phase to assess generalization during and after acquisition, but before fluency training was begun.

The evaluation in Figure 16 provides an illustration of ongoing assessment from Nat's case study. The skill shown is washing hands. Acquisition training was conducted in the classroom and school restroom. Weekly probes of generalization to a nontraining site were conducted at the fast food restaurant where Nat was learning to order lunch. After mastery of handwashing, Nat had not generalized this skill to the untrained site. Thus, the teacher, Ms. S., implemented instruction in this site and assessed another site for generalization (use of restroom while shopping). This is shown as the extended training for generalization.

While this training for generalization across sites was begun, Ms. S. also implemented fluency training in the school sites. If Nat "beat the clock" to get his hands washed, he could listen to music until the rest of the class was ready for the next activity (e.g., lunch). Once criteria for fluency were achieved,

Student: __Nat__   Period of break: __Christmas break 12/20__

Period of resumed program: __1/5__   Evaluation date: __1/12__

Check reason for break:

Illness _____   Vacation __✓__   Other (specify) _____

Programs (list)

Program priority and data trend Program priority	Toilet accidents*	Dress alone*	Pour pitcher	Prepare snack	Clean up snack	Pick up toys	Play Cross 4	Put on coat	Store belongings	Walk with adult*	Point to choice	Social interaction*	Total
1. Highest*	✓	✓					✓			✓	✓	✓	
2. Medium				✓	✓	✓		✓	✓				12 programs
3. Low			✓										
Postbreak data Prebreak													
4. Regression*	✓	✓	✓		✓		✓		✓	✓	✓		8
5. No change				✓			✓						2
6. Progress					✓			✓					2
Postbreak progress													
7. No/slow recoupment*	✓	✓			✓		✓		✓	✓		✓	6
8. Rapid recoupment			✓								✓		2
9. Progress above prebreak				✓		✓	✓		✓				4

Figure 15. Evaluation of student's graphs after program breaks. An asterisk after a program indicates that the data collected support extended school year eligibility based on the criteria of regression with poor recoupment in high priority skills.

Ms. S. implemented a maintenance evaluation phase in which she no longer set the clock or told Nat that he could listen to music if he finished on time. Nat had free access to a tape player after use of the restroom. Nat's fluency regressed. Then, Ms. S. taught Nat to self-evaluate whether or not he should use the tape player by prompting him to sign "fast" when he finished quickly and "no" when he dawdled. She then faded her prompting and Nat maintained his fluent

Behavior: __Wash hands.__ Name: __Nat__ Mastery: __100% for C, S, R__

	20	20	20	20	20	20	20	20	20	20	20	20	20	20	20	20	20	20	20	20
	19	19	19	19	19	19	19	19	19	19	19	19	19	19	19	19	19	19	19	19
	18	18	18	18	18	18	18	18	18	18	18	18	18	18	18	18	18	18	18	18
	17	17	17	17	17	17	17	17	17	17	17	17	17	17	17	17	17	17	17	17
	16	16	16	16	16	16	16	16	16	16	16	16	16	16	16	16	16	16	16	16
	15	15	15	15	15	15	15	15	15	15	15	15	15	15	15	15	15	15	15	15
13. Discard towel.	14	14	14	14	14	14	14	14	14	14	14	14	14	14	14	14	14	14	14	14
12. Dry hands.	13	13	13	13	13	13	13	13	13	13	13	13	13	13	13	13	13	13	13	13
11. Get towel or push blowers.	12	12	12	12	12	12	12	12	12	12	12	12	12	12	12	12	12	12	12	12
10. Turn off cold water.	11	11	11	11	11	11	11	11	11	11	11	11	11	11	11	11	11	11	11	11
9. Turn off hot water.	10	10	10	10	10	10	10	10	10	10	10	10	10	10	10	10	10	10	10	10
8. Rinse hands.	9	9	9	9	9	9	9	9	9	9	9	9	9	9	9	9	9	9	9	9
7. Put soap on back of hands.	8	8	8	8	8	8	8	8	8	8	8	8	8	8	8	8	8	8	8	8
6. Rub soap on palms.	7	7	7	7	7	7	7	7	7	7	7	7	7	7	7	7	7	7	7	7
5. Get soap from dispenser.	6	6	6	6	6	6	6	6	6	6	6	6	6	6	6	6	6	6	6	6
4. Rinse hands.	5	5	5	5	5	5	5	5	5	5	5	5	5	5	5	5	5	5	5	5
3. Turn on hot water.	4	4	4	4	4	4	4	4	4	4	4	4	4	4	4	4	4	4	4	4
2. Turn on cold water.	3	3	3	3	3	3	3	3	3	3	3	3	3	3	3	3	3	3	3	3
1. Walk to sink.	2	2	2	2	2	2	2	2	2	2	2	2	2	2	2	2	2	2	2	2
	1	1	1	1	1	1	1	1	1	1	1	1	1	1	1	1	1	1	1	1
%	0	0	0	0	0	0	0	0	0	0	0	0	0	0	0	0	0	0	0	0

Dates: Nov. 4 5 6 7 8 11 12 13 14 15 18 19 20 21 22
Settings: C S C S R* C S C S R R R C S R

Reviews

Date	Trend/mean	Decision
11-14-85	Mastery C, S, Not R.	Train R (restaurant).
11-22-85	Mastery C, S, R.	Train fluency
		(Begin duration data graph.)

Figure 16. Example of a graph showing generalization data during and after acquisition. (* = untrained site, C = classroom sink with paper towels and turn-knob soap dispenser, S = school restroom with paper towels and push-knob soap dispenser, R = restaurant with blow dryer and push-knob soap dispenser)

handwashing across the next month. Ms. S. also probed fluency in the community sites on a few occasions and found that even though the tape player was not present, Nat was finishing quickly and signing "fast." Ms. S. then discontinued data collection for this skill because she had evidence that it was acquired and extended to normalized use.

SUMMARY

This chapter has provided teachers with some guidelines for utilizing pupil performance data to make instructional decisions. These data-based decisions help the teacher to reap the investment of time and effort required to conduct ongoing assessment. The teacher who does not use data, but simply collects and graphs them, will probably soon tire of this exercise. However, with the help of data, the teacher can become more successful in instruction, and data collection is recognized as a valuable resource. This chapter has suggested a frequent schedule for ongoing assessment, and the use of equal interval graphs to summarize data. Decision rules were given to guide data review for accelerating and decelerating behavior. Suggestions were also given for evaluating extended use of a skill to meet normalized criteria. Once the goal of extended use has been achieved, the teacher can be more confident that the student not only has acquired a skill, but will use it in daily living.

CHAPTER 5

ASSESSMENT IN AND FOR THE HOME

DIANE M. BROWDER
AND JEFFRY FRIEDMAN

The home is an important and unique environment to consider when planning instruction to facilitate independence. Personal maintenance such as bathing, dressing, and grooming take place primarily in the home environment. Many leisure hours are spent with family, roommates, or alone. Housekeeping and food preparation activities also are performed on a regular basis. The home environment is also a place where individual expression and choice are especially appropriate. Families vary in their customs and traditions for leisure time, housekeeping, meals, and so forth. Within families, different members may vary in their choices about diet, clothing style, recreation, and friends. Even the physical facility called "home" reflects family and individual preferences, and may be an apartment, a large farm house, a duplex, a suburban ranch-style home, and so forth.

In planning for assessment of skills in and for the home, the teacher needs to develop procedures to help identify these differences in individual and family life-styles so that a student can be taught the skills appropriate for his or her current and future family. (The term "family" is used in this chapter to refer to people who live together and care for each other. They may be a biological family, foster parents and children, unrelated adults, or "houseparents" and "residents" in a group home. The term "caregivers" is used for the people who provide care to the person with severe handicaps, and may refer to the biological parents, foster or adoptive parents, a guardian, sibling, or paid houseparents.)

This chapter provides ideas for identifying skills needed by a student in his or her home environment, and for working with caregivers to prioritize skills for assessment and instruction. Before discussing specific skill assessment, the professional–caregiver partnership is described in further detail. Too often, a specialist conducts assessment with minimal caregiver contact and then pre-

Jeffry Friedman is a doctoral student in school psychology, Special Education Programs, School of Education, Lehigh University, Bethlehem, Pennsylvania.

scribes objectives to the caregivers. Even when the caregivers are staff members (e.g., group home staff), assessment is often conducted by a professional who will not carry out the instruction (Wetzel & Hoschouer, 1984). When such prescriptions are given to parents, who are not "on duty" with a special person but rather are coping with the many needs of their *total* family, follow-through may be negligible. How, then, can teachers improve their effectiveness in developing assessment so that it will yield home cooperation with caregivers?

COLLABORATION WITH CAREGIVERS

Caregivers obviously have the most information to share about their home environment, family customs, and so forth. As recommended in Chapter 2, initial assessment can be made more efficient by contacting caregivers to plan environments for assessment, and to begin setting priorities. A subsequent ecological inventory of the home provides further information on skills needed for the home environment. This collaboration with caregivers may be viewed as the minimum amount required to ensure that a student's curriculum has relevance to his or her caregivers and home setting. However, caregivers may also wish to collaborate in conducting the assessment (especially the ongoing assessment that will be used to make decisions about mastery of these home skills). However, such ongoing assessment requires skills in applied behavior analysis.

In numerous studies, parents have demonstrated their ability to implement applied behavior analysis strategies with their children (Beckman-Brindley & Snell, 1985; Snell & Beckman-Brindley, 1984). In these studies, a variety of problem behaviors have been successfully changed by parents and other family members. These problems have included aggression (Whitman, Hurley, Johnson, & Christian, 1978), noncompliance (Brehony, Benson, Solomon, & Luscomb, 1980; self-injury, self-stimulation (Hanley, Perelman, & Homan, 1979), seizures (Zlutnick, Mayville, & Moffat, 1975), feeding problems (Becker, Turner, & Sajwaj, 1978; Ives, Harris, & Wolchek, 1978), and fears (Matson, 1981). Skills taught have included self-care skills (Adubato, Adams, & Budd, 1981), mobility skills (Angney & Hanley, 1979), communication procedures (Salzberg & Villani, 1983), and academic competencies (Koegel, Glahn, & Nieminen, 1978). From these demonstrations of parents' use of applied behavior analysis, it is logical to assume that caregivers can also acquire the skills to conduct ongoing assessment. However, professionals need to consider the extent to which such collaboration is feasible.

According to Snell and Beckman-Brindley (1984), there are several setting events that can function to affect parental or sibling implementation of treatment programs (and, undoubtedly, assessment procedures, as well). These involve the nature of the family as a system or a unit in terms of its structure, function, and life cycle. Obviously, some families will have more time and skill for, as well as interest in, collaboration in assessment than others, because of such setting events. Beckman-Bell (1981) argues that stress factors unique to families of individuals with handicaps increase the difficulties of effecting behavior change. The presence of an individual with a severe behavior problem serves to compound the stress already deriving from such factors as worry about the individual's daily survival; guilt and/or anger about his or her future; interference with family activities such as leisure time, social activities, and sleep; and possible reduction of income when one family member must remain at home with the individual. These stresses may have an effect upon energy levels and belief in the possibility of change, which in turn will affect the level of commitment to change on the part of family members (Nordquist & Wahler, 1973). Thus, collaboration in ongoing assessment can be suggested, but needs to be realistic based on the family's values, its daily schedule, the interaction patterns among its members, and family members' willingness to use the assessment procedures suggested by professionals.

Professionals also need to remember that caregivers' primary responsibility is to maintain a nurturing and normalized environment for all members of the family, including themselves. Few homes interrupt the dinner hour, for example, to conduct task analytic assessment of eating with a spoon. However, many families encourage a member's acquisition of new skills. Caregivers may post evidence of progress in these skills (e.g., papers from school, a picture of performance of the skill). People trained in applied behavior analysis sometimes use more precise assessment in their families, but typically in unintrusive ways. For example, a checklist of family chores might be posted with each chore checked and initialed when completed by a family member. Or, a person might count the number of cigarettes in a pack in the morning and at night to assess deceleration of smoking across days. Similarly, when the teacher and caregivers decide to share assessment of skills used in the home, unintrusive procedures and schedules for assessment need to be developed that blend with the family's life-style.

Sometimes, collaboration will extend beyond the caregiver's assessment of the student's progress to include evaluation of the caregiver's implementation of procedures. As described in Chapter 9, student progress can be dependent on the consistency of instruction. Since caregivers often have received only inservice training in using treatment procedures, this evaluation of consistency can be especially important to ensure that student progress will occur (Budd, Green, & Baer, 1976; Wahler & Fox, 1980). Procedures to guide this evaluation are described in Chapter 9.

Given that caregivers' collaboration in both initial and ongoing assessment is highly desirable, but complicated by the many demands and stresses in families with a member who is handicapped, the teacher needs to communicate carefully with the family to set priorities for their participation. When the caregivers are group home staff who are paid to teach and assess, as well as provide care, a larger role may be played in conducting the assessment of home skills. In the more typical family where caregivers are parents or guardians, the teacher will probably assume the primary responsibility for assessment and instruction. Family collaboration may then include participation in skill selection, anecdotal reports of progress, and depending on family resources to participate, assessment and instruction of a few priority skills. The following sections describe how the teacher can plan these types of assessment in consultation with caregivers.

INITIAL ASSESSMENT TO DEVELOP THE CURRICULUM PLAN

In Chapter 2, a plan was outlined for the initial comprehensive assessment that focused on skills for the home, skills for the community, and related skills. Skills for the home can be broadly classified as: (a) personal maintenance, (b) recreation and socialization, (c) housekeeping and food preparation, and (d) preparation for community outings. The first step in developing this curriculum plan is to contact the parents to identify specific environments for assessment, and tentative priorities to guide the assessment plan. An illustration of a survey that might be sent to the parents to obtain this information on relevant environments and priorities was presented in Chapter 2 (Figure 3, p. 32). Assuming that this step has been completed, the next step in conducting the initial assessment is to select the skills for direct assessment through a review of previous records, completion of an adaptive behavior scale, and completion of an ecological inventory.

Selection of Skills for Assessment

Previous records will often reveal objectives not yet mastered that still have relevance for the student. Therapeutic and medical evaluations may also provide relevant details. For example, diet restrictions will need to be considered in planning food preparation instruction. Severe neurological damage may preclude independence in toileting, and require alternative management strategies. Allergies may require care in selection of cleaning products and detergents. In addition to this information gathered from previous records, the general information obtained in completion of an adaptive behavior scale often gives the teacher examples of the student's skills and deficiencies. While this information may not be specific enough to be used in writing the curriculum plan, it may guide planning of further assessment. Caregivers can play an important role in each of these preliminary steps. Often, the caregivers are the best source of information to complete the adaptive behavior scale (e.g., through interviewing the caregiver). Caregivers also may have more complete records of medical or other considerations. For example, in a caregiver interview conducted by the author, a mother produced complete documentation, including graphs, of the effects of different behavioral interventions on her son's eye contact and stereotypic behaviors. She had saved copies of all reports that had been sent to her by professionals across her son's years of school. By contrast, this complete documentation had not been retained in the student's school records.

Another important task in assessment planning is the development and implementation of an ecological inventory. This inventory can help the teacher begin to plan instruction that is relevant to a student's own home and family background. One way to design this home inventory is to use an open-ended guide such as the one shown in Figure 1. In this approach, the teacher visits the home to observe both the physical environment and family dynamics. The teacher interviews family members in a relaxed and informal manner during the visit to gather information about their preferences and priorities. Sometimes, caregivers have received overly pessimistic prognoses of a student's ability and may have difficulty imagining which life skills the student may acquire. If the teacher has completed the adaptive behavior scale, or uses this visit to also complete the scale with the parents, some ideas may be suggested from the scale.

Another approach to developing an inventory of skills needed in the home is to identify the daily routines that are followed in the home. Freagon et al. (1983) have described how to plan assessment and instruction in group home environments based on the use of a daily and weekly schedule. Such a schedule can also be a useful format for an ecological inventory. In this approach, the teacher asks the caregivers (either in a visit or mailing) to identify the family's weekday and weekend schedule so that skills can be selected from the family's typical routine. Figure 2 shows an example of this ecological inventory approach.

A third approach is to combine skill assessment and the inventory. By using either an adaptive behavior scale or a teacher's checklist, the caregivers can check whether the student possesses or lacks skills, and rate the importance of each skill for the home environment. While this can be a simple approach for both the teacher and parent, further communication may be required to find out more about specific family values and customs. For example, snack preparation may be a high priority to the caregivers, but what snacks would be acceptable in their home? An example of this third approach is shown in Figure 3.

From the skills identified by the ecological inventory, the adaptive behavior scale, and prior records, a long list of skill deficits may be generated. The teacher needs to set priorities for the skills that will be further assessed. At this point, it may help the teacher to list the skill deficiencies identified by the categories suggested: (a) personal maintenance, (b) recreational and socialization, (c) housekeeping and food preparation, and (d) preparation for community outings. Skills that have been identified by the caregivers as priorities should be starred. Then, the teacher will note which of these priorities require further assessment to identify the student's specific skill needs. Also, if one or

---

Student's name: Dennis   Date: September 8
Teacher: Ms. K.   Environment: Home
Source of information: Home visit to observe and interview Dennis's family

1. List characteristics of the physical environment that are relevant to instruction:
    — Kitchen table is wheelchair accessible; counters and sink are not.
    — Large family room accommodates whole family including Dennis.

2. What are some of the activities of nonhandicapped peers in this environment?
    — Dennis's brother, age 15, is responsible for carrying out the garbage, making the beds, and dusting. His favorite pastimes are listening to records and making models. He also plays football and rides his bicycle with friends.

3. What are the student's current skills in this environment?
    — Dennis currently is dependent on his family members for all of his choices and his care. His mother can sometimes determine his preference by watching his facial expression.

4. What problem behaviors interfere with full participation in this environment?
    — None.

5. What are the family's preferences and customs? What student preferences has the family observed?
    — The family typically eats together after Dennis has been fed. They like Dennis to sit with them. The family also enjoys crafts and outdoor activities.
    — The family has observed that Dennis seems to like easy listening music and television shows with laughter. He dislikes applesauce.

6. List ideas for further assessment and instruction:
    — Expression of choice about music, food
    — Participation in a family chore
    — Social communication for mealtime

Figure 1. Example of an ecological inventory for a home environment that uses open-ended questions to be completed through observations and family interviews during a visit to the home.

more categories reveal inadequate information (e.g., no information on recreational skills because the student has not had the opportunity to use many materials), more assessment may be planned. (The teacher may also wish to use the priority ranking form [Figure 7] that is presented in Chapter 2.)

Assessment of the Student

When more information is needed because of inadequate information, assessment may be conducted in several ways. The teacher may use task analytic

Student's name: Ann   Date: September 10

Teacher: Ms. P.   Environment: Ann's home

Source of information: Telephone interview with caregiver (group home staff person)

Weekday routine

A.M.

7:00	Caregiver wakes up Ann and takes her to toilet.*
7:30	Caregiver dresses Ann.*
8:00	Caregiver helps Ann eat breakfast.*
8:30	Caregiver brushes Ann's teeth and gets her belongings ready.*
9:00	Car picks up Ann; driver escorts Ann to car (9:00–3:00 P.M. at center).

P.M.

3:00	Car delivers Ann; caregiver escorts Ann to house, stores her belongings.
3:30	Caregiver takes Ann to toilet.
4:00	Ann watches television.*
5:00	Caregiver helps Ann eat dinner.*
5:30	Caregiver helps Ann carry her dishes to the sink.
6:00	Ann watches television; caregiver washes dishes and clothes.
7:30	Caregiver gives Ann a bath and dresses her for bed.
8:30	Ann watches television; caregiver helps roommates.
10:00	Ann is escorted to bed.

Weekend routine

A.M.

7:30	Caregiver takes Ann to toilet.*
8:00	Caregiver dresses Ann.
8:30	Caregiver helps Ann eat breakfast and brush teeth.*
9:00	Ann watches television; caregiver cleans house.*

P.M.

12:00	Caregiver helps Ann eat lunch.*
12:30	Caregiver takes Ann to toilet.*
1:00	Weekend special—caregiver takes Ann and roommates somewhere such as grocery store, movies, or for a walk. On Sundays, friends and family sometimes come for a visit at this time.
3:30	Ann watches television; caregiver cleans or cooks.
5:00	Caregiver helps Ann eat dinner.*
5:30	Caregiver helps Ann take dishes to sink.
6:00 on	Same as week nights

Figure 2. Example of an ecological inventory for the home that identifies skills needed by outlining the family's weekday and weekend routines. (* = activities that the teacher and caregivers identified as possible targets for Ann's instruction)

assessment (e.g., of use of new leisure materials), observations of the student that are guided by checklists or anecdotal notes (e.g., of independent eating), repeated-trial assessments (e.g., using pictures to follow a housekeeping schedule) or frequency counts (e.g., toileting accidents). Resources on instruction for students with severe handicaps provide many examples of the assessment and instruction of domestic skills (e.g., Falvey, 1986; Gaylord-Ross &

Student's name: Nat

Date: September 21

Teacher: Ms. S.

Environment: Home

Source of information: Survey mailed to caregivers

Please identify whether Nat currently performs the skills below. For each skill, please also rank how important you think this is for Nat at this time.

Skills	Performs the skill	Importance of skill
Personal maintenance		
1. Undresses.	yes	2
2. Dresses.	no	1
3. Eats finger food.	yes	3
4. Eats with spoon.	somewhat	2
5. Eats with fork.	no	3–4
6. Drinks (no spilling).	somewhat	2
7. Eats a varied diet.	no	3–4
8. Uses toilet.	yes	1
9. Has no toilet accidents.	somewhat	1
10. Selects clothes.	no	3
11. Selects food.	yes	3
Leisure/socialization		
1. Plays alone.	yes, too much	4
2. Plays with siblings.	no	1
3. Plays with toys.	somewhat	2
4. Has hobbies.	no	3
Housekeeping/food preparation		
1. Performs some chores.	no	3
2. Pours own drink.	no	2
3. Makes simple snacks.	no	2
4. Picks up belongings.	no	2–3
5. Sets table.	somewhat	2
6. Puts laundry in hamper.	no	2
Preparing for the community		
1. Obtains belongings.	no	2
2. Puts on coat.	no	1

Figure 3.   Example of an ecological inventory for a home environment that uses a skill checklist. This approach identifies both skill deficiencies and caregivers' priorities in one survey. (1 = top priority, 2 = important, 3 = somewhat important, 4 = not important)

Holvoet, 1985; Sailor & Guess, 1983; Snell, 1987; Wehman et al., 1985; Wuerch & Voeltz, 1982). Readers are encouraged to consult these resources for illustrations of task analyses for each area of home assessment that is discussed. In the following sections, examples of this initial assessment are illustrated by considering how each home category was addressed in the case studies.

Personal Maintenance   Personal maintenance is an area that is often included in adaptive behavior checklists. Sometimes, this information, combined with the home inventory to note priorities, is enough to plan personal maintenance goals for the 3- to 5-year curriculum. In other cases, the teacher may not have sufficient information in this area. Such was the case for Ann's skill deficiency in toileting. Ms. P. knew from the adaptive behavior survey completed by the group home staff and from her own work with Ann that Ann had toileting accidents. However, she did not have a clear impression of whether or not Ann had an elimination pattern that would make schedule training a realistic goal. Therefore, Ms. P. recorded both the frequency and schedule of Ann's elimination for 2 weeks. She recruited the assistance of the group home staff to fill in the schedule of elimination each day in the evening hours. To make sure that the staff conducted this assessment daily, Ms. P. asked them to send the copy of this schedule to her each morning. Each afternoon, she wrote a brief note to thank them for the previous day's schedule and included the current day's data form. Through this cooperative assessment, Ann's schedule of elimination could be evaluated. This is shown in Figure 4. From this information, Ms. P. concluded that schedule training should be attainable. Because this was a top priority for Ann, she made this a first-year objective. The group home staff agreed to continue recording Ann's schedule of elimination to provide ongoing assessment of Ann's progress in toilet-training in her home environment.

In Dennis's case, Ms. K. noted that his parents had difficulty suggesting goals for Dennis because they were discouraged by his lack of progress to date. The adaptive behavior scale had revealed that Dennis had virtually no skills in personal maintenance. Ms. K. felt that she needed to observe Dennis and his mother engaged in a care routine to identify potential responses that Dennis could make to participate to some extent in this routine. Ms. K. collected task analyses from books and from her own work on dressing, bathing, and eating to use as a guide in observing the responses that Dennis's mother currently performed, but that might be targeted for Dennis. She used a schedule to make notes of the order of activities so that she could plan for his participation in the transition, as well as the activities. A summary of her notes is shown in Figure 5. Dennis's mother was pleased with this assessment and felt that it acknowledged the many activities that she performed with Dennis that could be developed further for instruction and assessment. She offered to keep a calendar with notes on new responses that she observed Dennis attempt during the care routine. Ms. K. welcomed this anecdotal method to report generalization and to identify new responses as they emerged.

Nat's parents had asked Ms. S. to pay particular attention to Nat's dressing skills. Getting Nat dressed in the morning often created havoc in the family's routine because he neither dressed himself nor cooperated with family members' efforts to dress him. Ms. S. evaluated both Nat's dressing skills using task analyses for pants, shirt, shoes, and socks (on and off). She also used a discrepancy analysis to identify other skills that Nat needed to cope with this activity (e.g., communication of choice). This discrepancy analysis is shown in

Student's name: Ann   Date: October 1–7
Teacher: Ms. P.

	Sun.	Mon.	Tues.	Wed.	Thurs.	Fri.	Sat.
7:00							
7:30	U+		U−			U+	
8:00		U−		U−	U−		U+
8:30							
9:00							
9:30							
10:00	U−	U+				U+	
10:30			U+	U−	U+		U−
11:00							
11:30							
12:00						U−	
12:30	U+	U+	U+				U+
1:00				U−	U+		
1:30							
2:00							
2:30							
3:00	U+	U+				U−	
3:30			U−	U+			U−
4:00							
4:30							
5:00							
5:30							
6:00	B+	B+		B+			B+
6:30							
7:00							
7:30	U−		U+	U+	U−	U+	
8:00							U−
8:30							
9:00							
9:30							
10:00							

Figure 4.   Example of schedule of elimination used in assessment for toilet-training. (U+ = urination in toilet, U− = urination in pants, B+ = bowel movement in toilet, B− = bowel movement in pants)

Chapter 8 (Figure 5). Nat's father was especially interested in Ms. S.'s efforts to find new ideas for Nat. He wanted to observe these assessments and brainstorm with Ms. S. She negotiated times for Nat's father to observe and contribute (e.g., during a home visit, in a visit to the classroom) and also scheduled times to observe Nat during the daily school routine. (This schedule

Student's name: Dennis   Date: October 3

Teacher: Ms. K.

Schedule	Activity	Ideas for Dennis
7:00	Changes diaper	Greeting, indicate wet
7:30	Dresses Dennis	Head up to signal ready; indicate clothing choice
8:00	Prepares Dennis's food	Operate blender
8:30	Feeds Dennis	Indicate food choice
9:00	Cleans Dennis and wheelchair	Grasp cloth; wipe tray

Figure 5. Assessment of a caregiver's routine to identify responses for partial participation.

was shown in Chapter 2, Figure 8.) Ms. S. considered Nat's father's interest to be an asset to Nat, and planned to discuss with the father possibilities for ongoing home instruction and assessment.

Recreation and Socialization   Adaptive behavior scales often do not provide adequate coverage of home leisure skills. Ms. P. was especially concerned about Ann's home leisure. Since Ann typically used few leisure materials besides television and magazines, Ms. P. considered it important to evaluate both her interests and skills. She developed a checklist of home leisure skills, shown in Figure 6, by asking Ann's caregivers to suggest materials that Ann had tried or might learn to use. Ms. P. then gave Ann these materials and assessed her interest and skills in using them. Her results are shown in Figure 6.

Ms. K. noted that Dennis's home leisure materials were primarily toys designed for young infants (e.g., mobile toy animals, rattles). She wanted to help his parents find age-appropriate materials that required simple responses. Ms. K. assessed Dennis's use of a flipper switch to activate a toy bus by using task analytic assessment. Dennis moved his hand slightly against the switch after being shown that it would activate the bus. Ms. K. decided that this, or another switch, could be developed so that with training, Dennis would be able to operate battery-operated toys or a tape player. Dennis's grandparents were especially pleased with this new idea for Dennis and offered to buy new toys to be adapted with switches. This seemed to be another area that his mother might report anecdotally to the teacher on an ongoing basis.

Ms. M. discovered from John's previous records that he once enjoyed geographic magazines and writing simple letters. Since his loss of sight, his caregivers had obtained a radio that broadcast talk shows, the weather, news, and so forth. Because of his hearing loss, John listened to the radio with earphones. However, his attention span for these shows was short. Ms. M. wanted to assess John's listening comprehension to determine if such shows were meaningful to him. She read him passages from magazines and asked him questions about the passages. She discovered that John could only comprehend

---

Student's name: Ann   Date: October 7
Teacher: Ms. P.

Code for interest:
  Yes—Shows definite interest in material by, for example, smiling, laughing,
       holding material, using material
  Some—Shows some interest in material (e.g., looks at it; picks it up; touches it)
  No—Shows no interest in material or pushes it away
Code for skill:
  Yes—Uses material in its intended manner
  Some—Makes some of the responses to use the material
  No—Does not use the material

Materials	Interest	Skill
Radio		
—Upbeat music	Yes	Some
—Easy listening	Some	Some
Cassette player		
—Upbeat music	Yes	No
—Comedian/laughter	Yes	No
Simon game	No	No
Electronic self-playing piano	Yes	Yes
Photo album	Some	No
Camera	No	No
Stamp collection	No	No
Cards	No	No
Magazines	Yes	Some

Figure 6.   Example of an assessment of leisure skills and preferences for an adult.

passages that were simple and contained familiar information (e.g., passages about hits and runs in baseball, names of food, lists of familiar names). However, he enjoyed these simple, familiar passages. Ms. M. noted that John's independent leisure time could be enhanced if he learned to operate a tape player without help, and to use a selection of tapes that he understood and enjoyed.

Housekeeping and Food Preparation   When Ms. K. assessed Dennis's use of an adaptive switch, she got an idea for teaching him to participate in his food preparation. Dennis's food was blended because of his eating difficulties. Ms. K. talked with Dennis's parents about having a blender adapted to be used with a flipper switch so that Dennis could blend the food after a family member placed it in the blender. Dennis's mother thought this would be an exciting way to get him to participate more in his daily routine, so this was included in Dennis's curriculum plan.

In John's case, Ms. M. was surprised to learn that John's caregivers reported that John performed no housekeeping or food preparation activities. His caregivers were concerned about John's safety and did not allow him in the kitchen or laundry room nor allowed him to operate a vacuum cleaner. At work,

This teacher has adapted a favorite family recipe for bread pudding. She then assesses which responses a student with severe motoric impairments can make alone or with assistance.

John had learned quickly to clean the lunch table by moving from chair to chair and counting each chair until he reached the sixth one. Ms. M. decided that she needed to consult with a person who was independent in daily living, but was also blind, to help the caregivers understand what precautions were or were not appropriate for John. From this ecological inventory, Ms. M. concluded that John could be expected to learn to perform most of his housekeeping and food preparation routine. Safety could be taught concurrently with the activities introduced. Since Ms. M.'s curriculum plan was for an adult continuing education program that was primarily work oriented, she included housekeeping goals that were appropriate to the work setting but would also be useful to his home setting (e.g., sweeping, cleaning windows, making coffee). She recommended that the caregivers give John more opportunities to participate in his home routine, and noted that the skills he would be using at work would be good activities to expect John to perform at home. Since John's caregivers were paid staff who were responsible for teaching John home skills, Ms. M. gave the staff task analyses for several domestic activities that John might learn to perform, and shared her system of data collection.

Preparation for Community Outings A fourth category of home skills is preparation for community outings. This includes such skills as using the telephone to make an appointment, getting ready for work, consulting a bus schedule, or keeping an appointment calendar. Ms. P. noted that Ann needed skills in preparing to leave to go to her educational program on weekdays. Her caregivers reported that she sat passively until dressed in her coat and escorted to the van. Through her ecological inventory of the home, Ms. P. had identified the steps that Ann needed to perform to prepare to leave. These steps were identical to those needed to prepare to go home in the afternoon. Therefore, Ms. P. wrote a task analysis for preparing to leave and used it to assess Ann. The task analysis is shown below:

1. Go to coat room.
2. Put on coat.*
3. Put on hat.*
4. Put on gloves.*
5. Walk to refrigerator.
6. Get lunchbox.*
7. Walk to bathroom.
8. Get gym bag with spare clothes.*
9. Carry lunchbox and gym bag to car.

Ms. P. found that some steps required further specificity for ongoing assessment. These are marked by an asterisk. For example, step 6 (task analysis for getting lunchbox) is broken down into the following smaller steps:

1. Grasp refrigerator door handle.
2. Pull door open.
3. Reach and grasp lunchbox by handle.
4. Pull lunchbox from shelf.
5. Push refrigerator door closed.

These examples of the initial assessment conducted in each case study help to illustrate how this information is obtained. The specific skills selected for each student are shown in Appendix A at the end of this book. One of the most difficult steps in assessment is selecting the skills that will be the most important for the next 3–5 years, and those that should be taught the first year. Guidelines for setting priorities were given in Chapter 2. Some examples of prioritization from the case studies may also help to illustrate this point.

In John's case, Ms. M. was concerned about John's lack of participation in his home routine. But Ms. M. had an overall priority for John of increasing his vocational skills and productivity. Therefore, she only selected from his home routine those skills that were common to his work routine, and referred his home needs to his caregivers (who were paid to teach him, as well as care for him).

In Dennis's case, Ms. K.'s criteria for skill selection were to increase Dennis's active participation in his home routine, and to teach him to make choices about his personal care. Since Dennis's progress to date had been minimal, Ms. K. also wanted to build a repertoire of activities on a few responses to be trained (i.e., a "yes" response, movement of one hand, and holding his head erect). Therefore, she wrote a home environment curriculum based on using these few motoric responses to perform some part of each category of home skills.

For Nat, his preferences and his family's preferences gave Ms. S. some clear priorities for instruction. His parents' expectations for Nat were to learn to "pull his weight" in the family's busy early morning routine by learning to dress himself. His entire family wanted Nat to participate in their enjoyment of family leisure activities and conversations. Therefore, Ms. S. selected skills that would make Nat more independent in his routine sooner (e.g., dressing in elastic waist pants rather than snapping skills), and based Nat's leisure instruction on some of the family's favorite pastimes (e.g., taking walks together, box games).

ONGOING ASSESSMENT AND EVALUATION OF PROGRESS

The ideas for ongoing assessment and evaluation of progress described in Chapters 3 and 4 can be applied to skills needed for the home environment. Two specific challenges in making these applications for assessment in and for the home are: 1) writing analyses with adequate specificity for the task selected, and 2) developing collaborative assessment procedures to be shared with caregivers.

The routines typical of home skills can lead to long task analyses or analyses with steps that include many responses. For example, if the teacher is concerned with a student's acquisition of housekeeping, the task analysis could include all the chores to clean the house. However, for students with few skills, the task analysis may need to be as specific as the responses to turn on a vacuum and push the nozzle to vacuum a small area. In initial assessment, a general task analysis for a skill like vacuuming may help to verify the need for this skill. However, for ongoing assessment, the task analysis needs to be both task and response specific enough for assessment and instruction that shows progress. To illustrate how this can be accomplished for different students, Figure 7 shows a task analysis written three ways for preparing cereal for breakfast. The first "big chunk" task analysis might have been used in the initial assessment. This task analysis might also be specific enough for students who have some food preparation skills, but need to learn this specific task. The second "small chunk" task analysis identifies more specific responses. The advantage of this second version is that it provides more specificity for instruction and for

I. Less specific task analysis and instruction for independence

1. Get appropriate utensils (bowl, spoon, knife, napkin, glass), and place on table.
2. Get cereal from cabinet and banana from fruit bowl.
3. Get milk and juice from refrigerator.
4. Pour cereal into bowl.
5. Peel banana, slice into cereal, and throw peel away.
6. Pour milk into bowl.
7. Pour juice into glass.
8. Sit at table behind place setting and eat.

II. More specific task analysis and instruction for independence

1. Get bowl from cabinet.
2. Get spoon from drawer.
3. Get knife from drawer.
4. Get glass from cabinet.
5. Get napkin from napkin holder.
6. Set bowl on table in front of chair.
7. Set napkin on left side of bowl.
8. Set spoon on top of napkin.
9. Set knife on right side of bowl.
10. Get cereal from cabinet.
11. Get milk from refrigerator.
12. Get juice from refrigerator.
13. Place cereal on table.
14. Place milk on table.
15. Place juice on table.
16. Get banana from fruit bowl.
17. Bring banana over to place setting.
18. Pull one strand of banana peel to bottom of banana.
19. Pull second strand of banana peel to bottom of banana.
20. Pull third strand of banana peel to bottom of banana.
21. Toss peel in garbage.
22. Pick up box of cereal.
23. Pour cereal into bowl.
24. Pick up banana in left (right) hand.
25. Pick up knife in right (left) hand.
26. Slice banana over cereal bowl using upward motion of knife from underside to top of banana.
27. Pour milk into bowl, not exceeding brim of bowl.
28. Pour juice into glass, not exceeding rim of glass.
29. Pull chair out from table.
30. Place buttocks on chair.
31. Push chair into table.

(continued)

Figure 7. Examples of specificity of task analysis for preparing breakfast cereal.

III. Partial participation and highly specific task analysis

Caregiver	S^D	Student
1. Put utensils, cereal, milk, sliced banana, and juice on table.	Items on table	
2. Wheel student to table.	Bowl in hand	Grasp bowl.
	Bowl in front, glass in hand	Place bowl in front of student on table.
	Glass on top of bowl	Grasp glass, place glass on top of bowl.
	Napkin in hand	Grasp napkin.
	Napkin at left of bowl	Place napkin to left of bowl.
	Spoon in hand	Grasp spoon.
	Spoon on napkin	Place spoon on napkin.
	Cereal package in hand	Grasp cereal package.
	Cereal in bowl	Pour in bowl.
	Milk container in hand	Grasp milk container.
	Milk in bowl	Pour milk into bowl.
	Banana slices in hand	Grasp banana slices.
	Banana in bowl	Place slices in bowl.
	Pitcher in hand	Grasp juice pitcher.
	Juice in glass	Pour juice into glass. Eat meal.
3. Acknowledge that student is finished.		
4. Put away cereal, milk, juice.		

Figure 7. (*continued*)

assessment of progress. The third version shown is designed for a student's partial participation in this activity when independent performance is not a goal due to the student's physical limitations. Teachers may find that, with each home skill to be task analyzed, similar decisions must be made about the specificity of the task analysis to be used. In Chapter 3, further discussion of this issue of specificity is provided.

A second challenge, as discussed at the beginning of this chapter, is to develop assessment procedures for collaboration with caregivers. It can be difficult to develop techniques that will blend into the family's life-style. One caregiver might prefer the precision of traditional data sheets and grid graphs. Another might find such data collection intrusive, but be willing to complete a checklist. A third caregiver might enjoy using a system that involves the student in self-recording (e.g., putting chips in a container or coloring a bar graph). A fourth might provide descriptive notes that give adequate information for the

Parents and guardians: *Please find below a summary of your child's progress in the last 6 weeks. Beside each skill, the pattern of progress is noted. The decision made to maintain or improve this progress is also stated for each skill. At the end, anecdotal notes about the student's progress are also given. Please review this summary and use the space below for any comments or questions you have regarding your child's progress during this evaluation period. Thank you.*

Skill	Data pattern	Instructional decision
Pants on	Improvement	Continue instruction.
Socks on	Mastered	Teach shoes on.
Greeting "Hi"	No progress	Teach hand wave with "Hi."
Hang up coat.	Improvement	Continue instruction.
Follow picture schedule.	Regression	Vary pictures daily.
Play Connect 4.	Regression	Teach new game.
Pour drink.	Slow progress	Improve prompting.
Make snacks.	Improvement	Continue instruction.
Walk with adult on sidewalk.	Improvement	Continue instruction.
Purchase snack.	No progress	Use Velcro wallet.

Teacher's comments: Nat has begun to walk cooperatively by my side during community outings and does not lie down or pull on my arm. He likes the new student in our class and has given her a toy on several occasions. He showed me a new sign the other day—"bird"—while we were walking.

Caregiver's comments: I am generally pleased with Nat's progress, especially in dressing. I am concerned that you dropped the Connect 4 game because this is something he can do with the family. Can we talk more about the new game you selected?

Your comments: _____

_____

_____

_____

Figure 8. Example of a communication form to be sent to the parents approximately every 6 weeks to report progress.

teacher to judge the student's generalization of new skills to the home. The teacher may wish to develop a file of several examples of home–school communique. In working with caregivers to develop the curriculum plan, the issue of assessment in the home can also be discussed and these different models shared. The caregiver may also suggest his or her own system. If this system can provide the necessary information, the caregiver's choice may be the best version because he or she may be more likely to use a system that he or she designed.

In sharing progress in the program with caregivers, the teacher may need a slightly different communication form. One format for this communication would be to summarize measured progress for each objective and include anecdotal notes on other progress observed. The caregiver can be encouraged to respond to this communication with any comments or questions. Some teachers use this type of communication when report cards are sent home for students in the regular school program. An example of this communication is shown in Figure 8.

SUMMARY

Assessment in and for the home requires consideration of caregivers' interests and resources for collaboration in this assessment. This collaboration can be facilitated through teacher and caregiver communication to set expectations for the caregivers' participation and teacher's progress reports. Even if the caregivers cannot assess the student due to family stresses, the teacher will still want to invite their opinions about environments and priorities for the curriculum plan. The ecological inventory will be an important step in identifying the specific skills for the home environment. This inventory might be conducted through an interview, survey, or observation. However the information is obtained, it is important for teachers to respect the many differences in family life-styles in planning life skills instruction for this domain.

CHAPTER 6

ASSESSMENT IN AND FOR THE COMMUNITY

In the not-so-distant past, people with severe handicaps were often excluded from community settings because of their handicaps. Through litigation (e.g., *Halderman v. Pennhurst State School and Hospital*, 1977; *Lloyd v. Regional Transportation Authority*, 1977; *Pennsylvania Association for Retarded Citizens (PARC) v. Commonwealth of Pennsylvania*, 1972) and legislation such as PL 94-142, such discrimination has been discouraged. Full community integration has become the priority for education of individuals with severe handicaps.

Teachers who endorse the principle of community integration face a challenge in planning instruction to achieve this goal. The tradition of behavior analysis has developed primarily in private settings where clipboards, stopwatches, and other tools of the trade have been accepted. When these same analysis tools and procedures are transported to the community, the unresolved problem of social acceptance of behavioral procedures becomes an added burden to the teacher. Additionally, the students may have been victims of past discrimination and thus may lack the basic skills required to blend into community settings. For example, a teacher who received a client 2 days after his release from a 45-year long institutionalization at Pennhurst commented, "How can I measure his skills? He is overwhelmed by the many new sites and experiences of life outside the one building where he spent most of his years." Another teacher who has implemented frequent community-based instruction noted a different problem. He described the logistics of taking a small group of students into community settings (transportation costs, time, safety precautions) and questioned devoting this precious teaching time to assessment. Yet this same teacher noted that without evidence of progress, administrative support for the long trips away from the school would be discontinued.

This chapter is based on both the guidelines that have been developed in the emerging community instruction research, and teachers' experiences in developing assessment in the community when no guidelines exist. By carefully planning assessment in the community, the investment of time and energy required by community instruction may be appreciated.

CONSIDERATIONS FOR
PLANNING COMMUNITY ASSESSMENTS

It may be helpful for teachers to divide community assessment into two broad categories of skills: vocational skills, and other community skills including recreation, travel, and use of community facilities. Different issues arise in planning assessment for each of these categories. For example, in planning vocational skills assessment, it will be important to know the acceptable and required behaviors of employees in potential job sites. In recreational assessment, preference assessment becomes a priority because of the purpose of recreational activities to enhance enjoyment and relieve stress. Travel training requires critical decisions regarding criteria for independence. Evaluating usage of community facilities requires assessment of infrequent activities. These are a few of the differences that suggest benefits of defining these categories separately as follows in this chapter.

Social validation of assessment procedures is another consideration in planning assessment *in* (not just *for*) community settings. Two procedures that may be used for social validation are consultation with experts, and evaluation of normative behavior (Kazdin, 1977). If the term "experts" is used to mean those who are most familiar with the environment selected for assessment, then it may be possible to select employees or other individuals in the target settings for interviews about proposed data collection. For example, the manager of a fast food restaurant or store, the bus driver, the health clinic receptionist, and the shopping center security staff are all employees who may be able to predict which assessment methods will draw unwanted attention to teachers and students.

Another way to validate the assessment procedure is to collect data on the norms in a given setting. Teachers might make lists of the different ways that people in the setting record information. Some of the normalized data collection methods observed by this author have included calculators (across many settings), public opinion polls and petitions on clipboards (infrequent), and date books and small spiral notebooks (frequent). Also, portable tape players with headphones are currently popular. All of these systems might be adapted for data collection. Table 1 lists data collection systems that are designed to both provide adequate data and appear normal in community settings.

The suggestions in Table 1 can help the teacher plan data collection methods to minimize the effect of data collection and teacher presence on the student's normalized experience in the setting. However, the teacher may also need strategies for minimizing the effects of his or her presence. For example, a teacher who accompanied her class to a fast food restaurant was pleased that one nonverbal student approached the cashier on his own initiative and showed the cashier a card that said "Would you show me where the restroom is located, please?" Unfortunately, the cashier yelled across the restaurant to the teacher,

Table 1.   Materials for unobtrusive data collection in community settings

Task analytic or multiple skill data
1. *Checkbook*   Responses are written like check entries.
2. *Stenographer's spiral notebook*   Skills are written on the left and data marked to the right.
3. *Magazines, popular books*   Task analysis is clipped to a page. When not collecting data, teacher appears to carry reading material. If crossword or other puzzle books (e.g., find a word) are used, data collection may appear to be puzzle work.

Frequency counts
1. *Small spiral notebook*   (pocket size)
2. *Hand-held clicker*   Many grocery stores sell a hand-size adding machine for about two dollars. This can count two behaviors under 100 if the teacher uses the dollars for one and cents for the other.
3. *Calculator*
4. *Masking tape*   Tallies are marked with a pen on a piece of tape attached to cuff of teacher's sleeve.
5. *Pennies in pockets.*   A penny is transferred to a different pocket for each response.
6. *Wrist counters*   These look like watches and can be ordered through PRO-ED Enterprises.
7. *Old watch*   The minute hand is moved one number for each response.
8. *Wrist band with slip of paper*   A paper to tally responses is hidden in a wrist band.

Time-based data
1. *Walkman cassette player*   This can be used to give time cues for interval recording by an observer who is not teaching (e.g., supervisor).
2. *Stopwatch with neck strap*   Timing duration or latency is easiest with a stopwatch. With casual clothing and a jacket, the watch may not be obvious.

"Do you want to watch him do this, too?" Many teachers who have taken students into public settings for community instruction have experienced similar situations in which either people in the setting changed their behavior to try to please or help the teacher and students, or in which the student waited for the teacher to be watching before performing a skill. Two strategies for minimizing the influence of teacher presence to assess student performance in the normalized environment are: 1) to allow people in the setting to become acclimated to the presence of the teacher, and 2) to observe the student from a distance.

For example, in research, experimenters sometimes introduce a pre-baseline assessment period to allow the subjects to become acclimated to the data collection system. After this period, it is assumed that the subjects' behaviors return to their typical patterns and are no longer "reactive" to the presence of data collectors. When this acclimation does not occur, the observation may be made more unobtrusive, that is, designed to blend into the setting (e.g., by recording information in the same manner used by others in the environment). Repeated exposure and unobtrusive observations may be two methods to reduce the reactivity of both the student and the general public to data collection. If the teacher will be going to the same setting repeatedly, it may help to talk to the employees about the importance of the students performing skills in the same way that others do in that setting.

To assess what students will do when their teacher is not present, the teacher could ask persons unknown to the students to conduct the assessment, but this is usually impractical. An alternative way to observe the student "alone" is for the teacher to pretend to leave, but observe the student while partially or fully hidden. Or, the teacher may tell each student to "try it alone" and ignore attempts to gain teacher attention prior to completing the task.

ASSESSMENT IN AND FOR VOCATIONAL SETTINGS

Vocational placement is one of the highest priorities for adult or adolescent students. Most adults work outside their homes for wages. Others work in the home with other means of financial support (e.g., wage-earning family member) or work in the community without earning wages (e.g., volunteers). However, this pattern differs across age groups. Many young adults (ages

For an adult with few current skills, putting away belongings upon arrival at a work setting may be an important skill to assess.

18–21) continue to attend school. Most older adults retire from their primary wage-earning jobs and spend their days engaged in leisure activities, volunteer work, and/or new wage-earning pursuits. Vocational placement for adults with severe handicaps ideally would be similar to, or better than, typical wage-earning employment patterns. A "vocation" is a strong inclination to follow a particular activity or career. Ideally, teachers help students pursue a vocation, but pragmatically, teachers must prepare students for jobs available in the local community.

One of the most important factors for teachers to consider is the employability of students upon completing training. To enhance employability, students will need to receive training in skills for jobs that exist in community settings. If the real jobs for which students are trained have frequent openings, the chances of obtaining a job placement may also be improved.

Some teachers face a difficult challenge in considering vocational options for adult or adolescent students with profound skill deficits. Such students may not only have severe physical impairments, but may lack even basic communication systems, toileting skills, or self-care skills. It can be difficult to select the goal of job placement when such students' current skill needs are great. Hopefully, further research and demonstrations will provide alternatives for vocational training despite these challenges. For example, Renzaglia, Cullen, and Ruth (1985) have developed a technological adaptation that enabled a student with severe physical handicaps to perform benchwork assembly.

Currently, several alternative routes have been suggested for people who have been classified as profoundly mentally retarded with concurrent multiple disabilities or who have other special needs (e.g., medical complications). One route would be to find creative ways to make the student employable at minimum wage or above. This route should never be eliminated. Typically, the ability of students with severe handicaps has been underestimated. It is important not to set up invalid criteria for supported employment training. For example, in a follow-up study of job retention, Hill et al. (in press) found that having poor reading skills, being nonverbal, having a history of institutionalization, or needing intervention for behavior problems were *not* deterrents to job success. They also found that students with moderate mental retardation had better job retention than those with mild mental retardation. An important variable that Hill et al. (in press) found to be relevant to job success was previous training in community work crew–oriented programs. Thus, exposure to community integrated job training may be more important than many characteristics previously used to exclude people with severe handicaps from vocational opportunities.

A second route would be to place the student in an integrated work setting at a reduced wage (e.g., through application for the Handicapped Worker's Certificate). In this approach, people with complicated needs (e.g., medical or physical disabilities that preclude working at the expected pace or performing all tasks of a job) that make meeting employer expectations difficult may still earn more than a sheltered placement would allow, and have opportunities for normalized relationships with co-workers. Some researchers have suggested that meaningful work without wages may be preferable to segregated placements with less meaningful activities (Brown et al., 1984). Others argue that asking people to perform tasks without wages that typically are performed for pay sets up a dangerous precedent for discrimination (Bellamy et al., 1984).

If a student's current deficits and learning rate make acquisition of skills required in existing community jobs untenable, an alternative to unpaid job placements may be vocations that may be identified by interviewing non-handicapped people of a similar age group who do not work for pay. Meaningful alternatives for students who are not yet served in supported employment programs may be revealed in these interviews. These alternatives may include such "vocations" as volunteer work in churches or hospitals (e.g., delivering flowers), homemaking, senior citizen activities (e.g., tours, musical programs), pursuit of a hobby or art (e.g., painting, collections) or other activities that are often considered "leisure." Like nonhandicapped adults, adults with severe handicaps may also pursue these activities temporarily until paid work is obtained.

The importance and feasibility of wages, the type of work preferred, and the current job market all influence vocational decisions. When a student does not have the skills to observe and discuss a wide variety of vocational options, it becomes especially important for the teacher to work with the student and his or her caregivers to make the decisions required. Many job choices for people with severe handicaps will require years of training. Thus, it becomes important to begin assessment and instruction early in the student's school career. The following areas of assessment can help the teacher design vocational assessment for students who are at various stages with varying abilities and preferences. This assessment includes consideration of meaningful alternatives for people for whom supported employment does not yet seem feasible. However, teachers should carefully consider the advantages of paid employment for every student assessed, and encourage this goal in planning with caregivers.

Vocational Skill Selection

Vocational skill selection requires determining what jobs are available in the community, what the student wants to do, and what the job world requires the student to do. After obtaining this information, the teacher then begins to assess what the student can currently do. The first step of becoming familiar with jobs that exist in the community in which the student lives can be done by scanning the classified ads to identify positions that are frequently advertised, or obtaining employment listings from large companies and services (e.g., hospitals). In this screening, the teacher should note the general requirements for the job (e.g., license required).

Once the teacher has some idea about community job availability, he or she can proceed to the second step of assessing the student's preferences. This may require planning exposures to types of work available in a given geographic area, interviewing caregivers to determine their aspirations for the student, asking the student about different types of work that have been presented, and talking to past teachers about their observations of the student's preferences. Obviously, this selection process is longitudinal. An IEP objective for the elementary years might be for the student to communicate likes and dislikes about different types of work. As time becomes short (e.g., in programs for adults who do not yet have vocational skills), a more pragmatic approach may be needed in which the teacher presents the jobs currently available, and helps the student select from a limited list. Figure 1 presents a broad list of job types that the teacher may consider in designing preference assessment and caregiver interviews.

Job availability and the student's preferences are important starting points for the teacher in designing a vocational assessment. Once availability and preference are known, the teacher can begin the third step of assessment—conducting ecological inventories of potential employers to find out what skills will be needed to secure and maintain this type of employment. This inventory process has been well defined by Moon, Goodall, Barcus, and Brooke (1985) in their guide for job trainers that was developed based on their experience with the Virginia Commonwealth University supported work model. Their inventory process includes two analyses: an environmental analysis, and a job analysis. In the environmental analysis, the job trainer observes someone performing the job in its various phases. As the employee is observed, the job trainer notes the physical areas in which the job is performed, the major duties performed in each area, and skills related to each duty. The time spent in each work area is also noted. Once the job trainer has observed the job being performed, he or she then conducts a job analysis that consists of interviews with the employer and co-workers, and further observations. This analysis is conducted to identify specific skills needed, such as time management, mobility, communication, work initiation, and social behavior. It also includes questions about logistics such as the work schedule and transportation needed. The information obtained through this inventory clarifies what task analytic, work productivity, and vocationally related skills will need to be assessed for the student.

The well-defined Moon et al. (1985) method to conduct an ecological inventory with potential employers has been defined for adolescents and adults who will be placed in identified jobs for training. Teachers of younger students will want to identify skills for future placements. Since the teacher probably will not know the specific job that the young student will secure in the future, a broader array of skills may be targeted. To identify these target skills, the teacher of young children might replicate the job analysis approach across

	Student is familiar	Student prefers	Family prefers	Available	Adequate wage
Check which of the following apply for each job type:					
Job type					
1. Factory:					
Benchwork					
Assembly					
Bagging					
Machining					
Woodwork					
Clerical					
Custodial					
Other:					
2. Service (e.g., schools, hospitals):					
Food preparation					
Custodial					
Clerical					
Caretaking					
Other:					
3. Business (e.g., offices, banks):					
Clerical					
Custodial					
Other:					
4. Transportation (e.g., city bus, gas stations):					
Clerical					
Custodial					
Vehicle care					
Other:					
5. Arts, leisure:					
Food services					
Clerical					
Custodial					
Tickets					
Other:					
6. Stores:					
Stock storage					
Custodial					
Other:					

Figure 1. Vocational preference planning chart.

several jobs. While this would be initially time-consuming, this information could be used for planning across several years. Another approach to identifying employer expectations would be to review published surveys (Mithaug & Hagmeier, 1978; Rusch, 1983). The weakness of this latter approach is that some of the skills may be specific to the types of jobs and geographic areas surveyed. The obvious advantage is that the published surveys provide far more extensive information than is feasibly obtainable by a teacher. The results of two surveys reported by Rusch (1983) provide a checklist that could be used as the basis for either an interview or observation assessment for students (see Table 2).

Table 2. Competitive employment survival skills

	Skill	Percentage
1.	Recites verbally upon request full name	100
2.	Demonstrates basic arithmetic skills of addition	100
3.	Follows (1) one instruction provided at a time	100
4.	Recites verbally upon request home address	99
5.	Recites verbally upon request home telephone number	99
6.	Communicates such basic needs as sickness	99
7.	Maintains proper grooming by dressing appropriately for work	99
8.	Understands work routine by not displaying disruptive behaviors when routine task or schedule changes occur	99
9.	Responds appropriately and immediately after receiving one (1) out of every two (2) instructions	98
10.	Demonstrates basic arithmetic skills of subtraction	97
11.	Moves safely about work place by paying attention to where he or she is walking	97
12.	Works without displaying or engaging in major disruptive behaviors (e.g., arguments) more frequently than one (1)–two (2) times per month.	97
13.	Communicates such basic needs as pain	96
14.	Reaches places of work by means of own arrangement (walking, taxi, personal car)	96
15.	Maintains proper grooming by cleaning self before coming to work	96
16.	Initiates contact with co-workers when needs help on task	96
17.	Initiates and/or responds verbally in three (3) to five (5) word sentences	96
18.	Speaks clearly enough to be understood by anyone on the second transmission	96
19.	Maintains personal hygiene by keeping teeth clean	96
20.	Maintains personal hygiene by keeping hair combed	95
21.	Remembers to respond to an instruction that requires compliance after a specified time interval with one (1) reminder	95

(continued)

Table 2. *(continued)*

Skill	Percentage
22. Works without initiating unnecessary contact with strangers more frequently than one (1)–two (2) times per day	95
23. Communicates need to use toilet	94
24. Follows instructions with words such as "in," "on"	94
25. Continues working without disruptions when co-workers are observing	94
26. Initiates contact with supervisor when job cannot be done	94
27. Responds appropriately to safety signals when given verbally	93
28. Follows instructions with words such as "under," "over," "through"	93
29. Continues working without disruptions when supervisor observing	93
30. Writes three (3) to five (5) word sentences	93
31. Corrects work on task after second correction from supervisor	93
32. Communicates by means of verbal expression	92
33. Understands the purpose of money	92
34. Follows instructions with words such as "to your right/left"	92
35. Learns new job tasks explained by watching co-workers/ supervisors perform task	92
36. Responds to an instruction requiring immediate compliance within 90–120 seconds	92
37. Works without initiating unnecessary contact with supervisor more frequently than three (3)–five (5) times per day	92
38. Moves safely about work place by identifying and avoiding dangerous areas	91
39. Wants to work for money	91
40. Manages time by completing an assigned task on time	91
41. Follows four (4) to six (6) word instructions	91
42. Communicates such basic needs as thirst	90
43. Learns new job tasks explained by verbal instruction	90
44. Wants to work for sense of accomplishment	90
45. Works without initiating unnecessary contact with co-workers (who are working) more frequently than six (6)–eight (8) times per day	90
46. Recites verbally upon request age	89
47. Communicates such basic needs as hunger	89
48. Moves safely about work place by wearing appropriately safe work clothing	89
49. Learns to minimum proficiency new job task, provided one (1) to six (6) hours of instruction	89
50. Demonstrates understanding of rules (set down by supervisor) by not deviating from them more frequently than one (1)–two (2) times per month	89

(continued)

Table 2. *(continued)*

	Skill	Percentage
51.	Works without displaying or engaging in minor disruptive behaviors (e.g., interruptions) more frequently than one (1)–two (2) times per month	89
52.	Adapts to new work routine, achieving normal levels of productivity within one (1)–five (5) days	88
53.	Follows instructions with words such as "press," "hold," "twist"	88
54.	Recognizes the importance of attendance and punctuality by not being late or absent from work more than an average of once per month	88
55.	Maintains proper grooming by dressing appropriately after using restroom	86
56.	Answers the telephone appropriately for self	85
57.	Initiates contact with supervisor when a mistake is made	85
58.	Participates in work environment for periods of five (5)–six (6) hours	85
59.	Initiates contact with co-workers when needs task materials	84
60.	Completes repetitive tasks previously learned to proficiency within 25%–50% rate	84
61.	Works at job continuously, remaining on task for one (1) to two (2) hour intervals	84
62.	Reads 6 to 8 word sentences	83
63.	Recites verbally upon request name of previous employer	83
64.	Tells and follows time on the quarter hour	82
65.	Adapts to new work routine, with the number of supervisory contacts being three (3)–four (4)	82
66.	Maintains proper grooming by washing after using restroom	81
67.	Maintains personal hygiene by using deodorant	81
68.	Works alone and increases productivity on own	81
69.	Works continuously without leaving job inappropriately (not having a good reason) more than one (1)–two (2) times per day	81
70.	Responds appropriately to safety signals (e.g., buzzers, bells)	80
71.	Works alone and increases productivity when asked to complete job by a specified time	80

From Rusch, F. (1983). Competitive employment. In M. E. Snell (Ed.), *Systematic instruction of the moderately and severely handicapped*. Columbus, OH: Charles E. Merrill; used with permission.

While both the Moon et al. (1985) and the Rusch (1983) approaches to identifying skills needed in employment provide excellent techniques for students who have a repertoire of adaptive behaviors applicable to jobs, neither provides guidance for the teacher of students who have limited communication and mobility and who may not be able to care for themselves. For these students, the alternatives previously described need to be considered by interviewing people in the community who do not work for pay to identify other options in the student's community. If a vocation is viewed as a person's special interest and inclination to pursue a certain activity, new ideas may be found with an ecological inventory. Questions to help the teacher conduct ecological inventories to guide this process are given in Figure 2.

Assessment of Job Skills

In the job selection process, the teacher should first draw up a list of skills that the student will need for future job environments. The next step is to assess directly the student's performance of these skills. This may be done with checklist observations, task analytic assessment, and time-based assessments for latency or rate of learned skills. At this phase, the teacher does not try to make the assessment specific enough for ongoing evaluation, but rather, useful for skill selection. Table 2 (on pp. 145–147) provides an example of a list of skills that could be used in a checklist format. Over days, the teacher could present each task and note whether or not the student could perform it in the classroom setting. The teacher could note if the student has no skill, the mastered skill, or partial mastery of the skill.

A second type of checklist observation that might be performed is a daily routine assessment. The teacher could structure the day to follow the employer's typical routine, and assess whether or not the student could manage time and follow the schedule. Figure 3 presents an example of a schedule assessment.

The teacher also needs to conduct some task analytic assessments of the job skills identified (e.g., dishwashing, collating, assembly). For already mastered jobs, the teacher may also wish to assess: (a) the rate of productivity (e.g., for piece work), (b) duration for job completion (e.g., cleaning), or (c) latency to begin a job. This information can then be used when writing the individualized plan.

For the older student or adult who will be trained for specific jobs, it will be important to conduct this assessment in the job setting. A student who performs job skills in a familiar school setting may not generalize them to the employment setting. Even for the younger student who is receiving training for future placements, the teacher needs to remember that assessments of skills in simulated settings may not be indicative of performance in the actual community setting (see Snell & Browder, 1986, for review).

Ongoing Evaluation   For each objective on the individualized plan, ongoing evaluation is necessary. This assessment needs to be sensitive to subtle changes across days. For example, if the job is industrial dishwashing, the ongoing evaluation might be a breakdown of a big chunk task analysis into small chunk task analyses for dishes, pots, garbage, and material storage. Assessment of social and communication skills might be included in these task

Student's name: _____ Date: _____

Teacher: _____

Caregiver interview

1. Rank in order the importance of each of the following reasons for working:
   _____ Wages
   _____ Benefits
   _____ Friendships
   _____ Human service
   _____ Self-fulfillment
   _____ Other: _____

2. Which of the above would be your priority for this individual?

3. What special interests or abilities does this individual have?

4. Have you considered jobs for this individual? If so, what?

5. What alternative activities would you like to see this individual pursue if paid work is not obtained?

Nonhandicapped adult interview

1. Do you hold a job? If so, how did you select and train for your vocation?

2. What do you consider to be your "vocation"?

3. If you do not hold a job, what are your primary daily responsibilities and activities?

4. Please give a brief description of your daily schedule.

Student summary and planning

1. List special interests and skills.

2. Describe the results of any job exposures.

3. List priorities for vocational training and placement (e.g., wages, social interaction, human service).

4. List jobs in which the student might be trained to make one or more independent responses to fulfill priorities in #3.

5. List technological adaptations needed for #3.

Figure 2. Ecological inventory to identify vocational options for students with few adaptive behaviors.

Client's name: Nat
Week of: 9/3–9/7

Response

5—Begins next task within 3 minutes of set time
4—Moves to next area and waits
3—Looks at schedule and waits
2—Waits; does not consult schedule
1—Does not acknowledge schedule change (e.g., continues to work at previous task, wanders to nonwork area)

Times	Activity	9/3				
9:30	Snack preparation	2				
10:00	Snack	2				
10:30	Dress for P.E.	1				

Days

Figure 3. Schedule assessment.

analyses or scored on separate checklists. Figure 4 shows an example of a task analysis for initial job assessment with adaptations for ongoing evaluation. (See Chapters 3 and 4 for more examples of ongoing assessment and evaluation.)

Case Study Examples

The case study examples provided earlier can also be used to see how this vocational assessment procedure can be applied to various students. For each example, a brief description details how skills were selected, which procedures were used for initial assessment, and how ongoing assessment was developed for evaluation of progress.

Assessment for a Young Elementary Student: Nat Nat's case provides an example of planning for a young child who may be an excellent candidate for supported employment by the time he reaches high school, given longitudinal planning and instruction. Ms. S. began this longitudinal planning

Initial assessment task analysis for photocopying with self-feeding machine	Task analysis used for ongoing evaluation—Year 1: Grasp paper and push start.
	(Teacher removes staples.)
1. Remove staples from originals.	1. Slide fingers around stack.
2. Place stack in tray face up.	2. Move stack to tray face up.
3. Set number of copies.	3. Place stack on tray vertically.
4. Set paper tray choice.	4. Release grasp of stack.
	(Teacher sets all features)
5. Set automatic collate.	5. Extend index finder.
6. Press start.	6. Locate "start" button.
7. Remove each copy and insert it in electric stapler.	7. Push "start."
8. Place completed copy on shelf.	8. Grasp completed copy.
*9. Show communication card to secretary if machine flashes yellow words ("call key operator").	9. Move copy to shelf.
	10. Place copy on shelf horizontally.
	11. Release grasp of copy.
	(Teacher or another student staples and watches for machine breakdown)

Results: All steps were incorrect. Student did not look at machine. When guided to hold paper, student crushed it and tried to mouth it. Student did not have a pointing response to press buttons. Student had no visual discrimination of buttons. Teacher projected that mastery of this photocopying job could take 3–5 years. Student is 12 years old.

Figure 4. Example of revision of a task analysis used for initial assessment to adapt it for ongoing evaluation during the first year. (* = optional step)

by focusing on Nat's job exposure, work repertoire, and cooperation with teaching. To select skills for assessment, Ms. S. interviewed the parents to determine their priorities for Nat, used the survey shown in Table 2 (pp. 145–147) as a checklist for assessment, and interviewed the high school teacher to note skills needed in future vocational training. Vocational skills were not yet a priority for Nat's parents, but they agreed that Nat needed to develop independent work skills. Ms. S. spoke with the high school teacher and discovered that food preparation, custodial skills, and benchwork assembly were emphasized in that vocational program. From this information, she developed an initial assessment that included using the survey information (Table 2) as a checklist assessment, and conducting direct task analytic assessment for food preparation, food clean-up, and pen assembly. She also timed Nat's independent work on a known task. From this assessment, she wrote IEP objectives for making simple snacks, wiping a table, pen assembly, working alone, and stating personal information (name, age, address). Her ongoing assessment included task analyses for making a powdered drink, making peanut butter crackers, wiping a table, and pen assembly (the snack preparation tasks met Nat's domestic skill needs and contained components of the high school food preparation skills to be acquired such as unscrewing jars, stirring, and spreading with a knife). She timed his in-seat behavior with a stopwatch when assigned to work alone. For personal information, a repeated-trial assessment with generalization probes was used for social interactions with other personnel and students in the school.

Obviously, Ms. S. has targeted skills that will need to be generalized to later, real job settings. This generalization will be the focus of her extended performance objectives (see Chapter 4). For example, Nat will be taught to spread with a knife across types of spreads and breads, and to stir larger and thicker foods. Once he acquires benchwork assembly tasks, these tasks will be used to shape productivity and working for extended periods of time without teacher interaction. Once Nat enters high school, these skills will be probed in job settings. The extent of Nat's generalization will depend on how well the teacher has matched his longitudinal instruction in generalization to the actual stimulus and response generalization required in these settings. Thus, even though Nat is still young, the teacher needs to become familiar with the skills required in real job settings to plan longitudinal instruction.

Planning for a Student with Few to No Current Independent Adaptive Behaviors and Severe Physical Impairments: Dennis Vocational planning for Dennis required Ms. K. and the parents to do some creative thinking. To select skills for assessment, Ms. K. asked the parents about their preferences for Dennis. She also interviewed people with severe physical impairments who were employed, and some adults who were not employed due to disabilities but who had alternative vocations (i.e., meaningful activities to which they devoted time on a daily basis). The people Ms. K. interviewed who had physical impairments all had academic skills that enabled them to hold office jobs (e.g., vocational supervisor, computer expert). The two adults interviewed by Ms. K. who did not work (a disabled veteran and a man with a serious, chronic illness) spent their days involved in their hobbies (collections, ceramics), volunteer work (counseling at the veteran's hospital), and daily living (for both men, tasks such as dressing and cooking require extended time). The veteran viewed his activities as temporary while he continued to seek employment. The parents noted that Dennis's strongest preference was for music. In using the inventory shown in Figure 2 (page 149), the parents identified "self-fulfillment" as their priority for Dennis's vocation. Their second priority was human service. From this information, Ms. K. decided to expand her assessment of Dennis's recreational and domestic skills (described later in this chapter and in Chapter 5). A skill that seemed to provide potential for self-fulfillment and human service was use of a tape recorder. Ms. K. assessed playing a tape recorder with a flipper switch because Dennis could be asked to play musical selections for the family, for his class, and/or as a volunteer in nursing homes. Expression of preference for various musical tapes was also assessed by noting his reaction to tapes that were played. Ms. K.

designed ongoing assessment for partial participation in tape recorder use (task analytic) that included a communication step of signaling the need to change tapes. She and the parents noted the need to reevaluate Dennis's vocational options each year as his skills progressed and new technological advances were made that would enhance his participation in jobs.

Planning for a Student Who Will Enter Transitional Instruction for Supported Employment: Al Al was an excellent candidate for supported employment training. To select skills for Al, Mr. A. first noted job availability by scanning the classified ads and calling several area companies for job listings. He then conducted environmental and job analyses of two of Al's preferences that had real job availability: short-order cooking and custodial services. Al also expressed the specific preference for working in a bowling alley. Mr. A. spoke with the bowling alley manager about job availability, and decided to pursue this specific placement for Al. To enhance Al's success upon placement, however, Mr. A. decided to identify the jobs required in the bowling alley and assess them in the school setting (e.g., kitchen, restrooms) prior to beginning on-the-job training and assessment. Mr. A. would arrange transitional training for Al in the bowling alley to begin in the second year of his 3-year plan. For initial assessment, Mr. A. used task analyses of preparing an order of food, cleaning the restrooms, and cleaning the snack bar. He also used a checklist of social behaviors for interaction with customers, and another for time management. Mr. A. conducted most of his assessment during his class's short-order cooking program in the school. For ongoing assessment and evaluation, Mr. A. developed task analyses of each type of sandwich served, soda fountain use, dishwashing, mopping, restroom sink cleaning, and toilet cleaning. He was able to use his time management and social behavior checklists for ongoing evaluation without adaptation. For time management, he counted the number of work sessions correct (e.g., if he moved correctly to his next job or break.) For social behavior, he counted the number of customer interactions that met all criteria on the checklist (e.g., asks for order, ignores teasing or complaints about service, says "Thank-you" when giving check).

Planning for an Adult with Few Independent Adaptive Responses: Ann Because Ann was an adult with limited adaptive responses, vocational independence for her was improbable. However, Ann was in a job training program that gave her the opportunity to work for wages. To select skills for assessment, Ms. P. interviewed Ann's caregivers and two women who were the same age as Ann who did not hold jobs (one was a homemaker, the other had been unable to find a job for several years). Ms. P. asked Ann's caregivers about their priorities using the ecological inventory in Figure 2 (see page 149). Since Ann's income was limited, their first priority was for Ann to earn wages. The women interviewed by Ms. P. noted that they spent their days involved in domestic activities (cleaning, shopping), hobbies (sewing, gardening, reading, music), and civic activities. The woman who was seeking a job did odd jobs to earn money (e.g., housework, babysitting, yardwork, substitute school bus driver). Ms. P. also identified the entry skills for a supported employment office enclave. (An enclave is a program for adults with severe handicaps who work in an integrated site such as a factory or office with ongoing training and support.) Thus, she would plan for Ann to progress toward either the enclave or alternative vocations, and reassess her options each year. For initial assessment, Ms. P. made note of the need for expanded recreational and domestic assessment for Ann. She also decided to assess the wage-earning jobs that were most typically available at the center and that existed in the supported work enclave as possibilities for future placement. Then, she selected task analyses of the jobs with the best wage potential for Ann, which included mailing and photocopying. She also made a checklist of skills that would be needed for Ann to perform these skills in integrated settings (e.g., eliminate toileting accidents, communicate with less familiar people). From these direct initial assessments, she selected attaching labels and using a photocopier as the year's job priorities, and the related skills of communicating basic needs and becoming completely habit trained for toileting. These ongoing evaluations included task analytic assessment of the job tasks, frequency counts of toilet accidents (to be decelerated), and repeated, distributed-trial assessment of communicating basic needs with a picture book.

Planning for an Adult with Severe Regression in Adaptive Behavior Due to the Acquisition of Multiple Disabilities in Adulthood: John John had poor mobility and multiple sensory deficiencies, so Ms. M. had difficulty planning vocational options for him. To help her select skills for assessment, Ms. M. interviewed John's caregivers and two men with sensory impairments. One man was employed and one was not. She also obtained the entry criteria of the local office enclave supported work program. In an interview with his caregivers, Ms. M. found out that their priorities for John were self-fulfillment and earning wages. The enclave primarily performed mass mailings. John enjoyed receiving and handling mail, and he was able to state his preference when asked, so mailing was considered an excellent vocational choice for John. The men whom Ms. M. interviewed had very different life-styles. The man who was employed taught in an area high school and required few adaptations in his life with his family and in his profession. The man who was not employed had lost his sight in later life and retired early. This man spent his days involved with his hobbies (making rugs and other crafts) and socializing with his friends at the senior citizen center.

For initial assessment, Ms. M. designed a checklist of types of mailing jobs. She also developed a time management and social behavior checklist, since these were major problems for John. Independent ambulation in a familiar setting was also assessed by using a task analysis of walking to the restroom and break room. She made social integration a general goal to be developed in the months to come. Specific objectives were selected for the mailing tasks, time management, and ambulation to the restroom and break room. For ongoing assessment of the job tasks, Ms. M. used task analyses of affixing labels, folding letters, sealing envelopes, and stuffing flyers. For time management, she introduced John to a Walkman tape player with headphones and counted the number of times he left his seat before the Walkman cued him (to be decelerated). For ambulation, Ms. M. tested John's ability to find familiar locations by using the same task analysis as was used for the initial assessment.

The goal of identifying an activity of interest to be developed and pursued is being achieved for each individual. When students' motor deficits and age make them even more challenging than Dennis or Ann, enriched leisure may be their most meaningful vocation. However, wage-earning employment should be seriously considered for all individuals on an ongoing basis as new technological advances and research in employment training provide new opportunities for employment of people who previously could not secure jobs.

USE OF COMMUNITY FACILITIES

Initial Assessment

Living in community settings requires frequent use of public facilities to shop, receive health care, participate in recreation, and so forth. Some of the skills required for any of these settings are applicable to most of the other settings. Others (e.g., bowling) are setting specific. In developing the student's 5-year plan, the teacher may want to assess skills for recreation, for shopping, for health care, and for general public behavior.

Recreational Skills Recreational and leisure skills have become increasingly important in American society as technological advances for home care create more time for leisure pursuits. Even when an individual has long job hours, scheduling leisure time is important to maintain mental and physical health. For the person who has severe and multiple handicaps, leisure time is even more important. Often, vocational opportunities are limited and/or provide little stimulus for enjoyment. For individuals who do not work outside the home, community recreation provides opportunities for social interaction. In the previous chapter, a plan was developed for assessment of recreation in and for the home environment. This chapter focuses on recreation in community settings.

Community recreational skills selection will vary greatly across geographical areas. The teacher may begin the ecological inventory process by noting the types of recreation available, and by asking the caregivers about family outings. Sometimes, family outings will be limited by the student's current skill deficits. In other instances, accessibility of facilities will be a barrier to participation. While the latter problem is one that requires political and legal action, skill deficits can be addressed in assessment to improve both the student's and the family's access to community recreation. Figure 5 provides a community recreation inventory that is most applicable to small- to medium-size cities such as the Lehigh Valley area of Pennsylvania where this inventory was developed. In rural areas, community recreation often is centered around visits to friends, neighbors, and a prominent human service organization such as a church or civic group. Schools also provide the setting and impetus for special cultural or sports events.

Ideally, assessment of community recreational skills would be conducted by taking the student to the different settings and events and observing current skills. However, such assessment would rarely be feasible. Community recreational events are most often available after school hours and are often located some distance from the school. Also, many community recreational events are episodic (e.g., musical programs) or seasonal (basketball games). To make this assessment most feasible, the teacher may conduct an interview based on the inventory presented in Figure 5. An interview of the caregivers may reveal which skills that the student has. Sometimes, the student has had few community experiences because of behaviors not tolerated in public (e.g., grabbing people, toileting accidents). The teacher may be able to plan one community outing to assess related skill deficits as a supplement to the checklist. With the interview information and perhaps one observation, the teacher may then simulate some community activities to obtain direct assessment of recreational skills for selection of objectives to be taught. For example, a checklist such as that shown in Figure 6 may be used during a school assembly to assess participation in spectator events. Or, the school gymnasium might be used to conduct a broad task analytic assessment of participation in exercise classes such as those available at the YMCA or YWCA. An example of an initial assessment task analysis for an exercise class follows:

1. Dresses in appropriate clothes
2. Joins group before class begins
3. Stands in appropriate area
4. Imitates instructor for warm up
5. Imitates instructor for aerobics
6. Imitates instructor for floor exercises
7. Imitates instructor for cool down
8. Returns to dressing room when others do
9. Dresses in street clothes

If the student cannot perform any exercises, the instructor should be informed, and task analyses of each of the most frequently used exercises in the daily routines should be developed.

From this information, the teacher is ready to select one or two recreational objectives, and develop ongoing assessment.

Shopping Skills A frequent community activity is shopping, which may include small purchases at a convenience store, drug store purchases, grocery

Phase I. Selection of place and events

Type	List available places	Check if family participates	Check if a student preference
Spectator:			
1. Sports	————————		
2. Cultural	————————		
3. Movies	————————		
4. Other (e.g., rodeo)	———————— ————————		
Games and hobbies:			
1. Dancing (e.g., square dance)	———————— ————————		
2. Camping	————————		
3. Arts and crafts	————————		
4. Outdoor photography	————————		
5. Nature appreciation	———————— ————————		
Fitness activities:			
1. Swimming	————————		
2. Gymnastics, exercises	————————		
3. Ballgames	————————		
4. Walking, biking, hiking	———————— ————————		
Civic/social:			
1. Church	————————		
2. Scouts, clubs	————————		
3. Volunteer work	————————		
4. Educational classes	———————— ————————		
Friends' homes:			
1. Visits	————————		
2. Parties	———————— ————————		

(continued)

Figure 5. Ecological inventory for community recreation.

Phase II. Identification of activities and skills needed

List places identified with potential events for student's recreation. Check skills needed in each. Circle skills the student has not yet mastered (i.e., needs to acquire).

Places

		1. _____	2. _____	3. _____	4. _____
1.	Sit quietly.				
2.	Purchase tickets.				
3.	Show identification.				
4.	Purchase food.				
5.	Consume food.				
6.	Use restroom.				
7.	Communicate with people besides family.				
8.	Communicate with family.				
9.	Learn special skills (e.g., dancing, exercise).				
10.	Keep up with special equipment (e.g., camera).				
11.	Other				

Figure 5. *(continued)*

shopping, clothes shopping, and so forth. These various shopping activities share common responses that may be assessed and taught for generalized shopping skills to be acquired. In the ecological inventory to identify skills to be assessed, the teacher will identify specifics about the stores that are used by the student and his or her family. An example of an inventory completed for a shopping mall is shown in Figure 7.

Event: <u>Basketball game</u>

Skills	Check if typical of student during event	List student's socially unacceptable behaviors
1. Locates seat with minimal disturbance of people already seated	no	Pushed people aside to reach seat
2. Sits quietly if appropriate for event (e.g., movies, music programs	✓ Most of the time	Some stereotypic hand waving; some standing but sat when told to sit
3. Participates like non-handicapped peers (e.g., clapping, cheering)	✓ Imitated others cheering, clapping	
4. Looks at event	✓	
5. Communicates politely to request adjustment if disturbed by others (e.g., smoking, standing, sitting on belongings)	no	Cried loudly when someone sat on her jacket
6. Ignores rude and other socially inappropriate behaviors of others	no	Repeated angry voice tone and profanity at nearby spectator's comments about the referee

Figure 6. An example of a checklist that could be used to assess social skills during spectator events.

Following this inventory, initial assessment may be designed. Figure 8 provides an example of a checklist of shopping skills that may be used during an interview with caregivers, or during an observation in a shopping environment like the mall or grocery store.

Initial task analytic assessment may also be conducted for purchasing, giving a prescription to the pharmacist, grocery shopping, and so forth. Listed below is one such task analysis that is designed for direct assessment of purchasing a few items in a store with aisles and front checkout counters (e.g., grocery store, K-Mart, drug store).

1. Open door and enter store.
2. Walk across front of store to locate aisle.
3. Walk down aisle to correct item display.
4. Pick up correct item.
5. Walk up aisle to front carrying item.

Student's name: __John__   Source of information: __Observation/interview__
Relevant domain: __Community__
Environment: __Lehigh Valley Mall__   Date __10-30__

1. Environmental description:
   —Handicapped parking space at sidewalk to entrance (no street crossing necessary)
   —Shops include clothes store, restaurants, shoe store, drug stores, hair styling salon, sports shop, candy store

2. Activities of same-age nonhandicapped persons in the environment:
   —Buying both required and pleasure items, dining, socializing on benches, window shopping
   —Lots of older men were observed shopping and sitting on the benches.

3. Student's current activities in the environment:
   —Walks with sighted guide, consumes food purchased for him

4. Skill deficits that *must* be overcome for placement or further participation in the environment (e.g., loud screaming in a movie theater):
   —Sometimes has toilet accidents and screams loudly when confused about his activity or schedule

5. Family preferences/customs:
   —John's sister frequently shops in this mall but has never taken John with her.
   —John's sister usually has lunch at the drug store lunch counter when she goes.

6. Ideas for instruction:
   —Discriminate dollar to make a small pleasure purchase.
   —Learn the shopping routine of his sister so that he will not be confused about activities.
   —Purchase lunch in the drug store.
   —Get a hair cut.

Figure 7. Ecological inventory of a shopping mall.

6. Locate an open checkout counter.
7. Wait in line holding item.
8. Place item on counter.
9. Take out and open wallet.
10. Give cashier money.
11. Collect and pocket change.
12. Return wallet to pocket.
13. Carry bag to exit.
14. Open door and exit store.

From this task analysis, the teacher can select objectives, and design assessments of the specific skills that the student will be taught.

	Never	Sometimes	Most of the time
1. Walk in correct door.			
2. Manipulate shopping cart.			
3. Identify money; select item within budget.			
4. Determine items.			
5. Read aisle signs.			
6. Read shopping list.			
7. Give correct money.			
8. Carry bags.			
9. Take items out of cart, put on counter.			
10. Ask for information.			
11. Open refrigerator doors.			
12. Take clothes off hangers.			
13. Use elevators or escalators.			
14. Read numbers for floors.			
15. Read tags/labels.			
16. Use coupons.			
17. Return shopping cart.			
18. Try on clothes.			
19. Put clothes back on hangers.			
20. Read dates on items.			
21. Grasp item.			
22. Release items into cart.			
23. Walk and carry object.			
24. Take number for waiting.			
25. Climb stairs.			
26. Take free samples.			
27. Find appropriate places to sit (rest areas).			
28. Use restroom.			
29. Use pay phone.			
30. Use drinking fountain.			
31. Use tongs (means of selecting food).			
32. Knows not to sample merchandise.			
33. Be aware of other people (traffic).			

Figure 8.   Shopping checklist.

Health Care Students with severe and multiple handicaps often have health problems that require frequent visits to health care professionals. Sometimes, past unpleasant experiences cause the student to react to all visits to health care professionals with fear and resistance. Assessment of the skills needed to be an active participant in health care, and improve communication about procedures, may help the student tolerate these frequent visits. The parent interview can help the teacher know the types and frequency of health care appointments. An interview of one or more of the health care professionals in these settings may familiarize the teacher with the participation needed during examinations and treatments. From this information, the teacher may design a checklist for health care visits such as the one shown in Figure 9.

General Public Behavior, Mobility, and Travel Depending on the student's skills, different expectations may exist for the ways in which the student will use community resources. For some students like Al, further instruction may provide the skills to use resources alone or with companions who do not instruct or supervise. For other students, like John, brief opportunities may be made available for independently participating in an activity while an escort waits nearby (e.g., John might make a purchase in a convenience store alone but be driven to and from the store by an escort). Other students, like Dennis, will always have an escort while in public. To determine

| Place: _____ Purpose of visit: _____ | | |
| Student: _____ Observer: _____ | | |
Skill	*Check if typical of student during visit*	*Describe student's inappropriate behaviors*
1. Shows identification to receptionist	no	
2. Locates seat	no, escorted to seat	
3. Sits quietly; may view magazine	no	Screamed loudly and tried to leave
4. Follows nurse when name called	no	Continued to scream
5. Allows physician to conduct examination, treatments	no	Bit and hit physician
6. Communicates discomfort appropriately	no	Biting occurred when physician touched sore spot
7. Shows insurance information to receptionist	no	Ran out of office

Figure 9.   Checklist for health care visits.

the feasibility of using facilities alone, the teacher might use a checklist of skills required to be safely alone in public (see Figure 10).

Another important set of skills is needed for travel and mobility. Does the student have the skills to cross streets, locate a destination, use the city bus? For a student who will always be escorted, the teacher may note the student's cooperation with an escort in crossing streets, speed in exiting the bus, or head control while being pushed in a wheelchair on sidewalks. Figure 11 provides a checklist of travel and mobility skills that may be used in an interview or observation format.

Ongoing Assessment and Case Study Examples

After the teacher completes the initial assessment to plan a curriculum for community skills, the individualized plan is written, and ongoing assessment is developed. This should be done for each area of community skills. For instance, for recreational skills, specific ongoing assessment might include a

	Never	Sometimes	Most of the time
1. Recites verbally full name			
2. Recites verbally on request home address			
3. Recites verbally on request telephone number			
4. Uses telephone			
5. Communicates basic skills, sickness, and asks for restroom			
6. Uses restroom			
7. Enters and exits building			
8. Maintains proper grooming			
9. Reaches destination			
10. Communicates need for help			
11. Has pedestrian skills			
12. Waits in line			
13. Uses money correctly			
14. Responds to danger alarms (fire, etc.)			
15. Smiles if meeting acquaintances but ignores strangers			
16. Uses social pleasantries (excuse me, etc.)			

Figure 10. Assessment of skills needed to be in the community alone.

		Check skills student has:
I.	**Pedestrian skills**	
	A. Walking (escorted)	
	1. Walks with head erect	____
	2. Stays with escort	____
	3. Hands at side or carrying objects	____
	4. Quiet or communicates appropriately	____
	5. Crosses streets when prompted by escort	____
	6. Has stamina to walk to destination	____
	B. Wheelchair (escorted)	
	1. Rides with head erect	____
	2. Quiet or communicates appropriately	____
	3. Has stamina to ride to destination	____
	C. Orientation to destination	
	1. Walks or wheels self in correct direction	____
	2. Makes appropriate turns	____
	3. Arrives at destination	____
	4. 1–3 for simple, familiar destinations	____
	5. 1–3 for complex (several turns) familiar destinations	____
	6. 1–3 for new destinations with directions	____
	D. Street crossing	
	1. Waits if traffic approaches	____
	2. Crosses with light	____
	3. Crosses by observing traffic	____
	4. Stops if car pulls out or turns	____
	5. Crosses at appropriate speed	____
	E. Street types mastered (crossing stimuli)	
	1. "Walk" signs	____
	2. Traffic light (red, green, yellow)	____
	3. Stop sign for traffic	____
	4. Uncontrolled intersection	____

(continued)

Figure 11.   Checklist for assessment of travel and mobility.

task analysis of bowling or vending machine use. Task analyses might be more specific for students who learn slowly and have few entry skills, for example, a task analysis for grasping a soda can when assisted in purchasing a soda (see Figure 12), releasing a ticket to a ticket collector at a spectator event, or opening a wallet in a store. Frequency counts might be used for behaviors to be decelerated such as shouting or grabbing objects. The teacher might use some time-based data for assessment of fluency, such as latency in taking selected items to the checkout counter, or duration of time to use the vending machine. This specific assessment can be used to evaluate cross-time progress. For

    F. Street types mastered (traffic conditions)
1. One-way traffic   ____
2. Two-way traffic, two lanes   ____
3. Two-way traffic, four lanes   ____
4. Slow traffic   ____
5. Fast traffic   ____
6. Numerous vehicles   ____
7. Infrequent vehicles   ____

II. Car/van transportation
1. Enters/exits vehicle alone   ____
2. Fastens seat belt   ____
3. Does not touch door handle en route   ____
4. Operates window   ____
5. Has stamina to ride to community locations   ____
6. Sits quietly or communicates appropriately   ____
7. Communicates needs during travel (e.g., restroom, eating, too hot)   ____
8. (Wheelchair) Participates in transfer from chair   ____

III. City bus transportation
    A. Bus alone
1. Identifies correct bus   ____
2. Pays fare   ____
3. Quiet or appropriate communication on bus   ____
4. Locates destination and departs   ____

    B. Bus with escort
1. Waits at bus stop with escort   ____
2. Gets on/off bus at appropriate speed   ____
3. Inserts fare in slot   ____
4. Sits quietly or communicates appropriately with escort   ____
5. Sits with head erect   ____
6. Departs with escort   ____

Figure 11. *(continued)*

example, in Figure 12, the teacher is assessing the number of correct steps in a task analysis developed for early partial participation in grasping the soda. The figure also shows the decisions that the teacher made in evaluating the data trend. (The reader is referred to Chapter 4 for more information on evaluation of ongoing data.)

    Development of ongoing assessment is further illustrated in the following descriptions from the case studies.

    Nat When Ms. S. interviewed Nat's parents, it became clear that taking Nat into public was extremely difficult at that time because of his interfering behaviors and lack of alternative behaviors in public. Nat's problems in public limited the entire family's access to community events. Nat's parents' priorities were for Nat to accompany them safely and quietly in public. Ms. S. suggested

Behavior: __Grasp soda can.__ Name: __Ann__ Mastery: __100%/2 days__

Delay verbal

100	20 20 20 20 20 20 20 20 20 20	20 20 20 20 20 20 20 20 20 20
90	19 19 19 19 19 19 19 19 19 19	19 19 19 19 19 19 19 19 19 19
	18 18 18 18 18 18 18 18 18 18	18 18 18 18 18 18 18 18 18 18
80	17 17 17 17 17 17 17 17 17 17	17 17 17 17 17 17 17 17 17 17
	16 16 16 16 16 16 16 16 16 16	16 16 16 16 16 16 16 16 16 16
70	15 15 15 15 15 15 15 15 15 15	15 15 15 15 15 15 15 15 15 15
	14 14 14 14 14 14 14 14 14 14	14 14 14 14 14 14 14 14 14 14
60	13 13 13 13 13 13 13 13 13 13	13 13 13 13 13 13 13 13 13 13
	12 12 12 12 12 12 12 12 12 12	12 12 12 12 12 12 12 12 12 12
50	11 11 11 11 11 11 11 11 11 11	11 11 11 11 11 11 11 11 11 11
	10 10 10 10 10 10 10 10 10 10	10 10 10 10 10 10 10 10 10 10
40	9 9 9 9 9 9 9 9 9 9	9 9 9 9 9 9 9 9 9 9

8. Carry can. — 8 8 8 8 8 8 8 8 8 8 | 8 8 8 8 8 8 8 8 8 8
7. Stand erect. — 7 7 7 7 7 7 7 7 7 7 | 7 7 7 7 7 7 7 7 7 7
6. Lift can. — 6 6 6 6 6 6 6 6 6 6 | 6 6 6 6 6 6 6 6 6 6
5. Grab can. — 5 5 5 5 5 5 5 5 5 5 | 5 5 5 5 5 5 5 5 5 5
4. Curl fingers around can. — 4 4 4 4 4 4 4 4 4 4 | 4 4 4 4 4 4 4 4 4 4
3. Bend at waist. — 3 3 3 3 3 3 3 3 3 3 | 3 3 3 3 3 3 3 3 3 3
2. Lean toward machine. — 2 2 2 2 2 2 2 2 2 2 | 2 2 2 2 2 2 2 2 2 2
1. Extend hand. — 1 1 1 1 1 1 1 1 1 1 | 1 1 1 1 1 1 1 1 1 1
*********** % — 0 0 0 0 0 0 0 0 0 | 0 0 0 0 0 0 0 0 0 0 0

30 31 1 4 5 6 7 8 11 12 13 14 15 18 19 20 21 24 25 26

Dates: Oct./Nov.   Absent

	Reviews	
Date	Trend/mean	Decision
10/16/85 (not shown)	Acceleration; $\bar{x}$ = 10%	No change
11/12/85	Acceleration; $\bar{x}$ = 10%	Inadequate progress—improve prompts; delay verbal
11/14/85	Acceleration; $\bar{x}$ = 34%	No change

Figure 12.   Example of ongoing assessment for grasping a soda can. The figure shows the combination data collection/graph and data review described in Chapter 4. A slash (/) indicates the number of independent correct responses.

that Nat's interfering behaviors be decelerated by teaching Nat specific skills for family outings. The parents liked this idea.

To assess Nat's community skills, Ms. S. used the shopping checklist shown in Figure 8, and interviewed the parents to find out what Nat could do at that time. The parents said that Nat climbed stairs alone and grasped objects but did not put them in the cart or carry them. Nat also had no awareness of curbs or traffic, and was difficult to escort safely at street crossings and in the parking lots of shopping centers. Ms. S. took Nat shopping with her class and an aide, and observed his behavior in public. She also found that Nat was difficult to escort because he did not walk with her, but instead tried to pull away and run. Ms. S. also conducted a task analytic assessment for purchasing while at the store, but Nat performed none of the steps correctly.

Ms. S.'s long-term plan for Nat was for him to make purchases without help, and to accompany the class or his family in the store or restaurant. She targeted communication and walking with chosen objects as alternative behaviors to his running and pulling away from his escort.

For the next year, she selected in consultation with the parents the priorities of using a wallet to make a purchase under a dollar, communicating the purchase choice by pointing and signing, and walking while carrying a choice. Generalization training would be targeted for the grocery store and a fast food restaurant. For ongoing assessment, Ms. S. developed: (a) task analyses for wallet use and simple purchases, (b) a repeated-trial assessment for choice, and (c) a frequency count for leaving her side in public. The latter choice would be counted by using a hand-held grocery shopping clicker.

Al   Mr. A. began this part of his assessment with the assumption that Al would need the skills to be alone in public for long periods of time because of his competitive employment potential. Al also had some skills that could be shaped toward independent use of community recreational facilities. Al had mastered most of the skills required for city bus use and grocery shopping prior to this assessment but could not perform either activity alone.

In talking with Al's parents and the staff of a group home, Mr. A. concluded that Al's primary community environments outside his job would be the YMCA, a certain medical office complex, grocery stores, convenience stores, and a discount department store. Mr. A. knew Al's shopping skills from their previous work together. Al needed to learn to shop alone and to select items within his budget. By interviewing the parents, Mr. A. discovered that Al could not ride the bus to the medical complex and could not communicate well with the health care professionals. He also would annoy other people in the waiting room by repeatedly making inappropriate remarks to them. In conducting task analytic assessment on a class trip to the YMCA, Mr. A. discovered that Al dressed slowly and annoyed other people who were dressing by making inappropriate comments to them. He could use the exercise bicycle but had very poor fitness. He could not swim alone. Mr. A.'s long-term plan for

Al was for him to be able to work out at the YMCA with a nonhandicapped peer, to shop for a list of groceries alone, to improve his skills for medical visits, and to ride the bus to new destinations by following a bus schedule and calling for bus information.

For the first year, Mr. A., Al, and his parents selected locating bus destinations, using the grocery store alone, and selecting pleasure purchases within his $10 per month allowance. A nearby university gymnasium would also be used for improving cardiovascular fitness and acquiring appropriate gymnasium behavior (this less-public facility was chosen so that Al would not have bad social experiences at the YMCA during early learning). For ongoing assessment, Mr. A. designed a repeated-trial assessment for identifying the bus destination, a task analytic assessment for calling for information on the bus schedule, repeated-trial assessment for selecting purchases within his price limit, duration recording for time in the grocery store alone, a frequency count of appropriate and inappropriate social interactions in public, and pulse rate assessment for fitness training.

Dennis Ms. K. discovered that Dennis's parents frequently took him to public settings. However, they noted that he did not "do anything" anywhere they took him. Because of Dennis's feeding difficulties, they did not take him out to eat. His mother sometimes took him to a shopping mall but Dennis made no responses other than some visual orientation while there. Dennis's parents were active in a church. Dennis usually accompanied his parents to church functions where he received many social interactions to which he did not respond. He often did not hold his head erect when riding in the car or being pushed in public. Ms. K.'s long-term plan for Dennis was for him to communicate with his many friends at church and to participate to the greatest extent possible during shopping trips.

For the first year, Ms. K. chose communicating a social greeting, communicating choice by signaling "yes," keeping his head up while being pushed in the wheelchair, and improving visual orientation to objects in public environments. To assess these objectives, Ms. K. designed repeated-trial assessments for social interaction, communication, and visual orientation, and duration recording for keeping his head up.

Ann Ann's group home staff rarely took her to public settings because she walked very slowly, sometimes cursed loudly, and made few responses in these settings. Ms. P. used the shopping checklist, the checklist for health care visits, and the community recreational inventory. By interviewing the group home staff and taking Ann shopping, she discovered that Ann had no traffic awareness, attempted to eat coins if given them, and did not release objects that she grasped. In health care facilities, she wandered around the room and cursed loudly when sick. Ann could reach for choices and smiled when greeted.

Ms. P.'s long-term plan for Ann was for her to make simple purchases when escorted, to communicate distress using pictures or words, to cross streets safely with an escort, and to participate in community spectator events. For the first year, Ms. P. selected choosing and carrying an item in the store, using a wallet, and discriminating coins to use a vending machine (with supervision to prevent Ann from eating the coins).

John John enjoyed community outings and walked well with a sighted guide. Ms. M. interviewed his group home caregivers and learned that they took John out to eat, and to some special events. The caregivers found John difficult to manage because he would refuse to walk if confused about his destination and would roam around and yell if he wanted to leave a special event. Since John's vision loss, his inactivity had resulted in some weight gain and general deterioration of fitness. John had not ridden a bus since he lost his sight.

Ms. M. used a task analysis of bus riding to assess this skill. John had difficulty finding his coins and climbing the bus steps but otherwise enjoyed the experience and asked to repeat it. Ms. M. also used the task analysis for making purchases (see pp. 159–160) at a convenience store. John could make a selection and take money from his wallet, but could not select the correct amount. While being escorted, John frequently stopped to "catch his breath." Ms. M. asked John about his recreational preferences. John wanted to ride the bus and go to baseball games.

Ms. M's long-term goals for John were for him to use a cane to walk in public with an escort providing minimal assistance to find a destination; to ride a bus with an escort to help with the destination only; to select money to purchase pleasure items, clothes, groceries, and tickets at sports events; to communicate his need for information about departures and destinations and as necessary, wait for a group. If John's communication, money use, and mobility improved, it would be feasible that he might accompany a senior citizen group on a bus tour or to a baseball game with a peer escort.

For the first year, Ms. M. wrote objectives for improved cane use, increased distances for walking, discrimination of dollars and quarters, and making simple purchases at convenience stores. For ongoing assessment, she developed task analyses for cane use and making purchases, conducted repeated-trial assessments for money discrimination and communication, and measured distances walked (in city blocks) before John stopped to catch his breath. (The reader is referred to Appendix A for more information on the case studies.)

SUMMARY

People enjoy their communities as they learn more about the availability of preferred activities, develop friendships, and become familiar with routes and facilities. As people develop a vocation, self-fulfillment is enhanced and they become more financially independent. The purpose of assessment in and for community settings is to help students with severe handicaps enjoy their communities, meet their needs to use stores and services, make friends, and find a vocation. While some students will learn to cope without an escort, others will rely on lifetime companionship to open the door to community resources. The application of behavioral assessment helps the teacher identify specific objectives for community independence and to evaluate the effectiveness of instruction to achieve this goal.

CHAPTER 7

ASSESSMENT OF RELATED SKILLS
COMMUNICATION, MOTOR SKILLS, ACADEMICS

Traditional special education curricula have often focused on skills that are associated with daily activities, including communication, gross motor skills, fine motor skills, and functional academics. However, when these skills are addressed out of the context of their daily living use, the activities chosen for instruction often become nonfunctional, or have limited utility in daily activities. However, communication, motor, and academic skills can have more use for the student in his or her daily life if they are related directly to daily activities. For example, instead of teaching a student to identify coins with a tabletop activity, the teacher presents coin identification during vending machine, laundry, and shopping instruction. Instead of teaching a student to point to objects and sign their name in an isolated communication lesson, the teacher can have the student sign to request objects needed for lunch, self-care, work, leisure, and so forth. Instead of having a student improve fine motor skills with pegboards and bead stringing, the teacher can have the student focus on fine motor skills needed to play board games or prepare snacks. Thus, this chapter refers to the skill areas of communication, motor, and academic skills as "related skills" to emphasize the fact that these skills should be directly related to specific daily activities to enhance their generalized use in these activities.

Sometimes, to avoid identifying nonfunctional communication, motor, or academic skills, teachers have focused their assessments only on the daily activities. However, when assessment only focuses on the domains of daily living, these related skills may be underdeveloped. Often, when outlining skills needed for the home or work, it may not be readily apparent how communication will enhance skills in these environments. For example, a student may be able to perform job assignments with little to no social communication, but the development of this social communication can enhance the person's friendships in the work environment. This chapter provides guidelines for the teacher to assess related skills with the priority of selecting skills that will enhance the home and community activities considered most important for the student.

The first two skill areas, communication and motor skills, are often referred to a specialist (e.g., speech/language pathologist, occupational or physical therapist) for comprehensive assessment and treatment. Such comprehensive assessment is beyond the scope of this book. However, teachers are encouraged to work with these specialists in developing assessment and treatment plans in these areas. The teacher's contribution to multidisciplinary assessment of language and/or motor skills can be the identification of responses that will most likely be used and maintained in daily activities. Thus, the teacher often leads the planning of the language and motor "functions" to be targeted. Often, the advanced training of the therapist enables him or her to better identify the language and motor "forms" for these functions. Functions are the purposes for the language or motor responses to be acquired (e.g., to ambulate to the cafeteria, to cross a street, to open a drink can, to request items, to make choices). Forms are the topography of the responses used for these functions (e.g., self-ambulation in an electric wheelchair with a chin control, use of a picture communication book, manual signing). Obviously, both teacher and therapist will have ideas for form and function, but the teacher's knowledge of skills needed in the home and community make him or her especially aware of specific functions needed for acquisition of language and motor skills. This chapter is a guide for the teacher to follow in assessing functions for the related skills of communication and motor activities, with some discussion given to forms for these functions.

Academic skills also have many uses across daily activities. When targeting academic instruction per se, the teacher may become absorbed in "survival words" or computation, and lose sight of the purposes for this academic development. However, assessment of daily activities may not clearly indicate how skills like reading and math can and should be taught. This chapter gives the teacher guidelines for weighing the importance of academic skills in comparison to other skill needs, and for assessing those skills that are most closely linked to an individual student's environmental demands.

COMMUNICATION ASSESSMENT

Language has several characteristics that influence communication. These characteristics may be classified as components of form, content, and of pragmatic function. The components of form for *speech* are phonology, morphology, syntax, and semantics. Phonology is the study of the production and comprehension of speech sounds (e.g., the initial consonant "b" in the word "butter") and of prosadic features of speech (e.g., loudness, duration, pitch). Morphology is the study of the smallest unit of meaning in speech. "B" obviously has no meaning of its own. However, root words, suffixes, and prefixes do have meanings (e.g., -ing is used to mean a continuing process, as in "swimming"). Syntax is the study of production and comprehension of recognized sentence structures. Semantics is the study of the content of communication (e.g., vocabulary). While phonology, morphology, syntax, and semantics all are relevant to the specific form of communication, their importance is relevant to the extent that they help a person convey his or her purpose for communicating. Being able to convey one's purpose for communicating, and to obtain the desired response from others are the focus of the study of pragmatics. In this book, the term "function" will be used to refer to the purpose of communication. "Form" is used to refer to the mode, symbols, and rules to combine symbols and words in communication. The term "content" is used to refer to the vocabulary selected.

If a student uses a nonspeech form of communication, some of the speech forms of communication may not be applicable. For example, in picture communication, the study of phonology, morphology, and syntax do not apply unless pictures are sequenced into sentences (which probably is not necessary to convey meaning). In American Sign Language, syntax differs from spoken syntax, and individual speech sounds or letters are not signed for most words. Thus, consideration of form for nonspeech communication focuses on the mode and symbols for communication. Sometimes, syntax may be assessed and developed in the nonspeech form. In speech, consideration is also given to whether or not the student's production and comprehension of speech sounds and sentence structures are adequate for communication.

What is common to all systems of communication is that some mode is needed to convey a message (speech or nonspeech), some symbols are needed to differentiate meaning (e.g., words, pictures, codes), a vocabulary is needed that is adequate to the person's many reasons for communicating, and the person needs to be able to use these forms to achieve his or her purpose for communicating. In the following sections, consideration is given to the selection of the mode and symbols for communication, assessment of syntax when speech or written communication is used, and assessment of semantics and functional use of language. Following this general discussion, guidelines are given for developing assessment plans to consider both the forms, content, and functions of communication.

Selection of the Communication Mode and Symbol System

Figure 1 is a screening checklist to help the teacher make a referral to a speech/language pathologist or a speech and hearing clinic for further evaluation of the selection and development of a mode and symbol system for communication. As the figure suggests, this evaluation may be conducted to identify more than one form for instruction. It may be difficult to identify for a student with limited communication one form that will be applicable across functions. For example, signing may not be functional for ordering in a restaurant. A communication board will not be available to communicate the need for help during bathing, and may be too awkward for use during strenuous

I. Response mode selection

Check all responses that the student voluntarily makes. Circle any responses that the student makes frequently and consistently as well as voluntarily.

_____ 1. Speaks words
_____ 2. Speaks phonemes (e.g., baba)
_____ 3. Vocalizes sounds that are not recognizable phonemes
_____ 4. Nods yes or no (does not have to be used correctly yet)
_____ 5. Moves head other than nodding
_____ 6. Focuses eyes on objects
_____ 7. Focuses eyes on one picture or symbol in an array
_____ 8. Uses fingers independently (e.g., "OK" sign, shows age)
_____ 9. Points to objects
_____10. Uses hands to manipulate objects (e.g., pulls up pants, feeds self)
_____11. Moves arm and hand together across body and overhead
_____12. Slightly moves arm and hand together a few inches
_____13. Does not move hands, but can move other body parts independently (e.g., shoulder, foot, knee) (State part that can be moved.)
_____14. Other observable, voluntary responses (e.g., tongue clicking, eye blinking) (State response.)

II. Symbol selection

For each of the following symbols, note if the student: (a) responds to the symbol system (e.g., makes differential responses to spoken words), (b) uses the symbol system, and if so, the approximate number of symbols in the student's vocabulary, and (c) if the symbol system can be adapted to the student's response modes if not used currently.

(No. of symbols)	Responds to (yes/no)	Uses (no. of symbols)	May use adaptations (yes/no)
1. Speech			
2. Printed words			
3. Bliss or other symbols			
4. Pictures			
5. Photographs			
6. Objects (e.g., points to)			
7. Manual signs			

III. Other

_____1. Does the student come from a bilingual or non–English speaking home?
_____2. Should an electronic board be considered?

Figure 1. Communication forms to be targeted for instruction. The teacher may complete the checklist and share the information with therapists to aid selection of forms.

activities like exercising. Some combination of printed communication and signs or gestures would be applicable across these differing functions. A clinical evaluation can help the teacher and school-based therapist know whether or not speech is physiologically possible, if structural difficulties are influencing articulation, and if hearing is normal. If this clinical evaluation includes multidisciplinary assessment, the teacher may also learn from physical and occupational therapists augmentative forms for communication (e.g., feasibility of signing with impaired gross and fine motor ability), and how to position a student with physical handicaps for best expression of communication.

Assessment of Syntax

Sometimes, a student with severe handicaps has developed a sizeable vocabulary and may have some phrases and sentences in his or her expressive repertoire. The teacher may then be interested in expanding the syntactic repertoire of the student. Waryas and Stremel-Campbell (1978) describe how syntax can be assessed and trained along with semantics and pragmatics to improve a student's overall communicative ability. Using their language assessment, language objectives are targeted for functions, grammar, semantics, and nonlanguage behavior (i.e., tantrums). Grammatical training is an area in which it is easy to lose sight of the functional use for these improved forms. A student who masters plurals in daily sessions of 20 trials of stating the plural may make little use of this skill in other activities. Thus, grammatical training needs to be linked with language functions (e.g., stating requests for one cookie or two cookies). To help the teacher consider how to improve syntactical form, a skill sequence is given in Figure 2 to shape a student's form from nouns to sentences. This grammatical assessment might be applied to speech or to augmentative forms of expression that allow for expansion of syntax (e.g., Signing Exact English, Blissymbols, typing, or other printed word communication systems).

Assessment of Semantics and Functional Use

When the priority for assessment of communication is to target objectives to improve performance of daily activities, communicative function becomes the primary consideration. Consideration of semantics, and specifically, of vocabulary to be taught, should be linked to the activities in which communication will be required.

Warren and Rogers-Warren (1985) noted that functional language affects the listener in specific intended ways. The function of a communicative response is established when a person experiences the consequences for the response, and when these consequences are reinforcing. New forms are established when consequences are made contingent on their expression to achieve a function. McLean, Snyder-McLean, Sack, and Decker (1982)

Information for this checklist may be obtained by observing the student's communication and recording each word, or by testing the student's use of a vocabulary list that the teacher develops from the student's daily activities. For each category, note the number of words observed in spontaneous use, the number of words tested, and the percentage of words correct on the test.

	Number observed	Number tested	Percent correct on test
1. Noun imitation			
2. Nouns			
3. Verbs			
4. Noun–Verb			
5. Verb–Noun			
6. N–V–N			
7. "Wh" questions			
8. Prepositions			
9. Adverbs			
10. Negation			
11. Articles			

Figure 2.   Skill sequence checklist for assessment of development of grammar. (Adapted from Waryas & Stremel-Campbell, 1978.)

describe early nonlinguistic forms that have clear communicative functions. Sometimes, one form (e.g., crying) can serve several functions (e.g., to get help, to get attention). The child learns language as new forms are tried that achieve these and other functions that are reinforced by others in the environment. Thus, if the teacher assesses the functions of communication currently used by the student in either linguistic or nonlinguistic forms, and considers the functions and forms needed by current and future environments, communication objectives can be identified that will be related to daily use and improve the student's repertoire of forms and functions.

Several language experts have developed approaches to language that have either defined or implied procedures to assess functional use of language. For example, MacDonald (1985) developed a language curriculum that uses a conversational model. The conversation skills targeted include social recognition events, purposeful social contacts, joint activities, turn-taking, chains, initiations, responses, topic initiations, shifts, closes, and off-topic behavior. All behaviors can be verbal or nonverbal. Another approach to functional language is described in the Vermont Early Communication Curriculum (Keogh & Reichle, 1985). This approach concentrates on the language functions of requesting, rejecting, and describing. McLean et al. (1982) use the term "transactional" to describe their language approach that focuses on language function, content, and form. Each of these authors has described functions of language. To aid the teacher in developing assessment for various language functions, Table 1 lists language functions with definitions and illustrations that are based on several language resources. This list can help the teacher identify the student's existing functions and functions not observed or achieved in immature or inappropriate forms (e.g., tantrums, whining).

The content needed by the student for communication can be identified through consideration of the identified functions and through reviewing the ecological inventories that are used to identify skills needed in home, community, and work environments. Teachers often select vocabulary for nonvocal communication systems that is based on the functions of getting help or objects from caregivers (e.g., pictures or signs for "toilet," "eat," "drink"). By reviewing the many functions for communication, and the settings used to plan the student's curriculum, it will be obvious that this content, while important for self-care, is insufficient for the student's participation in daily activities. For example, social communication requires vocabulary to talk about activities and ask and answer questions.

To date, no single test has been developed to assist the teacher in assessing all students with severe communicative difficulties. Especially in the area of language function, published tests have limited utility. One reason why language function will always require some teacher-designed assessment is that it is dependent on the environmental demands on the student to communicate. The following communication assessment sequence combines several resources to help the teacher assess both language function and form.

An Assessment Plan for Communication

To design a plan for initial assessment of communication, the teacher might follow these steps:

1. *Review clinical and medical evaluations* of the student to identify speech, hearing, and motor abilities. If necessary, make further referrals to obtain information needed about the student's physiological capabilities as they relate to communication.
2. *Observe and record the student's language function and forms* during times that require or encourage frequent communication.
3. *Test the student's language* by using published or informal assessments to find functions and forms that were not observed, but that can be elicited.
4. *Review assessments of community and home activities* to identify specific communicative responses that are required by or can enhance these activities.

Table 1. Language functions: definitions and examples

I. *Instrumental functions:* Language that is used to obtain more than socialization. The person's intent is to get the listener to perform some action or to stop the listener from performing a proposed action.

1. *Request object.* Examples: "Please pass the salt," "More juice," manual sign to ask for food, pointing to a ball to get it.
2. *Request help.* Examples: crying to signal discomfort, pointing to untied shoes, saying "Help."
3. *Request permission.* Examples: saying, "May I go now?", pointing to a peer's toy to ask to play.
4. *Request action.* Examples: pulling at teacher's arm to get him or her to push the swing, pointing to picture to ask to dance.
5. *Get attention.* Examples: loud vocalizations to get teacher or caregiver to look, saying teacher's name to get him or her to look, tapping caregiver's arm.
6. *Get information.* Examples: asking, "What's this?", pointing to question mark on communication board in context of introduction of new item or activity, signing "What?"
7. *State a preference or choice.* Examples: sign "no" when asked if wants water, consent by pointing to "yes" when asked if peer can sit beside person, say "I want the cherry juice" when given a selection of drinks, say "Leave me alone."

II. *Social functions:* Language that is used for socialization. The speaker's primary intent is to engage the listener in an exchange that may be as brief as a polite greeting while passing, or an extended conversation.

A. *Initiations.* Language that is the first response in an exchange.
1. *Greeting.* Examples: saying "Hi," raising a hand in greeting, pressing a symbol on an electronic board that activates a voice to say "Hi, my name is John."
2. *Questions.* Examples: asking, "How do you like this weather?", signing "What is your name?", pointing to a symbol for "Would you like to talk awhile?"
3. *Declarations:* Examples: These may include jokes, compliments, and well-known social expressions that serve as conversation starters (e.g., saying, "It sure is hot," or signing, "Pretty dress.")

(continued)

5. *Conduct further observations, tests, or interviews* as necessary to assess current performance of communication in these daily activities.
6. *Select priority skills and plan generalization assessment.*
7. *Write the long-range (i.e., 5-year) and 1-year plans.*
8. *Develop annual ongoing assessment* to evaluate objectives for that year.
9. *Repeat steps 1–7 every 3–5 years.* Step 8 is repeated annually.

Review of Clinical Evaluations A review of Nat's and Dennis's case studies can illustrate how clinical evaluations may help the teacher develop communication assessment. In Nat's case, audiological evaluations had indicated normal hearing. His speech mechanism was also intact, but Nat had no

Table 1. *(continued)*

B. *Responses.* Language in response to another person's initiations.
1. *Answer.* Examples: saying, "My name is Sally," signing that you would like to talk for a while.
2. *Replies.* Examples: returning a greeting, saying, "Yes, it is hot," signing "thank-you" after a compliment.
3. *Social links.* Examples: asking "What else would you like to talk about?", touching the speaker's arm to ask him or her to keep talking.
4. *Closings.* Examples: signing "Good-bye," saying "I'll see you later," waving good-bye.

III. *Personal functions:* Language that is used for self-expression. It is intended neither to initiate a social exchange nor to get some desired object or action. However, this type of communication often occurs in the context of a social exchange.

1. *Express emotions.* Examples: pointing to symbol for "happy," signing "I'm sad," saying, "I'm angry."
2. *Label.* Examples: Saying, "This is a car," pointing to shoes when someone says the word "shoes."
3. *Rehearse.* Examples: Repeating the teacher's directions while performing an action, stating a sequence of steps aloud.
4. *Entertainment.* Examples: Repeating a word while playing, saying a rhyme to oneself.

Adapted from Lucas (1981); MacDonald (1981); McLean, Snyder-McLean, Sack, and Decker (1982).

history of using speech sounds. He had learned a repertoire of 10 signs in his preschool program. Given his chronological age and absence of speech sounds, the speech/language pathologist concluded in her last report that Nat might not acquire speech. Nat's motor skills were near age level. Instruction in signing encouraged Nat to use his motor ability to communicate. However, people who did not know Nat or sign language did not always understand him. Nat's teacher considered the need to assess Nat's comprehension of spoken language since his hearing was normal. She also planned to assess Nat's language functions and to consider augmentative forms to supplement his signing.

In Dennis's case, an audiological evaluation had revealed normal functioning, but it was uncertain how well Dennis comprehended different sounds or words. Dennis's oral muscular impairment precluded the development of speech. An occupational therapist's evaluation indicated that Dennis had some range of motion in one forearm. When Ms. K. first planned Dennis's assessment, he had no recognizable communication system.

After reviewing the information in the students' records, each teacher proceeded to plan the next step of the assessment—to observe the students' current communication during times when motivated to communicate.

Observation of Communication   One of the best methods to assess a student's current communication skills is to observe the student during periods when the motivation to communicate is high. For example, the teacher might introduce a recreational activity followed by a snack. During the activity, opportunities could be given to request new materials, to engage in conversation with the teacher and peers, to express feelings and preferences, and to describe the activity or give instructions. During this activity, the teacher might use one of two methods to record communication observed depending on the frequency and content of communication. If communication is brief and infrequent, the teacher might use a form such as the one shown in Figure 3. During the recreational session, the teacher would note the form and content of each communicative function observed, and would also note functions, forms,

---

Student's name: _____ Date: _____

Context in which communication was observed _____

Directions: *Select or set up a situation in one of the student's daily activities in which the need or incentive to communicate will be frequent. During the activity, note the forms, content, and functions that the student exhibits, and those needed by the student. Code for language forms observed by using the following abbreviations:* NL = *nonlinguistic (e.g., crying, whining, laughter, babbling, pulling someone toward an object),* G = *commonly understood gestures (e.g., pointing, motion for someone to come or go),* MS = *manual signs (e.g., American Sign Language, circle if approximation of sign),* P = *pictures,* C = *coded symbols (e.g., Bliss, numbers),* V = *verbal. For each utterance observed, code its length with a number. For example, a two-word phrase would be V2. If the student signed "my red coat," the code would be MS3.*

Functions	Observed		Needed, not observed	
	Form	Content	Form	Content
Instrumental				
1. Get object.	P2	*"Want cookie"*		
2. Get help.				
3. Get action.				
4. Get information.				
5. Get attention.				
6. State preference.				
Social				
1. Greeting.				
2. Ask question.				
3. Declare.				
4. Answer question.				
5. Reply.				
6. Social link.				
7. Closing.				
Personal				
1. Express emotion.				
2. Other.				

Figure 3. Form for observation of communication.

and content needed. MacDonald (1985) also recommends noting the communication provided by significant others. If feasible, the teacher might spend part of the activity watching and aide, parent, or nonhandicapped peer initiate communication with the student to note the types of communication that are typically presented to the student. Sometimes, because the student's communication is limited, the communication of others to the student is limited in frequency, form, and functions. This sets up a self-perpetuating cycle for limited communication. Thus, it may be helpful to note the opportunities that the student has to communicate, as well as the actual communication observed.

When a student has more frequent or lengthy communication, it may be helpful to record a *language sample*. A language sample is a verbatim recording of an exchange of spontaneous utterances between two people (Carrow-Woolfolk & Lynch, 1982). The use of language samples has had broad variation from collecting a sample of 3 minutes to samples of over 30 minutes, and from 50 to 1,500 utterances (Bloom, 1970; Brown, Fraser, & Bellugi, 1964; Lee, 1974; Muma, 1978). Carrow-Woolfolk and Lynch (1982) recommend collecting a sample of about 100 utterances. This goal may be too ambitious for assessing students with severe handicaps. However, to improve the chances of obtaining a representative sample, the teacher may collect samples across three or more 30-minute sessions, and combine these for analysis. Obviously, these sessions should provide motivation to communicate, as did the recreational activity described earlier. The best way to collect the sample is to tape-record it and later transpose what was said. However, if the communication is nonverbal, the teacher may prefer to make a written record or videotape during the observation. The analysis of the sample will depend on the level of expression.

One measure of linguistic achievement is *mean length of utterance*. This measure can show progress in language development across years that is more meaningful than age norms. Calculation of mean length of utterance (MLU) can be based on words or morphemes. One utterance is defined as a verbal string that is marked by inflection, either rising or falling. This verbal string may or may not be a grammatical sentence. The simplest method for calculating MLU is to count words (McLean & Snyder-McLean, 1978). The only components not counted as words in the language sample would be "fillers" (e.g., um, uh). Commonly connected words also count as one word (e.g., Burger King). Then, the total number of words is divided by the total number of utterances. This calculation is illustrated in Figure 4, as are other analyses that can also be performed for the language sample. These include: (a) listing the language functions observed (last column of Figure 4), (b) counting the vocabulary variety (count the first use of each word) (see count at bottom of Figure 4), and (c) noting correct and erroneous grammatical forms observed (see the "Grammar" column in Figure 4). For further discussion of the uses of language samples, the reader is referred to Miller (1980).

Student's name: Al   Date: 1/11

Context of sample: Al was shown photographs of his daily activities and asked to describe them to his gym teacher while the classroom teacher made this observation. Al then played basketball with the gym teacher.

	Grammar	Function
1. Al: "Mr. Sear!" Mr. S.: "Hey, Al."	N	S: Greet
2. Al: "Look my pictures." Mr. S.: "Nice. What are you doing in these pictures?"	V-PN-N	I: Get attention
3. Al: (as shows each picture) "cooking, cleaning, ride the bus, pay at K-Mart, count my money" Mr. S.: "That's nice. You stay busy."	N, N, V-A-N, V-P-N,* V-PN-N	S: Reply
4. Al: "It's a two. Pay three dollars." Mr. S.: "What? I don't understand."	PN-A-N V-Adj-N	P: Rehearse
5. Al: "You got any gum?" Mr. S.: "No, I don't."	PN-V-Adj-N	I: Get object
6. Al: (stares at Mr. S. and moves face close to his) Mr. S.: "Do you want to play ball?"	Nonverbal	S: Link*
7. Al: "Yeah!" Mr. S.: "Here, we'll play catch."	Affirmative	I: Choice
8. Al: "No. Basketball."	Negative-N	I: Choice

Vocabulary variety: 23 different words

Mean length of utterance: 3.5 (28 words in 8 utterances)

Comments: Al shows a variety of vocabulary and sufficient overall grammatical development to be able to communicate with an acquaintance.

Figure 4.   Example of the analysis of a language sample. (S = social; I = instrumental; P = personal; asterisks indicate potential needs for instruction including: omission of personal pronoun "I," failure to respond to listener's need for clarification, or need for an appropriate social link)

Language sampling has been developed to assess spoken language. Obviously, nonspeech communication can contain frequent and varied utterances. If the teacher considers the checklist shown in Figure 3 to be too limited for a student who has developed phrases and longer utterances, he or she may want to translate the nonspeech communication into a written record, and perform analyses similar to that suggested for a language sample.

Testing Language Skills   Many tests have been developed for language assessment that provide either norm or criterion-referenced scores. However, the utilization of these tests has several limitations. The first is that many of the available language tests do not analyze language skills to the extent that they can be utilized with students with limited language. Second, language tests are typically only oriented toward speech communication. Third, language tests may not provide information that is specific enough to plan intervention. Often, observations of communication as described in the previous section provide far more information than can be obtained on a test. For example, in research on children with language impairments, Blau, Lahey, and Oleksiuk-Velez (1984) found that more goals for intervention could be generated with a language sample than with a language test. Finally, a language test might not provide an adequate assessment of a student's language skills because the test format does not provide adequate motivation to communicate (e.g., many language tests use repeated trials of pointing to pictures).

Given these limitations, the teacher may want to focus primarily on observations of language use. However, tests may be used to try to identify language functions and forms that the student can use, but infrequently uses. When this testing approach is taken, the teacher needs to keep in mind the limitations described. Table 2 provides a list of some of the language tests available that may be useful for some students with severe handicaps (e.g., students like Al in the case studies). (The reader is also referred to the adaptive behavior scales listed in Chapter 2, Figure 5, for assessment of related skills.) The teacher may find it more beneficial to make his or her own tests that will focus on the specific assessment question that he or she wishes to address. For example, if the teacher wants to test language functions, he or she may think of activities or events to set the occasion for each function listed in Table 1, and note whether or not each occurred. If a specific grammatical form is the concern, the teacher may wish to design a repeated-trial assessment for the grammatical form. Vocabulary could also be tested in a repeated-trial format using pictures, objects, or activities, and asking "What is this?". The language observation will be sufficient for some students. For others, the use of one or two tests may provide information to supplement this observation.

Assessment of Language Needed for the Home and Community   The purpose of the language assessment is to identify language needed in home and community environments. The teacher begins by focusing on communication forms, content, and function per se, but then checks these against the demands for communication required in daily living. This may best be accomplished by first identifying the skills to be targeted for recreational, vocational, domestic, and community instruction. Each activity targeted for instruction can then be reviewed to identify communication that is required by each activity, and communication that can enrich each activity. By checking these against the language goals for the student, a language program can be developed that is e 2.   Examples of published tests to aid in the assessment of related skills

Language Tests

Peabody Picture Vocabulary Test
  American Guidance Service
  Publishers Building
  Circle Pines, MN 55014

Environmental Language Inventory
  Charles E. Merrill
  1300 Alum Creek
  Box 508
  Columbus, OH 43216

Receptive-Expressive Emergent Language Scale
  PRO-ED
  5341 Industrial Oaks Boulevard
  Austin, TX 78735-8898

Motor Tests

Milani-Comparetti Motor Development Test
  Meyer Children's Rehabilitation Institute
  University of Nebraska Medical Center
  444 South 44th Street
  Omaha, NE 68131

Peabody Developmental Motor Scales
  Teaching Resources
  50 Pond Park Road
  Hingham, MA 02043

Bruininks-Oseretsky Test
  American Guidance Service
  Publishers Building
  Circle Pines, MN 55014

both functional and enhances language development. This cross-planning process is illustrated in Figure 5. In this format, the teacher lists settings and activities that have been selected as priorities for the curriculum plan (see Chapter 2 for guidelines for this selection). Then, the teacher reviews these settings and activities to identify related skills needed in each, and determines whether the student has the skills. Finally, the teacher notes specific skills needed across activities that might be targeted for generalization training. Setting priorities and planning for generalization from this list of skills is discussed next.

Setting Priorities and Planning for Generalization   The assessment will probably generate many ideas for communication instruction. The next step of the assessment plan is to select priority goals for communication assessment. In setting priorities, the teacher may wish to review the guidelines described in Chapter 2. To set priorities for selection of related skills, the teacher will review both the general communication assessment for the student (e.g., Figure 3), and the verification that these skills and others are needed in priority daily

To assess social skills, a teacher will want to consider the skills typically displayed by others in the student's community environments.

activities (Figure 5). The prioritization process is illustrated by Nat's case study.

In Nat's assessment, the teacher was concerned with expanding his communication functions, developing forms to supplement signing, and increasing his comprehension of spoken language. Through observations using the checklist shown in Figure 3, Ms. S. noted that Nat needed to expand his communication functions. His current functions only included requesting and labeling objects. His current form was signing one-sign initiations or replies. His vocabulary was limited to a few common objects and needs (e.g., "go," "eat," "shoe," "brush teeth"). In reviewing the settings and activities that had been selected as priorities for Nat's home and community-related instruction, Ms. S. noted the specific need for the social function of communication to be developed, and observed that Nat needed vocabulary to request or refuse help and to describe his daily schedule in conversation. In planning for 5 years, Ms. S. targeted greetings (initiated by asking "what is it?"), expressing likes and dislikes, and short conversations based on questions about his daily activities. These priorities were endorsed by Nat's parents who were eager to see him communicate more in family conversations. Nat's teacher also targeted the use of pointing and pictures as forms to supplement his signing. Since spoken language would be used in his conversation training and throughout his daily instruction, no additional receptive language goals were targeted.

| Student's name: John | | | | Date: 10-4 |

Instructor: Ms. M.

Setting	Activity	Related skills needed		Student has skill (yes, no)
Snack bar	Purchase snack.	1.	Coin identification	1. No
		2.	Conversation with peers	2. No
		3.	Orientation and mobility to locate cashier and seat	3. No
Home	Plan social events.	1.	Read a schedule.	1. No
		2.	Read/follow calendar.	2. No
		3.	Use a talking clock.	3. No
		4.	Dial phone.	4. No
Work (mailroom)	Work on task.	1.	Ask for supplies.	1. No
		2.	Count inserts.	2. Yes, inaccurate
		3.	Sign checks.	3. Somewhat, writes off of check
Restaurant	Eat with friends.	1.	State order.	1. Yes
		2.	Greet friends.	2. No, hugs and kisses excessively
		3.	Wait for friends to eat.	3. No, wanders and screams
		4.	Converse.	4. No, inconsistent
		5.	Walk to restaurant.	5. No, shortwinded

Generalization planning—What related skills are needed across activities?

Communication: (a) Converse with other adults, (b) state need for supplies

Motor: (a) Orientation and mobility, (b) stamina to walk 3–4 blocks

Academics: (a) Identify coins, (b) follow schedule calendar, (c) follow talking clock, (d) sign checks, (e) count work pieces

Figure 5.   Example of cross-planning to identify related skills needed in daily living.

These goals reflect the use of several priority guidelines. The language goals have utility across both daily activities and Nat's lifespan. The responses targeted can enhance development of social interaction with his non-handicapped peers and his family. The goals also take an efficient approach by emphasizing functions while using simple forms like pointing and pictures to supplement signing. By contrast, the teacher did not plan to delay Nat's communication development by focusing on articulation of phonemes. Speech development would be a long and possibly unsuccessful procedure given Nat's age and clinical evaluation.

Another important step in developing a 5-year curriculum is to plan for generalization rather than hoping it will occur (Stokes & Baer, 1977). This can be planned in two ways. First, communication skills, as well as the other related skills, are targeted for use across daily living activities. Second, criteria for mastery are defined as generalized use of a response. For example, consider the generalization criteria that might be used for Nat's greeting response. If the teacher used the sufficient exemplar approach (Stokes & Baer, 1977), the criteria for generalization might be to greet two adults and two nonhandicapped peers who Nat has not been directly trained to greet. In addition to people as exemplars of the stimulus class that Nat is to master, settings might also be targeted. The criteria for settings might be to greet in two natural settings not used in training (e.g., playground, home neighborhood).

Another type of generalization that Warren (1985) targets focuses on linguistic structures for response generalization. These linguistic structures are selected from specific pragmatic categories (i.e., functions). For example, Nat has the goal of responding to social questions about his daily activities. One linguistic structure that might be targeted for this is the first person pronoun and a verb. For example, Nat would sign "I play(ed)," when asked "What did you do in school?" The pragmatic function that this form addresses is a social answer. Response generalization will have occurred when Nat uses some of the signs he now uses as labels as social replies. Thus, the criteria for generalization might be for Nat to make three untrained social answers using signs in his repertoire. This response generalization might be supplemented with some stimulus generalization goals. For example, the teacher might also target for Nat to give social answers to his parents, sister, and two nonhandicapped peers in a variety of settings. In the first criteria of generalization, the teacher might assess response generalization by using repeated, massed-trial assessment. For example, Ms. S. might have a conversation period at the end of the day in which she probes the students about their day. The second generalization criteria might be evaluated by keeping a tally of Nat's social replies throughout the day and/or by setting up situations in the natural environment in which someone asks Nat a question and the teacher observes his reply.

The Curriculum, Annual Plan, and Ongoing Evaluation   The curriculum charts and individualized plans at the end of this book illustrate how the assessment information is developed into instructional plans. Ongoing evaluation of communication warrants further discussion because of the complexity created by the cross-planning approach. In the domain areas of curriculum planning, ongoing assessment is straightforward. For example, a task analysis is developed for eating with a spoon. Or, productivity rate is used for packaging, a vocational task. Related skills are more complex because they are part of these other routines. The teacher might use several approaches for ongoing assessment of communication. *Whichever approach is used for assessment, it is assumed that instruction is scheduled during the activity in which the communication typically occurs.*

One approach to ongoing assessment would be to use massed, repeated trials for assessment of the acquisition of the target function and form, and to supplement these with checklist observations for generalization. For example, for Nat's use of "what," Ms. S. might spend 10 minutes presenting Nat with novel objects and pictures to give him 10 opportunities to ask "what" in a highly structured situation. She would also have a checklist of times when the use of "what" could be appropriate (e.g., with a peer at lunch who often brings toys and pictures from home, when a new vocational task is introduced, when a new material is introduced in the classroom). The teacher might then graph both number of responses in the structured probe, and percent use of "what" out of opportunities presented across settings. The first might be a graph of daily data to use the decision rules on rate of progress (see Chapter 4). The second might be a weekly graph of percent use of "what" out of opportunities targeted for use across a school week, and could be used to determine when mastery based on generalization has been achieved (e.g., used 2 out of 4 opportunities for 2 weeks).

A second approach to ongoing assessment might be to rely solely on assessment of use in context. Rather than using a probe approach, the teacher might plan 10 opportunities throughout the day when the use of "what" would be appropriate. For each opportunity, Ms. S. would record whether Nat used "what" alone or with prompts. The number of independent responses could be graphed each day and evaluated biweekly using the decision rules. This latter approach is simpler in that it only requires one graph. However, it calls for creating numerous "natural" opportunities to have enough responses for evaluation of early acquisition. Whichever approach is used, similar planning for ongoing assessment will also be needed for the other related skills—motor and academics.

MOTOR SKILLS

Motor skills, like communication, require careful interdisciplinary planning. The assessment described here is intended to assist the special education teacher in working with occupational and physical therapists to plan instruction for improving motor skills.

Prior to discussing this assessment plan, it may be useful to discuss the components of motor ability. While sensation and perception are related to motor ability, this chapter will focus on observable, voluntary motor responses that can be targeted for instruction. The therapist will often be concerned with involuntary responses (e.g., reflexes), sensation, and perception, as well as with voluntary responses. The teacher will want to work closely with the therapist to understand and implement recommendations related to discouraging abnormal reflexes and improving tolerance for sensory input. For more information, the reader is referred to resources that describe therapeutic approaches in further detail (Ayres, 1981; Bigge, 1982; Campbell, 1983; Fraser & Hensinger, 1983).

Observable responses that relate to motor ability can be classified using traditional terminology. Fine motor skills are movements that require small muscle groups such as those in the fingers and eyes, and those used for speaking. Gross motor skills are movements involving large muscle groups, such as those used in walking, dressing, or climbing a flight of stairs. Physical fitness is often associated with cardiorespiratory fitness. Fitness also includes strength, coordination, and flexibility. Posture is also an aspect of fitness.

Approaches to motor assessment often use tasks not encountered in daily living, but selected to evaluate specific motor responses. For example, stringing beads might be used to assess fine motor skills such as finger dexterity and eye-hand coordination. Unfortunately, such assessment also often leads to instruction using nonfunctional "fine and gross motor materials" such as balance beams, pegboards, obstacle courses, and so forth. By contrast, if the teacher avoids the use of such traditional motor development materials, it can be difficult to distinguish motor instruction from all other instruction since all responses are in fact motoric. But this lack of distinction between "motor" instruction and other instruction may be ideal since it focuses on motoric responses needed in daily living. Defining specific motor skills to be developed in other instruction may help to ensure that these are not underdeveloped.

The approach recommended here is similar to that suggested for language. The therapist's evaluation and recommendations will often provide the motor forms that need development (e.g., static balance). The teacher will then provide the functions for their use. To conduct assessment to identify functional motor skills instruction, a similar outline can be followed as suggested for language. That is, the steps to developing a *motor assessment plan* would be to:

1. *Review medical and therapeutic evaluations and treatment recommendations.*
2. *Observe motor skills.*
3. *Test motor skills.*
4. *Evaluate motor needs for daily living skills.*
5. *Conduct further testing as needed to assess performance of motor skills for daily living routines.*
6. *Set priorities and plan for generalization.*
7. *Develop the 3- to 5-year curriculum plan.*
8. *Write the first year's annual plan and develop ongoing assessment for each objective.*
9. *Conduct ongoing evaluation of data for each objective.*

Motor Assessment Plan

Review of Medical Evaluations and Therapy Plans   The first step in the assessment of motor skills is to review medical and therapy evaluations to obtain information related to planning motor development. Bleck and Nagel's (1975) medical atlas can be a valuable resource to help teachers understand this information. Discussion with the parents and the student's current physician and therapists may also be necessary to understand recommendations and any specific limitations of the student.

Motor difficulties often are associated with central nervous system damage, and may be manifested as a general delay in motor development or movement difficulties. Campbell (1983) has described evaluation of movement difficulties that is based on neurodevelopmental therapy. In her approach, the therapist assesses the basic processes underlying movement competence, including tonicity, patterns of movement (e.g., postural fixations), and quantity of movement. From this information, the therapist develops an individual education planning sheet. Such planning can then be shared with the teacher to be considered throughout instruction. Treatment strategies may include, for example, proper positioning of the student, proper use of adaptive equipment, the use of fast or slow movement when working with the child, and strengthening weak muscles.

Implementing the therapist's suggestions may require the teacher to work closely with the therapist to master the recommended procedures. In research on inservice training, Inge and Snell (1985) demonstrated two teachers' mastery of therapeutic interventions (e.g., transferring, positioning prone over a wedge, two-person lift) when the therapist used applied behavioral techniques to instruct the teachers. That is, the therapist used a task analysis, demonstrations, verbal and model prompts, corrective feedback, and praise to teach specific techniques with students whom the teachers had in their classrooms. When a therapist recommends a treatment that the teacher is to implement, the teacher may want to define it and ask for the therapist's assistance in mastering the technique.

Motor Skills for Daily Living: Observation and Testing Through interdisciplinary planning, the student's optimal motor forms can be identified and targeted for use across daily living skills. Similar to communication, the teacher will conduct general assessments of the student's motor forms and functions. Then, the teacher will note the motor forms and functions needed in the settings, and select activities for the curriculum plan (see Figure 5, page 186). Finally, the teacher will select priorities for instruction, and plan for generalization of motor responses that go across several activities.

To assist the teacher in working with the therapist in assessing and planning for motor development, Table 3 lists motor skills by traditional categories. Figure 6 provides illustrations of the grasps that are needed for fine motor skills. The list and illustrations may be reviewed in collaboration with therapists to select forms to teach to the student that would enhance motor functions that are absent or inefficient. For example, the student may be unable to open push bar doors because he or she lacks a firm grasp. The student's poor

Table 3. Fine motor skills and functional activities

	Skill	Activity
1.	Movement of fingers in any direction and with control	Turning book pages
2.	Individual finger use	Dialing telephone
3.	Individual thumb use	Clothes snaps
4.	Coordinated finger use	Typing, playing musical instruments, shoetying
5.	Arm placement	Placing arm on small table or in water basin
6.	Placing objects in/on other objects	Jar lids, box tops, records/tapes
7.	Using both arms for holding and carrying	Carrying cafeteria tray
8.	One hand holding, one hand manipulating	Painting, stirring, gardening
9.	Hook or shovel grasp	Toothbrushing, racquet sports
10.	Pincer grasp	Buttoning, zipping, sewing
11.	Lateral pincer grasp	Using scissors
12.	Spherical grasp	Throwing and catching, eating/drinking

From Bunker, L., & Moon, S. (1987). Recreational programming. In M. E. Snell (Ed.), *Systematic instruction of persons with severe handicaps* (3rd ed). Columbus, OH: Charles E. Merrill; used with permission.

grasp also may be apparent in other daily activities (e.g., grasping a bar in the restroom to sit on toilet alone). From this review, a tentative list of forms may be generated to be compared with functions that the student lacks.

The skills listed in Table 3, as well as many of the existing motor assessments, are most useful in identifying deficits in specific motor forms. Some of the commercially available tests are listed in Table 2. These instruments do not provide the most efficient approach to identifying motor functions needed by older students and adults (e.g., jumping and hopping would typically not be assessed for older students unless identified as components of a leisure skill such as dancing).

Motor functions have not been defined in the literature to the extent that language functions have. However, by reviewing the gross and fine motor demands of daily living, some common functions can be suggested. These motor functions are shown below.

1. **Ambulation**   This motor function is accomplished when an individual moves him- or herself across the floor or ground. *Examples:* walking, use of a wheelchair, crawling, walking with a walker
2. **Sitting/standing**   Many daily living skills require the function of moving into from sitting to standing, and vice versa. (Wheelchair use may bypass

ILLUSTRATION OF THE TYPICAL GRASPS

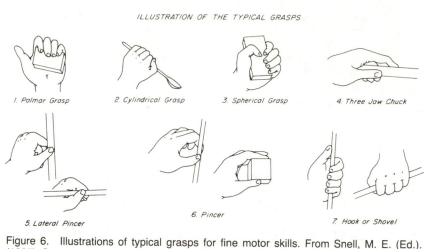

1. *Palmar Grasp* 2. *Cylindrical Grasp* 3. *Spherical Grasp* 4. *Three Jaw Chuck*

5. *Lateral Pincer* 6. *Pincer* 7. *Hook or Shovel*

Figure 6. Illustrations of typical grasps for fine motor skills. From Snell, M. E. (Ed.). (1987). *Systematic instruction of persons with severe handicaps* (3rd ed.). Columbus, OH: Charles E. Merrill; used with permission.

this function.) *Examples:* sitting on a bus seat, standing at a fast food restaurant counter, standing with the assistance of braces and crutches

3. **Negotiating changes in levels of landings** (e.g., stairs) This motor function has been accomplished if the individual safely reaches a different level of landing within buildings and walkways. *Examples:* ascension and descension of stairs, walking up and down ramps, walking up and down street curbs, use of an elevator

4. **Goal-directed ambulation (orientation)** When an individual can reach a near or far destination, he or she has achieved goal-directed ambulation. *Examples:* walking to the restroom in a workshop, walking to one's assigned seat in the classroom, using a cane or sighted guide to find the cafeteria, holding the teacher's arm to cross the street

5. **Opening doors** Most homes and community facilities require entering passageways by opening doors. *Examples:* turning a doorknob and pulling a door open, pushing a crossbar, walking on an automatic door opener

6. **Enter/exit vehicles** Community travel often requires movement in and out of vehicles. *Examples:* moving onto the seat of a car, stepping onto a van, walking up bus steps

7. **Open/close containers and fasteners** This function is achieved when the container needed is opened or closed, or when a fastener is used in dressing. *Examples:* opening a latch-type lunch box, opening a zippered gym bag, closing a thermos

8. **Object manipulation** Many daily living skills require manipulation of objects. *Examples:* grasp cereal box and release into cart, carry gym bag, grasp socks from drawer

9. **Locomotion and gross motor skills for recreation** Recreational activ-

ities require skills that are unique to specific sports and games. *Examples:* swimming strokes; hopping and jumping in aerobic dancing; ball skills such as rolling, throwing, catching

Figure 7 provides a checklist that the teacher can use to review the motor functions that the student has in his or her repertoire. The materials suggested to assess these functions are those encountered in adult living rather than those often found only in motor skills instruction (e.g., balance beams, stacking rings). By checking inefficient or inadequate functions with deficits noted in motor forms, the teacher develops a list of potential skills for instruction. However, these skills should then be checked against the settings and activities chosen for the curriculum plan (see Figure 5) to make sure that they are needed in, or can be used to enhance, these priority activities. The teacher may also wish to review the task analytic assessment conducted for recreational planning to further note the specific activities that can be used for motor instruction. (See examples of these task analyses in Chapters 5 and 6.)

Setting Priorities and Assessing Generalization   A review of one of the case studies can illustrate how consideration of priorities applies to the motor component of the assessment. As mentioned previously, Ann had limited independent responses. From her therapy and medical evaluations, Ms. P. learned that Ann had reduced strength and coordination in one arm due to a previous accident. Ann's motor development was generally delayed. She walked with an unsteady gait. Ann's range of arm motion was about half that typical of adults her age. Pronation of the pelvis contributed to her unsteady gait and limitations in range of motion. The therapist's treatment plan included exercises for Ann's arm strength and pelvis that she would implement, and a seat insert to encourage correct pelvic alignment. The occupational therapist was concerned that Ann learn to use her thumb and forefingers in opposition to learn tasks like snapping and zipping. In using the checklist in Figure 7, Ms. P. noted that Ann needed to improve the speed of her ambulation so that she could keep pace with a group of nonhandicapped adults during outings. Her goal-oriented ambulation was very poor to the extent that Ann could not find the restroom in the adjoining room of her educational center. She also could not open doors. Ann fed herself with a spoon using a spherical grasp, and drank from a glass using a palmar grasp. Neither grasp was efficient, and Ann had considerable spilling while eating.

In reviewing Ann's life domains, Ms. P. noted Ann's goals in the areas of eating, simple housekeeping, dressing, vocational assembly, leisure skills, and community travel that seemed especially relevant for concurrent development of motor skills. For the 5-year curriculum plan, Ms. P. recommended that Ann acquire a spherical grasp across pulling her pants up, drinking from a glass or soda can, and opening doors. She also targeted Ann's development of strength and use of a hook grasp to independently carry her gym bag, push a vacuum

Student's name: _____   Date: _____

Teacher's name: _____

For each of the following motor skills, note the level of assistance that the student needs to perform the skill. If necessary, provide an opportunity to perform the skill and observe performance. Scoring code:

    5—No deficiency
    4—Performs alone, but inefficient or slow
    3—Performs alone most of the time
    2—Needs partial physical assistance most of the time
    1—Needs full physical assistance

1. **Ambulation**
    ____Walks
    ____Walks with adaptive equipment (e.g., crutches, walker)
    ____Ambulates in a wheelchair
    ____Walks or wheels self length of average room*
    ____Walks or wheels self 1–2 city blocks*
    ____Walks or wheels self 3–5 city blocks*
    ____Walks, wheels, or jogs for 15 minutes*

2. **Sitting/standing**
    ____Sits and stands from armless chair
    ____Sits and stands from chair with arms
    ____Sits and stands from toilet
    ____Stands for 5–15 minutes (e.g., to wait for bus)

3. **Negotiating changes in levels of landing**
    ____Ascends stairs alternating feet
    ____Ascends stairs without alternating feet
    ____Descends stairs alternating feet
    ____Descends stairs without alternating feet
    ____Walks up/down ramp
    ____Ambulates wheelchair up/down ramp
    ____Uses elevator alone
    ____Steps up/down from street curb

4. **Goal-directed ambulation**
    ____Locates restroom in work setting or school
    ____Locates assigned seat
    ____Ambulates to van or bus
    ____Ambulates to community destination 2–3 blocks away

5. **Opening doors**
    ____Opens door by using key to unlock it
    ____Opens door with door knob
    ____Enters/exits door with crossbar by pushing
    ____Enters/exits door by pulling handle
    ____Enters/exits door that is opened by escort
    ____Enters/exits automatic door

6. **Enter/exit vehicles**
    ____Gets in/out of car
    ____Transfers from wheelchair to car
    ____Gets in/out of van
    ____Gets on/off bus

                                                 _____
                                                  (continued)

Figure 7.   Checklist to assess motor skills for daily living. (* = cardiorespiratory fitness)

194

7. **Open/close containers and fasteners**
   ____Opens/closes plastic lids on food, lunch containers
   ____Uses can opener to open cans when cooking
   ____Opens/closes plastic lunch bags
   ____Opens/closes latch-type lunchbox
   ____Opens/closes zippers on gym bag or pants
   ____Opens/closes Velcro on lunch bag or shoes
   ____Screws jar lids on and off

8. **Object manipulation**
   ____Grasp and release objects with both hands (e.g., grocery bag, basketball)
   ____Grasp and release hand-sized objects like socks, fruit
   ____Pour from a small jar or pitcher
   ____Grasp and release finger-sized objects like coins, comb
   ____Carry lightweight item like bag with small purchase
   ____Carry medium weight item like nylon suitcase
   ____Carry heavy item like vacuum cleaner
   ____Carry backpack or purse
   ____Grasp and pull clothing on/off
   ____Grasp and push mop or vacuum

9. **Locomotion and gross motor skills for recreation**
   (Student only needs enough of these skills to participate in targeted leisure and fitness activities)
   ____Run or jog
   ____Jump in aerobic exercises or dancing
   ____Hop in games or exercises
   ____Roll a ball
   ____Catch a ball that is rolled
   ____Throw a ball
   ____Catch a ball that is thrown or hit
   ____Strike a ball with a bat or racket
   ____Kick while swimming with assistance
   ____Kick and stroke to swim without assistance
   ____Pedal a stationary bicycle
   ____Ride a regular bicycle

Figure 7. *(continued)*

cleaner, and carry her laundry basket. The plan also targeted use of a pincer grasp (modified if necessary) to pick up coins to use a vending machine, perform collating tasks, and zip her pants and gym bag. Ms. P. also selected the specific fine motor skill of opening plastic lunch containers. Increased distance, speed, and direction were chosen to improve Ann's fitness and independence in ambulation, with generalization targeted across: (a) walking to the restroom alone, (b) walking to the van alone, (c) keeping pace with the group to walk from the van to a store (about 2 blocks), and (d) taking a leisure-time walk for 3–4 blocks with a companion.

Ongoing Assessment and Evaluation of the IEP Similar to the ongoing assessment utilized for language, motor objectives might be assessed in the context of other activities (e.g., as one or more steps of a task analysis), or

Behavior: Spherical grasp   Name: Ann   Mastery: 90%/2 days

New Prompt Fading

	100																			
		20 20 20 20 20 20 20 20 20 20	20 20 20 20 20 20 20 20 20 20
	90	19 19 19 19 19 19 19 19 19 19	19 19 19 19 19 19 19 19 19 19
		18 18 18 18 18 18 18 18 18 18	18 18 18 18 18 18 18 18 18 18
	80	17 17 17 17 17 17 17 17 17 17	17 17 17 17 17 17 17 17 17 17
		16 16 16 16 16 16 16 16 16 16	16 16 16 16 16 16 16 16 16 16
	70	15 15 15 15 15 15 15 15 15 15	15 15 15 15 15 15 15 15 15 15
		14 14 14 14 14 14 14 14 14 14	14 14 14 14 14 14 14 14 14 14
	60	13 13 13 13 13 13 13 13 13 13	13 13 13 13 13 13 13 13 13 13
		12 12 12 12 12 12 12 12 12 12	12 12 12 12 12 12 12 12 12 12
	50	11 11 11 11 11 11 11 11 11 11	11 11 11 11 11 11 11 11 11 11
E = Grasp door.		10 10 10 10 10 10 10 10 10 10	10 10 10 10 10 10 10 10 10 10
L = Grasp glass.	40	9 9 9 9 9 9 9 9 9 9	9 9 9 9 9 9 9 9 9 9
R = Grasp pants.		8 8 8 8 8 8 8 8 8 8	8 8 8 8 8 8 8 8 8 8
R = Grasp door.	30	7 7 7 7 7 7 7 7 7 7	7 7 7 7 7 7 7 7 7 7
R = Grasp pants.		6 6 6 6 6 6 6 6 6 6	6 6 6 6 6 6 6 6 6 6
R = Grasp door.		5 5 5 5 5 5 5 5 5 5	5 5 5 5 5 5 5 5 5 5
L = Grasp glass.	20	4 4 4 4 4 4 4 4 4 4	4 4 4 4 4 4 4 4 4 4
R = Grasp door.	10	3 3 3 3 3 3 3 3 3 3	3 3 3 3 3 3 3 3 3 3
R = Grasp pants.		2 2 2 2 2 2 2 2 2 2	2 2 2 2 2 2 2 2 2 2
V = Grasp soda.		1 1 1 1 1 1 1 1 1 1	1 1 1 1 1 1 1 1 1 1
************	%	0 0 0 0 0 0 0 0 0 0	0 0 0 0 0 0 0 0 0 0

Dates: January 4 5 6 7   8 11 12 13 14 15 18 19 20 21 22 25 26 28 29 30
(Absent)

Reviews

Date	Trend/mean	Decision
1/17/86	Flat/x̄ = 14%	Inadequate progress—
	(same x̄ as 1/3/86)	improve prompt fading
1/30/86	Acceleration/x̄ = 50%	No change

Figure 8.   Example of cross-evaluation for the specific motor skill—a spherical grasp. The teacher evaluated the use of this grasp in the context of the activities listed on the vertical axis, but summarized this specific response to assess generalized use. The teacher's evaluation of progress and decisions are also shown. (V = vending, R = restroom, L = lunch/snack, E = exit building)

summarized across activities for evaluation of a specific motor skill. Figure 8 shows a self-graphing data sheet on which Ann's generalized use of a spherical grasp has been summarized. The vertical axis shows the activities in which the grasp was assessed. The teacher would also have task analytic assessment graphs for each of these activities. As mentioned for communication, such cross-evaluation is a time-consuming task. This method of evaluation is not feasible for all related skills targeted. For some, evaluation of their use in the context of activities will suffice. For one or two priority related skills, this cross-evaluation might be utilized. Figure 8 also shows the decisions that Ms. P. made in evaluation of Ann's progress on the acquisition of this motoric response. While the first evaluation showed minimal progress, revision of prompting enhanced performance across the time period used for the second evaluation. (See Chapter 4 for more information on data evaluation.)

FUNCTIONAL ACADEMICS

Many daily living skills can be performed without mastery of academic skills like math or reading. Browder and Snell (1987) describe three approaches to academic instruction for students with severe handicaps. The first is to teach generalized academic skills (e.g., functional literacy). The second is to teach specific limited academic skills as they arise in planning daily living instruction (e.g., the prices on a drink machine). The third is to teach the use of academic prostheses that minimize the skill complexity (e.g., a money-matching card). In addition to these instructional approaches, Browder and Snell (1987) note that many students with severe handicaps have skill needs of higher priority, and that academic tasks might be performed for the student by the teacher and caregivers (e.g., handing the student coins needed to purchase a soda).

The assessment of the math and reading skills needed for literacy are beyond the scope of this book. However, the teacher might consider some specific academic skills that are often encountered across daily living tasks. These include the use of money, use of a calculator, telling time, sight-reading words, and writing a signature. A skill checklist for these specific functional academics is shown in Figure 9.

As Figure 5 illustrates, academic skills are also considered in cross-planning to enrich the instruction of life skills (see comments at bottom of figure for "Academics").

SUMMARY

Communication, motor skills, and functional academics may be under-developed if a teacher focuses only on life domains in assessing a student to design an individualized curriculum. However, when these skills have been taught, instruction has too often been isolated from their functional use. That is,

Student's name: _____   Date: _____
Teacher's name: _____

Check the academic skills that the student currently demonstrates in at least one activity of daily living. Circle any items that the student needs to acquire, improve, or generalize across activities that have been identified in recreational, vocational, domestic, or community skill planning.

1. **Sight reading**
   ____ 1. Performs action shown in one picture
   ____ 2. Follows series of picture instructions
   ____ 3. Follows instructions with pictures and words
   ____ 4. Discriminates between edible/nonedible groceries when shown packages
   ____ 5. Selects given product from grocery shelf
   ____ 6. Selects food from picture menu or cafeteria food line
   ____ 7. Selects food from printed word menu
   ____ 8. Selects soda choice by pushing correct button
   ____ 9. Identifies numbers to use phone, bank machine
   ____10. Selects purchases from picture store fliers
   ____11. Uses grocery store aisle names or numbers
   ____12. Locates bus or street by sign
   ____13. Locates correct restroom
   ____14. Discriminates cleaning products by label

2. **Signature**
   ____1. Writes name
   ____2. Makes distinctive mark with pen or pencil
   ____3. Uses rubber name stamp

3. **Money use**
   ____1. Uses a 1-dollar bill for small purchase
   ____2. Uses quarters for vending machines
   ____3. Discriminates need for dollar versus quarters
   ____4. Uses 10-dollar bill for larger purchase
   ____5. Discriminates need for 1- versus 10-dollar bill
   ____6. Counts 1-dollar bills to pay close to price under $10
   ____7. Counts 10-dollar bills to make large purchase
   ____8. Reads prices to select purchase within budget

4. **Time management**
   ____1. Follows others' activities to stay on schedule
   ____2. Matches printed schedule and digital clock or watch to follow schedule
   ____3. Uses digital watch to follow unwritten, familiar schedule
   ____4. Uses digital watch to make unfamiliar appointment time
   ____5. Punches in at a time clock before time to begin work

5. **Computation/math**
   ____1. Adds prices with a calculator
   ____2. Subtracts prices with a calculator
   ____3. Uses calculator to follow budget while shopping
   ____4. Uses calculator to plan purchase within budget
   ____5. Identifies numbers to dial phone, use bank machine
   ____6. Counts items for vocational assembly

Figure 9.   Checklist for functional academics. (Adapted from Browder & Snell, 1987.)

people do not communicate in isolation (e.g., in repeated trials about "What is this?"), but rather, they communicate about their daily lives in the context of other activities. Similarly, motor and academic skills are typically embedded in the routines of daily living. To meet the dual goals of developing these related skills and planning functional use of these skills, cross-planning is needed. The teacher first plans the student's life domain skill needs, then plans related skill needs, and finally compares these assessments to see how communication, motor skills, and academics can be taught in the context of other instruction. Sometimes, to make sure that these related skills are not lost in other instruction, the teacher will keep separate graphs of skills such as signing, but will not necessarily teach these in isolation from other activities. The individualized curriculum charts at the end of this book show the results of this cross-planning (see Appendix A).

CHAPTER 8

ASSESSMENT OF SOCIAL SKILLS AND INTERFERING BEHAVIOR

Interpersonal skills, or the ability to relate to others, greatly influence a person's friendships and job success. Examples of these skills include responding to social invitations, greeting acquaintances, and handling conflicts. Unfortunately, the segregated settings in which people with severe handicaps have often lived and learned are not conducive to learning the social interactions typical of an individual's age and cultural group. In fact, follow-up research on people with mental retardation who have left institutions reveals that social skills deficiencies often interfere with vocational and community living success (Gaylord-Ross, 1979; Greenspan & Shoultz, 1981).

Regrettably, research and practice have often focused on problem behaviors as isolated sources of social exclusion. For example, a program to decelerate self-abuse or stereotypic behavior may be implemented with no concurrent instruction in alternative adaptive behaviors. Unfortunately, for some of these individuals, "maladaptive" behaviors may comprise most or all of their leisure and social behavior repertoire. It is not surprising that deceleration programs often must be intensified or directed to new problem behaviors when a deceleration approach is taken without concurrent instruction in skills that the individual can use to get access to reinforcement (e.g., social attention).

Behaviors that are different from those exhibited by most people are not necessarily problems. Many individuals have minor quirks or bad habits that have no effect on friendships, jobs, and community acceptance (e.g., nail biting, jewelry twirling, smoking, messiness, odd-spoken expressions). Evans and Meyer (1985) describe this "normal" deviation as follows:

> Sometimes we choose to change such behavior, but often we do not. We may choose not to do so because the behavior is difficult to change (that is, it is a habit), and we may "depend on it" for some reason. For example, a person who attempts to give up nail biting may experience an increase in generalized anxiety such that she or he finds it more difficult to deal with everyday situations . . . In some

Placing a call to inquire about a job requires appropriate social skills as well as telephone skills.

cases, the behavior itself is not as difficult to tolerate as would be an intervention program to change it! (p. 59)

Similarly, social competence varies across age and cultural groups. Small-town southern friendliness may be perceived as foolish by a New Yorker (e.g., waving at everyone who passes one's house). The behavior of teenagers often differs considerably from that of adults.

The assessment of social skills needs to be approached with three points in mind. First, individuals with severe handicaps have limited skill repertoires. An educative social skills instructional approach best meets the need to build these repertoires. That is, students with severe handicaps will often need direct instruction in appropriate social skills. This direct instruction should be selected whether the student only has skill deficits or behavioral excesses (i.e., problem behavior) as well as deficits. Second, the acceptability of behavior that is "different" varies. Assessment will need to determine the cost that an atypical behavior has for the student in order to determine if an alternative response should be taught. Third, social skills have age and cultural variation. Ecological inventories to select skills for instruction should be conducted with a student's similar age and cultural group. Considering these three points, the assessment plan will need to include: (a) rationale to pinpoint certain behaviors as "interfering" with the student's community living, (b) procedures to identify social skills deficiencies that impede social integration, (c) initial assessment of these behavioral excesses and deficiencies to pinpoint objectives for instruction, (d) ongoing assessment, and (e) evaluation of ongoing assessments.

SKILL SELECTION

Identification of Interfering Behavior

Behavior is often considered problematic if it causes physical harm to the student or to others, or if it seriously disrupts the teacher's overall instruction and classroom management (Gaylord-Ross, 1980; Sulzer-Azaroff & Mayer, 1977). However, not all behavior that is viewed as problematic meets the criteria of being dangerous or seriously disruptive to the learning environment. Sometimes, teachers and parents are concerned with behavior that interferes with the student's attainment of friends and general use of public facilities because it is repulsive or frightening to others. Evans and Meyer (1985) have developed a decision model that classifies deviant behavior into three levels. *Level I* is *urgent behavior that requires immediate social attention*. These rare, excessive behaviors are clearly evident to the student's caregivers and teachers and are likely to result in death or permanent physical damage. *Level II* is *serious behavior that requires formal consideration*. This consideration is only made when an individualized plan of instruction has been developed. These problematic behaviors exist despite implementation of a well-designed educational program. These behaviors may interfere with the rights of others or with the student's instruction, can become more serious without intervention, and may be of great concern to caregivers. *Level III* is *excess behaviors that may reflect "normal deviation."* Often, these behaviors will not be targeted for instruction because modifying them creates more of a disturbance in the learning environment than does tolerating them. However, these excesses may be targeted if they create negative social consequences for the student. The questions posed for each category of problem behavior are shown in Figure 1.

At this phase of the assessment procedure, the teacher is simply reviewing the rationale for focusing on a behavior that is of concern to him or her or to the caregivers. By reviewing the checklist in Figure 1, the teacher and caregivers may decide that the behavior is an individual difference that does not require further attention (Level III). In this case, no data would be collected on the behavior, and the assessment process would proceed to consider needed social skills. If the behavior is categorized and identified as a problem because it interferes with the student's life or community integration (Level II), the teacher will define and measure the interfering behavior. If the behavior is life-threatening (Level I), an immediate treatment is needed (see Evans & Meyer, 1985 for recommendations regarding life-threatening behavior). Whether or not the behavior is Level I, II, or III, the teacher proceeds to begin the social skills assessment planning while collecting data on the interfering behavior.

Level I. Urgent behaviors requiring immediate social attention

____1. Is the behavior life-threatening or does it cause irreversible physical harm to the student?

If yes, implement instruction to train incompatible skills, prevent the occurrence of the behavior, and if necessary, decelerate behavior through DRO or negative consequences. Also, define, measure, and analyze the behavior and begin social skills assessment.

If no, consider Level II.

Level II. Serious behaviors requiring formal consideration

____1. Does the behavior interfere with learning?
____2. Is the behavior likely to become serious if not modified?
____3. Is the behavior dangerous to others?
____4. Is the behavior of concern to caregivers?

If yes, define, measure, and analyze the behavior, and begin social skills assessment.

If no, consider Level III.

Level III. Behaviors that reflect "normal deviation"

____1. Is the behavior not improving or getting worse?
____2. Has the behavior been a problem for some time?
____3. Does the behavior damage materials?
____4. Does the behavior interfere with community acceptance?
____5. Would other behavior improve if this behavior improved?

If yes, define, measure, and analyze the behavior, and begin social skills assessment. Consider the cost versus benefits of decelerating this behavior.

If no, consider this to be "normal deviation." Informally monitor its existence as other skills are developed.

Figure 1. Checklist to identify and classify problem behavior. (Adapted from Evans & Meyer, 1985.)

Identification of Social Skills for Assessment

Social skills assessment will be important whether or not problem behaviors are also being considered. Before conducting assessment of social competence, it will be necessary to identify what skills are critical. One approach to this identification would be to conduct ecological inventories to identify the social skills needed for community environments. Often, these will have been identified or implied in inventories conducted to plan instruction in and for the home and community. The teacher can review these inventories to begin to generate a list of skills to assess. To supplement this list, the teacher might consult resources on social skills instruction to generate an expanded list (e.g., Cartledge & Milburn, 1980; Certo, Haring, & York, 1984; McClennen, Hoekstra, & Bryan, 1980; Renzaglia & Bates, 1983; Voeltz, McQuarter, & Kishi, in press). This list can then be validated by the caregivers who can be asked to rate the importance of the social skills listed. If a student is being trained for a specific job, the employer might also be asked to respond to the list of suggested social skills.

An instrument that is currently in development that provides a scale of validated social skills is the *Assessment of Social Competence (ASC): A Scale of Social Competence Functions* (Meyer et al., 1985). This scale provides directions for directly observing a student's skills to initiate, self-regulate, follow rules, provide positive feedback, provide negative feedback, obtain cues, offer assistance, accept assistance, indicate preference, cope with negatives, and terminate interactions.

Language and social skills obviously tend to overlap. The social functions of language identified in Chapter 7 are also included in the teacher's developing list of social skills to be assessed for curriculum planning. Figure 2 is a form for conducting an ecological inventory of social skills needs that can be completed by caregivers or employers.

INITIAL ASSESSMENT

Initial Assessment of Social Skills

Once the social skills and any serious interfering behaviors have been identified, initial assessment can be conducted to develop the 3- to 5-year curriculum plan (as described in Chapter 2). Social skills assessment and instruction may be the only treatment needed to decelerate problem behavior. Assessment of the concomitant change in interfering behaviors might be conducted to document the effect of the social skills training on these problems. Further analysis of the interfering behavior can also help pinpoint specific alternative skills to replace interfering behaviors.

The simplest procedure to assess social skills would be to complete a published checklist to summarize skills that have been observed. The *Assessment of Social Competence* (Meyer et al., 1985) provides a comprehensive scale for an initial assessment. This scale is based on social functions that can be achieved by using varying forms that may differ across situations: The functions are intended to represent a hierarchy of increasing social sophistication. For example, in the function to "Provide Positive Feedback," the simplest level of the function is that "Positive occurs, but is not consistently related to social events." An example given for this level is that the individual "smiles or laughs inconsistently in response to events involving people and activities or objects." The highest level is "engages in nonpreferred activities and shares highly preferred, limited resources on reciprocal basis." An example of this level is that the individual "in order to save enough money to buy a present for a family member or close friends, restricts personal spending for leisure activities, snacks, and so forth." The ongoing validation of this instrument suggests that it will be an excellent tool for social skills assessment.

As discussed for language assessment, a more complex but informative assessment of social skills might involve observations of the student in his or her community and home environments. A checklist such as the one shown in

Student's name: _____ Date: _____
Teacher: _____

I. (to be completed by the caregiver or employer)
Directions: Please take a moment to note the importance of each of the following social skills in your home or business. Please rate each as:
    1—Very important
    2—Important
    3—Somewhat important
    4—Not important
    5—Would not be appropriate in my setting

_____ 1. Greeting others with wave or brief communication
_____ 2. Greeting acquaintance with hug or touch
_____ 3. Shaking hands with new acquaintance
_____ 4. Engaging in conversation
_____ 5. Sitting or standing at an appropriate social distance
_____ 6. Giving compliments
_____ 7. Patting back of acquaintance
_____ 8. Looking at speaker when called by name
_____ 9. Walking to speaker when called by name
_____10. Smiling when praised or in pleasant social exchange
_____11. Accompanying caregiver or employer upon request
_____12. Staying near group during activities
_____13. Waiting for turn or activity to begin
_____14. Initiating leisure activities with peers
_____15. Participating in leisure activities with peers
_____16. Responding appropriately to criticism
_____17. Requesting assistance
_____18. Asking others to stop an annoying behavior
_____19. Avoiding unwanted social attention
_____20. Avoiding abuse or abduction
_____21. Choosing activities
_____22. Managing his or her own schedule
_____23. Staying busy
_____24. Using social amenities ("please," "thank-you")
_____25. Dressing like others in the environment
_____26. Sharing things
_____27. Making complaints

II. (to be completed by teacher)
Review the above list and circle any skills identified as important by the cargiver or employer that the student does not have. Star any skills identified as "very important." Also, list any social skills deficits identified or implied in ecological inventories conducted for skills needed for the home and community.

Figure 2. Ecological inventory to identify social skills for assessment and curriculum planning.

Figure 2 can be adapted as an observation checklist by scoring: (a) if the student has the opportunity to make the social response, and (b) if the social response is made. This observation can be repeated across social situations that typically arise in the student's daily living to identify skills needed in each. Some of the skills listed in Figure 2 have not been well-defined (e.g., "responding appropriately to criticism") since the acceptable behavior is situation specific (e.g., offering an apology for damaging someone's property versus ignoring insults or criticisms about one's personal values or appearance). If, in using the checklist as an observation guide, the teacher notes a lack of response when one is needed (e.g., failure to apologize), or a clearly socially unacceptable response (e.g., running from the room or striking the speaker), then, the next step can be to operationalize a correct response based on consideration of what the student's nonhandicapped peers would do in that situation (e.g., after damaging materials, the student communicates, "Sorry.").

More structured observations might be used to identify potential skill needs. To measure specific properties of the behavior, the response would need to be operationalized. For example, the teacher might count the number of times that a student makes eye contact when spoken to, or measure the latency of responding when the student is called by name. This more specific assessment will be required for ongoing assessment of instruction, but might be used during initial assessment to note if the behavior is similar to that of nonhandicapped peers.

Testing social skills is difficult for students with severe handicaps. Social skills testing typically utilizes simulations of social situations through role play, game formats, and so forth. Such simulations require complex communication about the social events to be assessed. For example, the teacher would ask, "What would you do if . . . ?" Even if the student could perform well in such a simulation, it would be uncertain whether generalization would occur in the actual situation. Observations of the defined social responses in the natural environment have the advantages of measuring generalization, and eliminating the need to design simulations. Thus, observations will be the most frequently used method to assess social skills. Unfortunately, some social responses cannot be assessed through observation, because the events that require their use are infrequent (e.g., a mistake that requires an apology) or private (e.g., social sexual behavior). If such responses have been selected for assessment in the ecological inventories of the student's environments, the teacher probably can identify the specific situations that would occasion their use (e.g., bumping someone in the hallway while pushing a cleaning cart, refusing a sexual advance). Such situations might be assessed with "confederates"—people unknown to the student but instructed by the teacher to set up the events that would occasion the target response (e.g., the confederate positions himself so that the student bumps into him, or asks the student personal questions about sex). The teacher could probably think of hundreds of such potential situations. The important point to remember for keeping social skills assessment manageable is to use the ecological inventory to identify the specific skills that are important, and design procedures to measure these specific responses.

Example of Al's Social Skills Assessment   Al's case study provides an example of social skills assessment. Because the goal for Al is competitive employment, Mr. A. considers social skills a high priority for Al. In using the checklist in Figure 2, the bowling alley manager noted that he did not want his employees bothering the customers with hugging or handshakes. He also considered it important to use social amenities, avoid unwanted social attention, avoid abuse or abduction, and stay busy. Mr. A. observed Al during the school-based vocational training times and counted the number of handshakes and hugs (goal would be none) and social amenities. He kept anecdotal notes on incidents of teasing and other inappropriate social advances (usually from other students in the school), and Al's reactions to them. Mr. A. also asked teachers in the school who were familiar and unfamiliar with Al to invite Al to leave his work and go with them. Mr. A. would intervene to tell him not to leave a job assigned by the boss, or not to go with strangers. From this assessment, Mr. A. noted that Al never hugged and rarely shook hands except to appropriately greet a new acquaintance. He also said "please" and "thank you," unless he was angry. However, he complied with requests for him to go with familiar and unfamiliar people, and reacted to teasing or stares with loud swearing. The social skills of refusing to leave a job assigned by the boss, refusing to go with strangers who did not know a special code word (selected by Mr. A. and Al's parents), and ignoring unwanted social attention by walking or looking away were selected for Al's 3-year curriculum plan.

Initial Assessment of Interfering Behavior

In the initial assessment of interfering behavior that has been determined to need formal consideration, the teacher wants to determine potential variables that influence the student's behavior, and identify alternative behaviors. Gaylord-Ross (1980) developed a planning guide that provides an excellent sequence for this assessment. Specific ways to gather this information might include an ABC (Antecedent-Behavior-Consequences) analysis (Sulzer-Azaroff & Mayer, 1977), a discrepancy analysis (Evans & Meyer, 1985), or a functional analysis of behavior (Durand, 1982; Iwata, Dorsey, Slifer, Bauman, & Richman, 1982). The following paragraphs describe resources for assessing interfering behavior. A summary of this asessment planning guide is shown in Table 1.

Medical Referral   One of the first assessments that the teacher needs to make is to rule out medical or health problems as causes for the problem behavior. Students with severe handicaps often do not have adequate communication to describe illness or chronic pain. Intense crying, head banging, and screaming may all be reactions of physical discomfort. Sometimes, medical treatment will eliminate both the discomfort and the behavior of concern to the teacher and/or caregivers. Such occurrences also may suggest the need for instruction in communication (e.g., to sign "hurt" and point to a body part). Sometimes, the interfering behavior continues after the discomfort has been alleviated because of the social attention received while ill. In some cases,

Table 1. Assessment planning guide for interfering behavior

The following assessments are listed in order from those that require the least teacher planning and implementation time to those that require the most time. By following this plan sequentially, the teacher may identify simple solutions to problem behaviors, and avoid investing unnecessary time to develop complex intervention plans.

Step 1. Document that the behavior requires formal consideration.

Use checklist to identify and classify problem behavior. Proceed to Step 2 when and if documentation is available to support formal consideration.

Step 2. Obtain medical evaluation if appropriate.

Refer to physician if onset of behavior is recent, or if the student has not had a recent physical checkup. Proceed to Step 3 when potential medical problems have been resolved, or when physician recommends that the student be taught to cope with physical discomfort that cannot be alleviated.

Step 3. Review and make simple environmental changes.

Use checklist for simple environmental changes and/or ABC analyses to identify changes to be made. Proceed to Step 4 if and when simple environmental changes have not adequately decreased the problem behavior.

Step 4. Conduct a discrepancy analysis.

Compare student's responses in specific environments to that of non-handicapped peers to identify discrepant skills to be taught. Proceed to Step 5 if and when instruction in discrepant skills has not adequately reduced or eliminated the problem behavior.

Step 5. Conduct a modified functional analysis.

Collect and summarize data on the target problem behavior for different situations that may set the occasion for the occurrence of the behavior, or for potential naturally occurring reinforcement of the behavior. If Step 5 does not lead to effective, educative intervention, consultation may be required for observation and analysis of the behavior.

chronic pain may not be completely treatable, and the teacher will need to help the student learn to cope with daily routines despite discomfort. In either of these situations, a physician's evaluation is needed to help the teacher make decisions about instruction and further assessment. A referral for a medical examination would be especially appropriate if: (a) there has been a recent onset of new and intense behavior such as crying, self-abuse, or general refusal to participate in all activities, (b) the student has not had a recent checkup, (c) previous medical examination reports suggest uncertainty concerning whether or not the student's behavior is related to medical problems, or (d) previous medical reports note the existence of pain that cannot be fully controlled through medication but give no guidelines for the type of activities that should be restricted or encouraged.

Simple Environmental Evaluations Sometimes, a problem behavior can be eliminated by making simple environmental changes. Thus, the next step of the assessment of interfering behaviors is to conduct simple evaluations of the student's environment. This may be done by considering a set of questions about variables in the student's environment, or by filling out an ABC analysis each time the behavior occurs. Figure 3 is a checklist of variables that can easily be changed to eliminate a problem behavior prior to designing a formal instructional plan. Figure 4 gives an example of an ABC analysis that is conducted for each occurrence of the problem behavior to see if any of the

---

Check any change that the teacher will implement to decelerate problem behavior.

_____ 1.   Minimize "dead" (noninstructional) time by using group instruction and reorganizing the schedule for better teacher time management.

_____ 2.   Provide a variety of materials that the student can obtain and use without teacher assistance during times when the teacher must work with other students individually (e.g., toileting).

_____ 3.   Vary the materials provided during independent time.

_____ 4.   Vary the activities or materials used in instruction to promote both generalization and motivation.

_____ 5.   Eliminate lessons that set the occasion for problem behavior if they are not clearly required for independent living, or modify required activities to include more reinforcement (preferably increased access to naturally occurring contingencies like frequency of pay for vocational tasks).

_____ 6.   Self-monitor the schedule of social reinforcement being given to the student for engaging in alternative adaptive behavior versus the schedule of negative attention for the problem behavior. Increase the schedule of reinforcement for alternative behavior and eliminate or minimize interactions during or immediately following problem behavior.

_____ 7.   Improve the general comfort level of the room and the student. Check temperature, furniture, lighting, schedules for meals and snacks, and so forth.

_____ 8.   Modify the schedule to reduce fatigue (e.g., shorter lessons), or improve motivation (e.g., schedule preferred activities to follow nonpreferred activities).

_____ 9.   Review the student's progress across instructional programs to note overall performance. Modify curriculum plan and instructional procedures as necessary to enhance the student's correct responses in lessons.

_____10.   Talk to the parents or caregivers and previous teachers to identify simple ways to decelerate the problem behavior.

_____11.   Give the student instructions to engage in alternative responses to interrupt a chain of maladaptive responding (e.g., when student begins to whimper at onset of tantrum, prompt to communicate "help").

_____12.   "Teach through" problem behaviors so that the student can be prompted to get access to reinforcement with alternative responses. In future lessons, "up the ante" for reinforcement so that the student must make the response without engaging in the problem behavior to get access to reinforcement.

Figure 3.   Checklist for simple environmental changes that may reduce or eliminate problem behavior.

Student's name: John   Date: September 15

Teacher: Ms. M.   Environment: Snack bar

Description of activity: John's group was given the opportunity to take a coffee break in a snack bar that was a popular location for other adults. Ms. M. escorted and assisted each adult in making a purchase at the vending machines while an assistant sat and talked with the group. The group had performed this activity on numerous other occasions. John's screaming had occurred on most previous occasions. Once, when he became very loud, the group had been asked to leave. John is totally blind and partially deaf.

Antecedents	Behavior	Consequences
John had purchased and finished his coffee and cookies. Ms. M. was assisting another student to use the vending machines. The assistant was helping one of the adults to open his package of crackers.	John stood up, pushed in his chair, and began to say "let's go."	Ms. M. and the assistant ignored John and continued to assist others.
	John began to scream and grabbed the arm of an unfamiliar adult who was sitting nearby.	Ms. M. went to John and told him to sit and wait for the group. She escorted him to his seat.
	John stood and screamed and reached out to find someone.	Adults at surrounding tables left the snack bar. Ms. M. escorted John out of the snack bar and the group and assistant followed.

Comments: John had nothing to do once he consumed his snack. He could not see or hear the other adults in the environment. He had no way to anticipate how long the break would last. The teacher's efforts to calm him and escort him out could be reinforcers for screaming.

Figure 4.   Examples of an ABC analysis completed for John's screaming.

variables listed in Figure 3 or other variables are influencing the target behavior. Again, the purpose of this level of the assessment process is to see if the behavior can be eliminated with simple manipulations of the environment. (See pp. 216–217 for an illustration of how Ms. M. handled John's behavior outbursts.)

Discrepancy Analysis   If no simple environmental problems are identified, or changes to improve the environment are not successful, the teacher then must find out what the student needs to learn to do as an alternative to the problem behavior. Evans and Meyer (1985) describe a discrepancy analysis to identify skill deficiencies that coexist with problem behaviors. An example of their discrepancy analysis is shown in Figure 5. As shown in the figure, the

Student's name: Nat   Date: November 2

Teacher: Ms. S.   Environment: Dressing room

Description of activity: Ms. S. teaches Nat to undress and dress in a private area of the classroom that has been designed to simulate his bedroom at home. This activity precedes Nat's adaptive PE lesson. Nat puts on a sweat suit and sneakers for class. This lesson is taught to a group of two boys so Nat observes a classmate dress and then is instructed to dress, or vice versa.

How information on nonhandicapped peer obtained: Interview of a parent of a young elementary-age boy

Typical performance of nonhandicapped peer	Nat's responses	Discrepant skills
Puts on pants alone Asks for help when shirt gets stuck over head	Cannot put on shirt or pants until physically guided through a task analysis of each	Dressing skill acquisition of one or two steps that can be learned by watching model (e.g., peer)
Refuses mother's attempt to help with shoes by pulling away and saying, "No! I'll do it by myself."	Cries loudly when guided; continues to cry for duration of lesson	Communicating "Let me do it."
Puts on shoes alone	Can take off shoes alone; needs physical guidance for shoes on; when tries to put shoes on alone and fails, crying escalates to screaming	Communicating "Help me."
Jokes with mother when finished	Lesson ends with Nat upset	Initiating enjoyable social exchange

Figure 5.   Example of a discrepancy analysis conducted for Nat's dressing program.

teacher observes the occurrence of problem behaviors in the context of functional daily activities, and notes what a nonhandicapped peer would do in that activity, what the student does, and the discrepancy between the two. The advantage of this approach is that it helps the teacher identify functional, age-appropriate alternatives to interfering behavior. It also provides a way to evaluate clusters of problem behaviors that coexist because of a problem situation. It also avoids defining problem behavior outside of its environmental contexts (e.g., to label a child as self-abusive overlooks the skill deficits in specific situations that set the occasion for self-abuse). For most interfering behavior, this discrepancy analysis should be adequate to write the curriculum plan and first year's objectives. The plan will typically focus on the acceleration of the discrepant skills. An objective often will also be written for the deceleration of the problem behavior(s), but these behaviors may only be measured as discrepant skills are taught. Resources on management of problem behaviors provide further guidelines for deceleration when skill instruction is not enough (Evans & Meyer, 1985; Gaylord-Ross, 1980; Renzaglia & Bates, 1983).

Functional Analysis of Behavior The most complex evaluation of an interfering behavior would be to conduct a functional analysis of behavior. In this approach, the behavior is measured under different environmental conditions that are believed to be potential contributors to the problem behavior. A functional analysis might be conducted after a discrepancy analysis has been used to identify alternative skills to teach. However, if instruction in these skills has failed to reduce the interfering behavior to acceptable levels, then the teacher may want to identify the variables in the environment that set the occasion for the interfering behavior and maintain it (i.e., serve as reinforcers) to plan interventions that are related to these variables.

One formal way that a functional analysis is conducted is to define variables that may influence the target behavior, and introduce these variables in controlled sessions. Setting up these conditions and precisely measuring the behavior usually requires more than one professional. However, this analysis can provide critical information to plan treatment to eliminate urgent behavior. The research of Iwata et al. (1982) exemplifies a functional analysis. Iwata and colleagues have developed several conditions that are used in a medical setting to identify the environmental variables controlling self-abusive behavior. In their comprehensive assessment, the student is assessed when alone, when instructed in a highly demanding lesson, and when social attention is given for self-abuse. This analysis can provide clues for treatment (e.g., if social attention for self-abuse maintains it, a high rate of social attention could be given for performing independent leisure or other skills and not given for abuse). Because self-abuse can be life-threatening, such an analysis may not be feasible without the involvement of medical personnel, as is the case with Iwata's work at Johns Hopkins Hospital in Baltimore. Parental permission will also be critical for an evaluation of a serious behavior under conditions that could temporarily increase it.

An alternative approach to conducting a functional analysis that may be more feasible for teachers is to collect data on the occurrence of the behavior in different naturally occurring situations (e.g., with new adults and familiar adults, with classroom activities and community activities, with well-known lessons and difficult or new lessons, when teased by peers, when peers are loud or disruptive). This data can be graphed in trend lines or as bar graphs of cumulative responses to compare these different conditions. Figures 6 and 7 illustrate a modified functional analysis of behavior (described later in the case

Definition of behavior: whining, screaming, or crying that lasts more than a few seconds

Measurement: frequency of occurrence or nonoccurrence within each defined activity across the day using a tally sheet, duration of each occurrence using a stopwatch

Conditions for analysis:

1. Physical assistance—Nat receives 10 minutes of physical guidance from the teacher to help him perform an unknown response in his life skills instruction (varied activities).
2. Short lesson, no physical assistance, variation—Nat receives instruction (gestures, modeling, verbal instruction, stimulus cues, but not physical guidance) for 10 minutes.
3. Long lesson, no physical assistance, variation—Nat receives instruction (gestures, modeling, verbal instruction, stimulus cues, but not physical guidance) for 30 minutes (measure tantrums at end of lesson to have a 10-minute sample).
4. No variation—Nat receives 10 minutes of instruction that utilizes the same materials, activity, and instructions (not physical guidance) every day.

Sample data:

Lesson	Condition	Frequency	Total duration
Shoes on	1	1	4'32"
Clean up	2	0	0
Snack preparation	3	2	4'11"
Set table	4	1	0'45"
Pants off	4	0	0
Legos (toy)	1	1	4'5"
Toy play	2	0	0
Picture recognition	3	4	3'2"

Figure 6. A modified functional analysis of Nat's tantrums.

studies). This type of analysis can help the teacher identify skill deficits that were not obvious in the discrepancy analysis or that go across numerous situations (e.g., the student has no way to communicate the need for help when annoyed by others). To conduct a functional analysis, the teacher has to have some ideas about what could contribute to the problem. The investment of this cross-time evaluation to find out which idea is correct would be reserved for occasions when: (a) simple environmental evaluation has provided no clues, (b) the problem continues to exist despite skill instruction based on the discrepancy analysis, and (c) the urgency of the problem justifies the investment of time to clarify what events set the occasion for this behavior.

ONGOING ASSESSMENT AND EVALUATION

Once the target behaviors have been selected for the long-term curriculum plan and the annual plan, the teacher will develop methods to measure ongoing

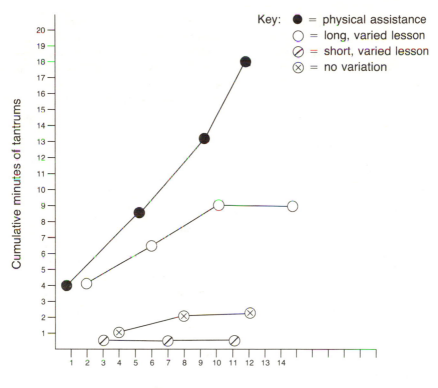

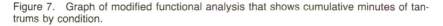

Successive school days

Figure 7. Graph of modified functional analysis that shows cumulative minutes of tantrums by condition.

progress. Often, the assessment of social and interfering behaviors in research utilizes complicated time sampling procedures that are difficult or impossible to replicate while teaching. (For a discussion of the pros and cons of time sampling procedures, see Chapter 3.) Therefore, teachers typically rely on simple frequency counts of the target responses. Sometimes, other characteristics of the behavior can also be evaluated. Through use of a stopwatch, a teacher can time latency (e.g., of a social response) or duration (e.g., of screaming), and continue to teach. Qualitative judgments may also be used to evaluate the intensity of an outburst or the appropriateness of a social initiation like touch. (See Chapter 3 for more information on methods of ongoing assessment.) Whichever measurement procedure is utilized, it will be important to define the target response in clear, measurable terms. The teacher will then need to decide how to get the best representative sample of the response. Some teachers record every occurrence of serious behaviors (e.g., hitting others) throughout the day by using portable methods of data collection (e.g., clicker, masking tape on sleeve, pocket transfer of coins). Social responses may also occur at a rate that makes frequency counts across the day feasible. For example, the teacher could easily count occurrences of smiling when greeted by familiar people in the school and community across the day. The occasions for smiling may be as few as four or five per day. A behavior like spitting may occur much more often, but still be easy to count. For example, the student may spit at peers and the teacher several times in a 15-minute lesson. Each occurrence could be tallied on paper, counted with a clicker, and so forth. (Obviously, the teacher would arrange seating so that the student's peers were at minimal risk of being spit on until this behavior was eliminated.) However, some responses may not be amenable to all-day frequency counts. The teacher may then select representative times for data collection (e.g., social responses during children's recess or adults' coffee break).

As mentioned, interfering behaviors may be measured and graphed even if the treatment choice is to teach alternative skills and not to direct treatment to the interfering behavior per se. Such measurement allows the teacher to note the collateral changes in interfering behaviors as skills increase.

For each social and interfering behavior objective, evaluation of instruction and treatment will be important. Evaluation is discussed in Chapter 4. The reader may wish to review the suggested guidelines for both evaluation of acceleration and deceleration of behavior presented in that chapter.

CASE STUDY EXAMPLES

A review of the case studies illustrates how teachers utilized these levels of assessment for students with interfering behaviors. In each example, the hierarchy of interventions suggested is followed to try to identify the least intrusive, and most educative approach to the problem.

Planning for an Adult with Behavior that Disturbs the General Public: John

Ms. M. was concerned with John's screaming and grabbing people in public. When she reviewed the checklist shown in Figure 1, Ms. M. decided that this was a Level III behavior but that it warranted formal consideration because of public reaction to it (the class had been asked to leave a public facility on some occasions). In the initial assessment, John's medical checkups were current. Ms. M. also had a hunch that John's screaming was related to his skill deficits in new environments. In reviewing the simple environmental evaluation, Ms. M. noted that John had nothing to do on public outings for coffee breaks or lunch, once he had consumed his food. He could not see or hear what was going on in the environment, nor could he follow time to know how long he had to wait for his companions to be finished. Ms. M. tried giving John a portable radio with headphones on outings and having him place his order after the rest of the group had obtained their food. While these simple changes reduced the number and intensity of outbursts, John still needed time management skills. Ms. M. developed a plan to teach John to follow time (his cassette tapes were coded with time cues). She also kept ongoing frequency counts of his incidents of screaming to see if these outbursts would decrease as his time management skills improved.

Planning for a Young Student's Tantrums: Nat

In Nat's case, Ms. S. and Nat's parents were concerned about his tantrums (loud, prolonged crying), which had existed for years. Ms. S. concluded that this was a Level III behavior, but one that required intervention because of the parents' concern and social reaction as Nat became older and larger. Ms. S. noted that Nat's medical checkups were current and indicated no cause for discomfort. In a review of simple environmental changes, Ms. S. could find no changes to be made. Ms. S.'s schedule involved Nat most of the day. His lessons incorporated functional skills, and were designed to end in reinforcing events. Ms. S. also used a high rate of praise for responses that Nat made during instruction, and made many positive remarks to him during transitions. Ms. S. had completed an ABC analysis for each tantrum for several weeks, so she now began to look at specific activities when tantrums occurred. One such activity was a group lesson in dressing. When the teacher guided Nat to pull up his sweat pants when dressing for exercise, he would begin to cry. If she continued to try to help him, his cries became screams, and lasted for up to an hour. Her other ABC analyses revealed similar patterns. Ms. S. decided to complete a discrepancy analysis. To identify discrepant skills, she talked to a teacher who had a young boy about her nonhandicapped son's dressing skills. She learned that this teacher's son could dress without help for most items. When he could not put something on, he came and asked her to do it. The teacher mentioned that her son also had often resisted her help when he was first learning to dress. The teacher noted that Nat's discrepancies were in dressing and signaling the need for help (he had no sign for "help"), or to be allowed to try alone (he had no sign for "I'll do it"). Since dressing was a valuable skill for Nat to acquire, Ms. S. decided that it was important to design instruction that motivated Nat to learn this skill with her. She selected objectives in dressing and communication and decided to time tantrums in this and other lessons.

Although the dressing lesson improved, Nat continued to have tantrums throughout the day. His parents noted that their family life was seriously disrupted by Nat's continuing tantrums. Ms. S. decided to invest the time in a simplified functional analysis. She began to graph her data according to ideas she had about the variables maintaining Nat's tantrums.

She classified each tantrum by antecedents. She noted that tantrums occurred when Nat: (a) could not perform a response and the teacher was assisting him, (b) had been engaged in instruction on a skill for over 20 minutes, or (c) had received instruction on the same activity for over 2 weeks. She also measured the duration of the tantrum. Using cumulative minutes of crying,

Ms. S. noted the highest number of minutes when Nat could not perform a response and the teacher was assisting him, and when the lesson was long. However, Ms. S. noted that Nat's noncumulative graph on number of minutes of crying per day had shown a sharp acceleration and now was decelerating. Ms. S. concluded that by continuing to teach Nat to sign the need for help or to try alone, selecting small amounts of behavior for Nat to learn in each lesson, and ignoring him when he cried instead of signing for help or to try alone, his tantrums would continue to decrease. Ms. S.'s functional analysis data for Nat is shown in Figure 6.

SUMMARY

Because students with severe handicaps have limited skill repertoires, deceleration of behavior alone is rarely an appropriate goal. Rather, the teacher seeks to identify alternative skills to be taught that help the student gain access to natural reinforcers in the environment. Sometimes, problem behaviors are easily eliminated by simple manipulations of the environment to make it more comfortable or interesting to the student. In other cases, the problem behavior is related to the student's skill deficiencies (e.g., to request help or attention, to engage in leisure activities). The teacher's initial assessment may include the use of a checklist to consider the rationale for intervention, medical referrals, a checklist to consider simple environmental changes, an ABC analysis, a discrepancy analysis, or a simplified functional analysis of behavior. Ongoing assessment may include measurement of the problem behavior, even if intervention involves general skill instruction and not a specific deceleration plan.

Adaptive social skills should not be overlooked when considering unacceptable social behaviors or general life skills needs. Social skills are often an important variable in a student's acceptance in integrated settings. Social skills encompass many responses and may be difficult to operationalize or measure if viewed in isolation. However, the teacher can use ecological inventories of community environments that address social as well as daily activity skill needs. These inventories can then help the teacher develop assessment procedures that target specific social responses in specific situations. The best way to measure such responses will usually be to observe their use in naturally occurring situations. The teacher may sometimes have to create these situations by prompting other people to approach the student when the social skills to be assessed occur infrequently.

For each social and problem behavior selected for intervention, the IEP should include specific objectives. Like other related skills, these behaviors should be included in cross-planning for instruction in and for each life domain. (For a further description of cross-planning, see Chapter 7.) A checklist to evaluate the adequacy of planning for problem behaviors is presented in the next chapter (Chapter 9).

CHAPTER 9

AN ASSESSMENT PLAN FOR SUPERVISORS

DIANE M. BROWDER AND MARYANN DEMCHAK

Throughout this book, guidelines have been offered to teachers for developing an assessment plan for comprehensive educational evaluation. Through this careful planning, teachers identify priorities for instruction, and evaluate progress toward these priorities. Similarly, supervisors who work with teachers in programs for people with severe handicaps need to set and evaluate priorities for the overall program quality. This chapter offers suggestions for supervisors to plan teacher appraisal and program evaluation.

Supervisors often have the responsibility of evaluating teacher performance. Unfortunately, this evaluation may be the only assessment conducted to judge program quality. Teachers find that this kind of evaluation provides little information to help them improve their performance because it is vague, unrelated to their community-based instructional efforts, and episodic (e.g., conducted twice per year). However, if supervisors develop a program evaluation plan, teacher performance appraisals can be valuable in shaping the quality of a program.

To develop a program evaluation plan, supervisors need to identify the priorities for the program. This cannot be done "from an armchair," but must be based on information about practices identified through research, as well as priorities of the teacher and needs of the student. From these priorities, supervisors can develop assessment procedures to measure the extent to which priorities are being addressed. These procedures will often create a more interactive role between supervisors and teachers as both successes and problems are identified. If supervisors use the data obtained in this evaluation to help teachers improve, this interaction can become enjoyable and inspirational for both teacher and supervisor. However, a word of caution is needed. Teacher

MaryAnn Demchak is a research scientist, Special Education Programs, School of Education, Lehigh University, Bethlehem, Pennsylvania.

experiences with supervisor observations often have produced the opinion that data will be used to make judgments, not to prescribe and support improvement. At the end of this chapter, suggestions are given for establishing ground rules with teachers about the use of program evaluation data so that the most favorable results are accomplished.

SELECTING PRIORITIES FOR PROGRAM EVALUATION

In the 1980s community-based services for people with severe handicaps have experienced considerable growth. Concurrently, professional literature about service provision has expanded greatly and has established a number of program priorities including: (a) an emphasis on instruction *in,* as well as *for,* community settings, (b) selection of skills that are age-appropriate and relevant to student current and future environments based on ecological inventories, (c) encouragement of integration with nonhandicapped students through the physical location of services and instruction to encourage integration, (d) utilization of applied behavior analysis to design instruction and evaluate progress, and (e) applications of educative procedures to decelerate problem behaviors (e.g., Falvey, 1986; Gaylord-Ross & Holvoet, 1985; Sailor & Guess, 1983; Snell, 1987; Wehman et al., 1985; Wilcox & Bellamy, 1982). Support for the appropriateness of these priorities can be found in the research literature. For example, numerous studies exist in which students with severe handicaps acquired age-appropriate life skills through instruction that utilized applied behavior analysis procedures. (For examples of this research, see Snell & Browder, 1986.) Support for these priorities can also be provided by examining the logic behind them. Donnellan (1984) describes this logic as the "criterion of the least dangerous assumption." That is, it is probably less dangerous to assume that direct instruction of life skills in real settings will enhance community independence than to assume that students will generalize from artificial activities and settings to achieve this goal.

The Urban Training Model of the Philadelphia School District has applied the priorities of community-integrated instruction to program policy for a large, urban school district. Philadelphia's priorities have been explicitly stated as criteria for their program (see Table 1). These criteria were selected after considerable collaboration among professionals from across the nation. They reflect not only the trends mentioned above, but operationalize these trends so that program evaluation can measure the degree to which each has been achieved.

These criteria can serve as a starting point for other programs to select and define their priorities. Identifying priorities might be achieved through meetings with parents, teachers, and administration to establish a program's goals for a future period. For example, many school districts and adult service programs develop 5-year plans that state the goals to be achieved by the

Table 1. Quality program checklist components.

Program area	Components	Program area	Components
Assessment	Assessment tools and procedures are appropriate for the characteristics of the student and lead to the identification of functional skill needs.		are structured, consistent, and occurring throughout the school day in every instructional environment.
	The student's current performance and educational needs for increased independence and participation in the home, school, and community are specified.		Responsibilities of all paraprofessionals and student teachers providing instruction to the student are defined.
	Comprehensive assessments are completed for each student twice a year.	Program implementation	Instructional cues are effectively used and faded.
IEP	Annual student goals on IEPs reflect functional life skills leading to increased independence in the home, school, and local community.		Student-specific therapeutic techniques that are required for obtaining optimal performance in educational activities are used.
	Student objectives on IEPs are behavioral, measurable, and include the conditions required for successful performance.		Teaching techniques specific to student learning needs and current level of performance are effectively used.
	All students have complete and current IEPs with plans for providing related services, interactions with peers who are not handicapped, special therapeutic or adaptive equipment, and evidence of parent involvement.		Reinforcers which are effective and natural are systematically provided.
			Attention to student behavior is given when that behavior is appropriate rather than when it is inappropriate.
Parent involvement	Parent input on the student programs is solicited and feedback to parents on student progress is provided.		Generalization and maintenance of acquired skills is promoted by providing training in more than one activity, in more than one setting, and with more than one staff member.
	Regular communication is maintained with parents.		Each student's method of communication, as indicated on the IEP, is consistently used in all routine and structured activities.
	Parent involvement in student programs is facilitated.	Program evaluation	Data are collected on all objectives for all students.
Program organization and management	Instructional environments include classroom, school, and nonschool (community) settings.		Data are graphically plotted to evaluate the effectiveness of the instruction.
	The classroom is arranged to promote the learning of age-appropriate, functional skills in areas that simulate natural environments.	Integration	The class participates in the normal school routine.
			An activity to promote interaction with nonhandicapped peers is planned and conducted.
	The materials are those naturally used in the performance of the activity.		Information, attitudes, and appropriate interaction methods are modeled to regular education staff and students.
	A master schedule which includes instructional activities, responsible staff members, and learning environments is designed and posted.	Transdisciplinary services	For students receiving related services, collaboration occurs between the teacher and specialist for planning and evaluating programs.
	Written instructional and emergency procedures are posted in the areas where they are used.		For students with therapeutic goals, techniques are carried over into educational activities with input from the therapist.
	Opportunities for student learning		

From McGregor, G., Janssen, C. M., Larsen, L. A., & Tillery, W. L. (1986). Philadelphia's urban model project: A system-wide effort to integrate students with severe handicaps. *Journal of The Association for Persons with Severe Handicaps, 11,* 61–67; used with permission.

programs. Rather than developing a plan with a vague list of goals, identifying priorities might be an excellent method of defining specific criteria for program quality to be achieved over the next 5 years.

This chapter describes the program evaluation developed at Lehigh University for the Life Skills program of Centennial School and Lehigh

Continuing Education for Adults with Severe Disabilities. This evaluation was field tested with numerous teachers in these model programs, and replicated by supervisors in area school districts who are program graduates. The criteria for this evaluation are shown in Table 2.

RATIONALE FOR DATA-BASED SUPERVISION

As the criteria in Table 2 suggest, the recommended form of evaluation is based on direct assessment of both written plans and teaching outcome. Before considering procedures for this assessment, it is important to review the rationale for this direct, data-based approach in contrast to the more subjective, anecdotal evaluation frequently used in supervision. While anecdotal evaluation often accompanies the feedback given to the teachers in the data-based approach, observations typically include direct assessment of one of the program's criteria for quality.

Teacher supervision at both the preservice and inservice levels should check to ensure that adequate teaching occurs to produce student learning. Unfortunately, teacher supervision in special education has been imprecise compared to the precision of instruction expected of teachers (Markel, 1982). In particular, behavioral assessment of teaching, with concurrent measurement of student behavior change, has been rare (Csapo, 1981). For teachers of students with severe handicaps, teacher trainers have advocated and empirically supported the advantage of using data to make instructional decisions about students (Holvoet, O'Neil, Chazdon, Carr, & Warner, 1983). Ironically, these same teacher trainers and supervisors often neglect to base teacher evaluations on observational data.

Collecting precise data on teacher performance has advantages over anecdotal note strategies. First, and most important, observational data can help to validate the relationship between teacher behaviors and student behavior change (Fredericks, Anderson, & Baldwin, 1979; Koegel, Russo, & Rincover, 1977). Second, ongoing data on teacher performance can document specific teaching behaviors or techniques (such as prompting) that are acquired and maintained. Another advantage of collecting data is that the data can form an objective basis of information provided to staff concerning their work behavior.

An examination of the Koegel et al. (1977) study provides a practical demonstration of two of these advantages. Koegel et al. (1977) focused on establishing a procedure to assess and train teachers in the application of behavior modification techniques to teach new skills to children with autism. Specifically, the investigators taught 11 teachers the correct use of discrete-trial instruction. In discrete-trial instruction, the teacher presents defined antecedents and consequences for each opportunity that the student has to respond. Typically, the term has been used in conjunction with massed, repeated-trial

Table 2. Priorities for services for students with severe handicaps used at Lehigh University to guide program evaluation

Priority	Defined goal	Type of evaluation
1. Age-appropriate, community-relevant plans	At least six objectives based on ecological inventories across each domain and related skill; comprehensive assessment at least every 5 years	Checklist for IEP Checklist for comprehensive assessment
2. Objectives and instruction operationally defined for each target behavior	Every lesson has a written plan that meets checklist criteria	Checklist for written plan
3. Instruction matches operational definitions on plans	90% of the observed teaching behaviors match definitions for three observations across lessons and bimonthly maintenance	Data-based observation of instruction
4. Community-based and group instruction well-planned and taught	Same as #2 and #3 across one group lesson and one lesson in the community	Same as 2, 3. Supervisor goes with group in community to observe instruction.
5. Teachers interact with all students positively, and encourage adaptive behaviors both in and between lessons	Teachers use praise and attention as consequences for adaptive behaviors. For maladaptive behaviors, they give instruction, ignore, or reprimand (or use defined contingency). The goal is for attention for adaptive behaviors to exceed any necessary attention for maladaptive behaviors by 3:1, and a balance of attention across students.	Data-based observation of general behavior management
6. Plans for problem behaviors follow an educative and least-to-most instrusive hierarchy	Plans written for each problem behavior meet checklist criteria	Checklist for problem behavior plans

(continued)

Table 2. *(continued)*

Priority	Defined goal	Evaluation
7. Instructional plans are revised to improve student progress	(a) Data collection for each objective at least 3 times week (b) Data collection 80% reliable (c) Graph meets checklist criteria (d) Data evaluation 90% reliability (e) Changes implemented within 1 week	(a) Graph (b) Reliability observation (c) Graph checklist (d) Data-based decision review (e) Change line on graph
8. Students progress in skills that are important to them and their caregivers	At the end of a year of service, graphs show progress for at least half of the objectives for each student. Caregiver survey indicates satisfaction. Students' data reflect motivation.	Annual summary of progress, caregiver survey

instruction. Koegel et al. (1977) defined the components of discrete-trial instruction as follows: (a) presenting the discriminative stimuli, (b) prompting, (c) shaping, (d) providing consequences, and (e) presenting trials with a distinct onset and ending. After intervention, which included written materials and opportunities for practice with feedback, the teachers used the procedures with 100% accuracy, demonstrating a marked increase over baseline levels. Data collected concurrently on students' behaviors revealed that their task mastery improved remarkably after the teachers mastered the targeted teaching procedures. Interrater reliability was 94.6%, which showed that it was possible to evaluate with confidence the teachers' use of behavior modification techniques.

As previously stated, precise data can communicate to staff the accuracy of their teaching behavior. This feedback, in isolation or in conjunction with reinforcers (e.g., supervisor praise), may be provided through a variety of methods that include verbal, privately written, or publicly posted feedback. Verbal feedback, which is a verbal description of the observed behavior and verbal praise regarding specific staff behavior, has been demonstrated to be effective in improving staff behavior (e.g., Brown, Willis, & Reid, 1981; Realon, Lewallen, & Wheeler, 1983). A second type of feedback involves written messages concerning performance provided privately to individual staff members (Repp & Deitz, 1979; Shoemaker & Reid, 1980). Feedback can also be publicly posted in an area visible to all staff involved. This posted feedback,

In a data-based approach, the supervisor reviews the teachers' written plans and also observes and evaluates instruction related to these plans.

in graph or chart form, can represent behavior of either individuals or groups. Public posting has been demonstrated to be effective in improving the behavior of both institutional staff and teachers (Greene, Willis, Levy, & Bailey, 1978; Hutchison, Jarman, & Bailey, 1980; Whyte, Van Houten, & Hunter, 1983). However, publicly posting staff data is sometimes associated with negative staff reactions (Whyte et al., 1983).

The studies above clearly demonstrate the advantages of using data-based feedback to improve specific instructional skills of teachers. Since the goals of supervision are to help teachers improve and evaluate their performance, supervision based on data regarding valid (i.e., empirically supported) behaviors can provide objective rather than idiosyncratic and subjective guidance.

Even though it has been demonstrated that feedback can improve teacher behavior, the technology of data-based supervision is not well developed. Translating teacher behavior research into supervision practice can be difficult. However, the need for objective appraisals requires that supervisors develop adequate observation procedures. Resources to guide this practice have begun to emerge. For example, Stowitschek, Stowitschek, Hendrickson, and Day

(1984) have described procedures for supervisors to observe direct instruction. From research on direct instruction procedures that produce student learning, they have developed supervisory observational procedures. Page, Iwata, and Reid (1982) also used validated teacher behaviors (i.e., procedures that facilitate student learning) in their research on supervisors' use of an observational system. The results of the Page et al. (1982) study support the feasibility of implementing data-based supervision with a staff of supervisors.

The data-based supervision procedures that are presented in the remainder of this chapter have been developed through review of research on instruction and behavioral supervision. As mentioned, these have been field tested at Lehigh University in the model programs for individuals with severe handicaps. In one of these model programs, a yearlong evaluation examined the effect of data-based supervision on student and teacher behavior change. Results provided evidence that teachers improved when given this feedback, and that this improvement also influenced student progress (Browder, Mace, D'Huyvetters, & Ambrogio, 1984). Subsequent research was focused on teacher use of data-based instructional decisions, and provided a demonstration of the effectiveness of teacher self-management to improve this criteria for program quality (Browder, Liberty, et al., 1986). In summary, empirical support for the proposed data-based supervision model is emerging, but incomplete. Its application in model programs with frequent reliability checks between supervisors has led to annual revisions to improve the assessment procedures. Therefore, readers are encouraged to adapt procedures to their own defined criteria for program quality, and to conduct field testing to evaluate the reliability of the specific methods developed for use.

ASSESSMENT PROCEDURES FOR PROGRAM PRIORITIES

The assessment procedures for each of the stated criteria in Table 2 are discussed here along with other alternatives for evaluating program quality. These criteria can be generally divided into the areas of: (a) written plans for curriculum and instruction, (b) instruction that matches the written plan, (c) techniques for general management of behavior and problem behaviors, (d) community-based instruction, (e) ongoing evaluation of student performance (i.e., data-based instructional decisions), and (f) annual evaluations of progress.

Written Plans for Curriculum and Instruction

The first area that supervisors should assess includes the written plans of the teachers. Written plans that are unclear, or plans not based on the program's overall goals for community-integrated instruction, will become evident during observations of instruction or data evaluation (i.e., a teacher probably will not instruct well with a poorly written or conceived plan). Therefore, to give teachers the best chance of demonstrating the program's goals while working with students, the supervisors should be sure that written plans reflect these criteria. The three levels of plans that can be reviewed include the comprehensive assessment plan conducted to write a curriculum chart, the 1-year individualized plan, and the instructional plan for each lesson.

Comprehensive Assessment Plan   Throughout this book, recommendations have been given for planning and implementing a comprehensive assessment to develop a 3- to 5-year curriculum chart. This assessment is critical to longitudinal planning for students to achieve the skills that are top priorities for each of their environments. Given the effort this assessment requires, and its impact on the students' education for several years, it may be worthwhile for supervisors to evaluate this assessment. In Figure 1, a checklist is provided to

---

Teacher: _____   Supervisor: _____

Date: _____   Student: _____

I. **Evidence of a well-planned assessment**
  ____ 1.   Relevant previous records are summarized briefly.
  ____ 2.   Parents have been contacted for initial information on student, parental preferences, and relevant environments.
  ____ 3.   Ecological inventories have been conducted.
  ____ 4.   An adaptive behavior scale or alternative skill checklist has been used.
  ____ 5.   Priorities and supporting rationale are stated.

II. **Assessment of the student**
  ____ 1.   Teacher-made assessments include clear directions and scoring.
  ____ 2.   Testing is related to priorities stated.
  ____ 3.   Testing supplements skill checklists used in screening so that information is available on skills in:
        Related skills
        ____ communication
        ____ motor skills
        ____ academics (optional)
        Home skills
        ____ housekeeping
        ____ personal maintenance
        ____ recreation and socialization
        ____ community preparation
        Community skills
        ____ vocational skills
        ____ community recreation
        ____ other

III. **Preparation of a 3- to 5-year curriculum plan**
  ____ 1.   Skills are listed for each area above (see II-3).
  ____ 2.   Chart is organized so that skill areas and subskills are easily read.
  ____ 3.   Skills chosen reflect assessment results and priorities.

Figure 1.   Evaluation checklist for comprehensive assessment.

guide supervisors' evaluation of this assessment. The criteria in the checklist are based on the model for comprehensive assessment described in Chapter 2 and illustrated in Chapter 5–8. Supervisors will probably want to revise these criteria to reflect the expectations of a specific program's assessment approach (e.g., the teachers might be expected to utilize an existing life skills curriculum or school–district developed skills checklist at an early phase of the assessment planning).

Individualized Education Program   For school-age children, the Individualized Education Program (IEP) is developed annually as a guide for instruction. In this book, an individualized plan is also suggested for adult continuing education. In a review of IEPs for students with severe handicaps across the state of Pennsylvania, Browder, Lentz et al. (1984) found that most IEPs contained objectives too vague for measurement or life skills planning. While annual goals were applicable to almost any student (e.g. "improve communication"), short-term objectives lacked behavioral terms, conditions for performance, and criteria for mastery. If Pennsylvania IEPs are typical of others across the nation, teachers obviously need guidance and feedback in writing behavioral objectives with a life skills orientation. In Figure 2, a checklist for IEPs is given that is based on the operational definitions used by Browder, Lentz, et al. (1984) in their research. By using these definitions, they were able to obtain 98% agreement across the evaluation of hundreds of objectives.

Written Lesson Plans   Another important part of planning is writing instructional plans for each lesson. Because this book has focused on assessment, guidelines for writing instructional plans have not been described. However, other resources on the education of people with severe handicaps provide information and examples for writing these plans (e.g., Snell & Grigg, 1987). The written plan is not only critical to evaluating whether or not lessons meet the criteria designated in the curriculum plan and IEP, but also provides the focus of supervisor observations. Therefore, it is important that the plan operationalize the procedures to be followed in teaching the specified lesson.

Typically, the written plan is reviewed prior to conducting an observation. Supervisors notify teachers about the upcoming observation and either ask for an instructional plan to observe at a specified time, or ask for a time to observe a specified procedure. If supervisors observe instructional plans, teachers submit that plan in a pre-observation conference so that supervisors can evaluate it as well as obtain the necessary information for the observation (e.g., methods of prompting, schedule of reinforcement). The instructional plan will be completed on a form such as that shown in Figure 3, and supervisors can use the form shown in Figure 4 to evaluate the plan. One purpose of reviewing the written instructional plan is to assess the teachers' planning skills. Since the actual planning is not observed, the permanent product (i.e., the written instructional plan) resulting from the planning is evaluated.

Teacher: _____   Supervisor: _____
Date: _____   Student: _____

I. Evaluation of complete behavioral objectives
Code each objective if it meets each of the following criteria:

"A" (Antecedent)—The objective states the environmental stimuli that should set the occasion for the behavior to be performed. The setting is assumed to be the classroom unless stated otherwise.

> *Examples:* "When escorted by the teacher or parents to McDonalds"
> "When given leisure time and a selection of toys"
> *Nonexamples:* "John will brush his teeth." (No condition)
> "When given the cue" (Nonspecific condition)

"B" (Behavior)—The objective states a measurable, observable response or responses. These responses cannot be vague across time trends (e.g., "improve").

> *Examples:* "Point." "Grasp." "Say."
> *Nonexamples:* "Experience." "Develop."

"C" (Criteria)—The objective states the degree to which the behavior should be performed for mastery.

> *Examples:* "By performing all steps of the task analysis independently for 2 out of 2 observations"
> "Within 5 seconds on 5 out of 6 observations across 2 days"
> *Nonexamples:* "Tie his shoes 90% accuracy" (impossible to tie shoes 90%; 90% of what?)
> "With physical guidance" (not a student criteria—relies on teacher behavior)

II. Evaluation of normalized, functional objectives
Code each objective if it meets each of the following criteria:

"S" (Setting)—If not stated, skill must be appropriate to classroom performance (e.g., dressing is not). If stated, the setting should be the natural setting or a stated simulation.

> *Examples:* "At the grocery store, will buy"
> "Will put lunch away" (no setting, appropriate for classroom performance)
> *Nonexamples:* "Take off and put on pants" (no setting, not appropriate for classroom performance)

"M" (Material)—If stated, material must be the actual item used for a real life activity, or must be stated as a simulation. Therapy equipment is a nonexample for teacher's objectives (acceptable for therapist's objectives to be implemented by teacher).

> *Examples:* "Zip his pants." "Buy a soda." (not stated, assume will use real money and vending machine)
> *Nonexamples:* "peg boards" "zipper block" "busy box"

"Ac" (Activity)—Activity stated in the objective is appropriate to the student's age and is the "real life" activity for the target behavior.

> *Examples:* "grocery shopping" "dresses for gym class"
> *Nonexamples:* "String beads." "Point to body parts when asked by the teacher."

_____
(continued)

Figure 2.   Evaluation checklist for 1-year individualized plan.

Summary
Number of objectives that meet all criteria _____
Total number of objectives _____ Percent correct _____
Areas of deficiency:
    Number with A _____, B _____, C _____, S _____, M _____, Ac _____

Figure 2. *(continued)*

Another reason for inspecting the written instructional plan is to complete the pre-observation form (Figure 5, p. 235). Supervisors use this form to clarify the exact discriminative stimuli, prompts, reinforcements, and error correction procedures to be used. The form also permits teachers to identify particular questions or areas of concern for which they would like specific feedback.

Observation of Instruction

As outlined above, a complete review of the written plan is necessary to identify the teaching behaviors to be observed. The current research on instruction of students with severe handicaps does not suggest one specific way to design this instruction, but rather provides demonstrations of various procedures that can be effective. In reviewing research on community-integrated instruction, Snell and Browder (1986) noted various prompting procedures, trial presentations, and locations for instruction that have proven effective (e.g., prompt hierarchies, time delay of a single prompt, whole-task instruction, chaining, *in vivo* instruction, simulated instruction). Given the current diversity in research, it follows that teachers will also vary their instructional plans. It would be beyond the scope of this chapter to describe assessment procedures for the many instructional plans that might be utilized. Instead, an example is provided for an instructional plan that utilizes task analytic instruction.

Observation of task analytic instruction is emphasized for two reasons. First, many skills required for daily living are taught and used as chains of behavior (Snell & Browder, 1986). Second, although task analyses are widely used, supervision of task analytic instruction is rarely presented in the literature. A brief description of task analytic instruction is provided.

Much of the research on individuals with severe handicaps who have acquired new skills has been conducted using a discrete-trial format (e.g., Matson, DiLorenzo, & Esveldt-Dawson, 1981). The discrete-trial format has been applied to task analytic instruction by treating each step of the task analysis as the discriminative stimulus of the next step, and by providing prompts and consequences as necessary for each step of the task (Cronin & Cuvo, 1979; van den Pol et al., 1981). One prompt system that has been successfully replicated in several studies is a prompt hierarchy that provides progressive assistance from a verbal direction, to a model, to physical guidance depending on the help that students require to perform each step of the task analysis (Cronin & Cuvo, 1979; Cuvo et al., 1978; Johnson & Cuvo, 1981;

Specific skills: _____ Client/student: _____
Materials/equipment needed:_____
Instructional objective:
   Antecedent: _____
   Defined response: _____
   Criteria for mastery: _____

Assessment: _____
Method: _____
Schedule: _____

Task analysis:	Teaching procedures: Antecedents (e.g., preresponse prompts)
	Consequences (e.g., reinforcement, correction)

Explanations/modifications

Instructional guidelines:

Modifications (date each):

Figure 3. Instructional format.

	Yes	No
A. General information		
1. Is the skill identified?	——	——
2. Are the student's first and last names given?	——	——
B. Instructional objective		
1. Is the objective functional?	——	——
2. Is the antecedent defined?	——	——
3. Is the response in observable and measurable terms?	——	——
4. Are the criteria for mastery specified?	——	——
C. Materials/equipment		
1. Are the needed materials/equipment listed?	——	——
2. Are the materials appropriate for the objective?	——	——
3. Are the materials functional?	——	——
4. Are the materials age-appropriate?	——	——
D. Assessment of progress		
1. Is the method of assessment listed?	——	——
2. Is the schedule for assessment provided?	——	——
E. Instructional plan		
1. Is the skill task analyzed?	——	——
2. Is the discriminative stimulus listed?	——	——
3. Is the prompt procedure identified?	——	——
4. Is one prompt example given?	——	——
5. Is the response latency specified?	——	——
6. Is the type of reinforcement identified?	——	——
7. Are the criteria given for receiving reinforcement?	——	——
8. Is the reinforcement schedule provided?	——	——
9. Is an error correction procedure specified?	——	——
10. Is an example of an error given?	——	——
11. Are the codes for recording independent responses, prompts, and errors provided?	——	——

Teacher: _____ Date: _____

Supervisor: _____ Plan: _____

Figure 4. Evaluation checklist for instructional plan.

Tucker & Berry, 1980). Based on this kind of research, the components of instruction of a task analyzed skill are: (a) using a task analysis, (b) presenting the trial (i.e., the discriminative stimulus), (c) prompting, (d) fading prompts by using a prompt hierarchy, (e) specifying reinforcement procedures, and (f) specifying error correction procedures.

Definitions for Task Analytic Instruction In order to determine teacher competency in task analytic instruction, the above-listed components must be defined. The *use of a task analysis* refers to the written list of task components needed to perform a task, and designates the subskills for instruction if chaining is used. The teachers provide step-by-step instruction on the task analysis such that all designated steps are taught in the specified sequence. The written task analysis and the instructed subskills have a one-to-one correspondence (i.e., no critical step is omitted).

In task analytic instruction, the trial is presented through the use of a *discriminative stimulus* that is clear and discriminable. The discriminative stimulus should be appropriate to the task. Since the discriminative stimulus should be presented only once at the beginning of the trial, students should be attending to the teachers or to the environmental cue and should not be engaged in overtly disruptive behavior.

The *prompts* to be used in the instruction should be specified prior to beginning the instruction. The prompt(s) should be provided after the defined response latency (e.g., after 3–5 seconds) or to interrupt the initiation of an error, and should not be given after a correct response. If a prompt hierarchy is planned, the prompts should be given in the specified order. If the prompts have been *faded* over prior instruction, no prompt should be provided that exceeds the assistance level defined for the current fade level (e.g., no further prompts should be given if the student needs only a verbal prompt).

Reinforcement should be given only for correct responses, and should be delivered immediately (i.e., within 3 seconds) after the desired response. Reinforcement should be clear (e.g., teachers do not frown while praising the student), and teachers should label the behavior being reinforced (e.g., "That's good walking "). Reinforcement should be consistent in that it should follow the schedule and be of the type planned by the teachers.

If students make an error on a response, *error correction* should occur immediately (i.e., within 3 seconds). Error correction should be contingent on errors (i.e., given only for incorrect responses), and consistent. As with reinforcement, error correction should be clear (e.g., the teachers do not smile), and the behavior performed incorrectly should be labeled with "no" or "don't."

Collecting Data on Task Analytic Instruction   The data collection technique used in task analytic instruction research can provide the basis for development of teachers' observation instruments. As stated earlier, in task analytic instruction, the chain of behaviors required to perform a target skill is defined and written as a task analysis. Teachers define the discriminative stimulus for the initiation of the chain, and the response latency for each behavior in the chain. To assess students on the chain of behaviors, teachers provide the discriminative stimulus to students and score the students' behaviors on each step of the chain. When prompting is used, the type of prompt required for each step of the chain is recorded. If possible, this recording should take place immediately after the step occurs. If the number of responses in the chain are few, with short latencies, teachers may score the behaviors at the end of the chain. Since the use of task analytic instruction will vary across students and lessons, the specifics of the procedure should be discussed in a pre-observation conference with the teachers.

To further develop this data collection system for teacher observation, teacher behaviors (providing the discriminative stimulus, prompting, reinforcing, and correcting errors) can be scored as correct or incorrect according to the teachers' written instructional plans and the definitions in the previous section. After the teachers provide the discriminative stimuli to begin the chain, they may provide from zero to several prompts and may also provide reinforcement or error correction on each step of the chain. The supervisors will record all of the defined teacher and student behaviors for each step immediately after their occurrence. Figures 6 and 7 provide examples of data collection sheets that score discrete-trial instruction on a task analyzed skill. The observation instrument in Figure 6 is designed specifically for supervisors' use, while the form in Figure 7 is the one that the teachers would use to record student data, but is shown adapted for supervisor use.

An Observation of Task Analytic Instruction Figures 6 and 7 show sample data for task analytic instruction of two different skills (i.e., buying and drinking a soda, and cleaning the toilet, respectively). The pre-observation forms in Figure 5 contain the information (e.g., the prompting system) that supervisors need before observations. Figure 6 shows the data for a teacher instructing a student to select and drink a soda. Susan, the teacher, presented the discriminative stimulus correctly and within 3 seconds. Sam, the student, selected a soda. Susan correctly praised Sam (Step 1 in Figure 6). Sam did not pick up the soda within 3 seconds. Susan correctly gestured and waited 3 seconds. When Sam did not respond, Susan gave him verbal directions. However, when he still did not respond, Susan did not model the response and mistakenly implemented the error correction procedure (Step 2). The third step was one Susan performed for Sam in this phase of instruction. On the fourth step, Susan used the three prompts correctly, and Sam performed the step. Susan then waited 3 seconds, and when Sam did not independently raise the can to his mouth, she mistakenly gave a verbal prompt. Susan mistakenly praised Sam for a prompted correct step (Step 5). Sam performed the sixth step independently and Susan correctly praised him. On the final step, Sam again performed independently, but Susan did not praise him.

In Figure 7, Jane, the teacher, correctly presented the discriminative stimulus, and John, the student, performed the first five steps independently. Jane mistakenly praised the second step (reinforcement was only to be delivered on the starred steps according to Jane's plan), but correctly praised Step 5. On Step 6, John did not respond within 3 seconds and Jane correctly provided a gestural prompt. On Step 7, John did not respond within 3 seconds and Jane omitted the gestural prompt and gave him a verbal direction. John independently completed Steps 8–10. On Step 11, John did not respond within 3 seconds and Jane correctly provided a gestural and then a verbal prompt and praised John when he completed the step. John independently completed Step 12 but did not continue to Step 13; Jane provided three prompts correctly. The

1. Skill: Buying and drinking a soda
2. Write task analysis on observation form.
3. Observation date: January 30   Time: 2:00   Place: Lounge
4. Materials: _____
5. Trial components:
     Discriminative stimulus: "Buy a soda."
     Response latency: 3 seconds
     Code for unprompted correct: +
     Prompts (in order): Gesture   (G)
                   Verbal direction   (V)
                    Verbal and model   (M)
     Reinforcement: Type: Praise
                   Criteria: Perform steps without prompt.
                   Schedule: All steps
                   Error correction: Example: Does not imitate model prompt (student has good imitation skills).
                                       Type: "No, that's not how you buy a soda" (physically guide).
6. Teacher's concerns/questions: _____
_____
_____
_____

1. Skill: Cleaning a toilet
2. Write task analysis on observation form.
3. Observation date: February 1   Time: 10:00   Place: Bathroom
4. Materials: Brush, sponge, cleaner
5. Trial components:
     Discriminative stimulus: "Clean the toilet."
     Response latency: 3 seconds
     Code for unprompted correct: +
     Prompts (in order): Gesture   (G)
                    Verbal direction   (V)
                    Verbal and model   (M)
     Reinforcement: Type: Praise
                   Criteria: Performs starred steps without errors
                   Schedule: Starred steps
                   Error correction: Example: Does not imitate model prompt
                                       Type: "No, that's not how you clean a toilet" (physically guide).
6. Teacher's concerns/questions: _____
_____
_____
_____

Figure 5. Pre-observation forms for task analytic instruction.

Teacher: Susan   Observer: Diane
Student: Sam   Date: January 30
Skill: Buying and drinking a soda   Time: 2:00
Discriminative stimulus: "Buy a soda" S^D correct: X   S^D incorrect: ___

Task analysis	Teaching							Total trial correct?	Comments
1. Press selection panel.	+	1	2	3	4	R	E	Yes	
2. Pick up soda.	+	1	2	③	4	R	X	No	
3. (Instructor opens can.)	+	1	2	3	4	R	E		
4. Grasp can with thumb below drink hole.	+	1	2	3	4	R	E	Yes	
5. Raise can to mouth.	+	①	X	3	4	R	E	No	
6. Take sip of soda.	+	1	2	3	4	R	E	Yes	
7. Put can down.	+	1	2	3	4	®	E	No	
8.	+	1	2	3	4	R	E		
9.	+	1	2	3	4	R	E		
10.	+	1	2	3	4	R	E		

Key: + Student's independent response or initial response latency
       1 = Gesture
       2 = Verbal
       3 = Verbal and model
       4 = (only three prompts in this system)
       R = Reinforcement
       E = Error correction

Figure 6.   Example of an observation form for task analytic instruction designed for the supervisor's use. (slash (/) = correct response, circle (○) = omitted response, X = incorrect response)

next two steps were completed independently and followed by Step 16, which required a gestural prompt; Jane correctly praised John for completing the step. John completed Steps 17 and 18 independently, but required a gestural prompt to complete the final step of the task. Again Jane correctly praised John for completion of the step.

Providing Feedback to the Teacher   After the observation is completed, the teacher and supervisor should meet in a post-observation conference to discuss the observation. The basis of this discussion would be the data collected during the observation. Since the supervisor completes a written post-

Teacher: __Jane__   Student: __John__   Date: __1/30__   Environment: __Bathroom__

Discriminative stimulus: __"Clean the toilet."__

Correct: __yes__   Incorrect: _____

Task analysis

Task components		
1. Obtain supplies.	+	
2. Go to toilet.	+	Ⓡ
3. Lift seat.	+	
4. Flush.	+	
5. Put cleaner in bowl (one squirt).*	+	R
6. Scrub bowl with brush.	G	
7. Flush.	◯	Ⓥ
8. Rinse brush.	+	
9. Put brush away.	+	
10. Pick up sponge.	+	
11. Put cleaner on sponge (one squirt).*	G	V R
12. Wipe around lip of bowl.	+	
13. Wipe under seat.	G	V M
14. Put seat down.	+	
15. Wipe seat.	+	
16. Wipe back and sides.*	G	R
17. Wipe top.	+	
18. Wipe base.	+	
19. Return supplies.*	G	R

Key: + = correct without help   M = verbal and model

G = gesture   R = reinforcement

V = verbal prompt   * = steps designated for reinforcement

Figure 7. Example of an observation form for task analytic instruction that adapts the teacher's data collection form for the supervisor's use. (circle (◯) = omitted response, circled letter = incorrect response)

237

observation summary (see Figure 8) as well as meets with the teacher, the teacher is receiving both written and verbal feedback. In order to have a maximum effect on teacher behavior, this feedback should be paired with praise or approval for appropriate teaching behaviors (Brown et al., 1981; Cossairt, Hall, & Hopkins, 1973; Realon et al., 1983). Any particular concerns or questions that teachers have regarding the observation should be addressed. Before terminating the post-observation conference, supervisors and teachers should work together to establish goals for the teachers, and to schedule a date and time for a follow-up observation. Throughout the observation process, it is essential that supervisors remember that teacher data should be confidential and shared only with the teacher who was observed.

Additionally, supervisors should be prepared to work with teachers to identify effective teaching techniques and apply them to a particular lesson. This assistance could be offered through several different forms. Supervisors might provide instructions, either verbally or in writing, regarding a specific technique. A technique might be modeled for teachers, or teachers and supervisors may engage in role-playing situations. Thus, data-based supervision should be related to on-the-job training.

Observing Behavior Management Techniques

Behavior management consists of general management techniques, as well as procedures for eliminating or handling specific problem behaviors (e.g., differential reinforcement of an alternative behavior). This section discusses methods for evaluating both aspects of behavior management.

General Management of Behavior Teachers can respond to student behavior in a variety of ways. For example, teachers can ignore students; converse with students; or provide instructions, reinforcers, reprimands, or assistance. Much of the time, teachers are involved in instruction, and follow the specifics of the instructional plan to provide prompts, reinforcers, or correction procedures. However, there are many other times (e.g., transition from one activity to another) during which instructors can interact on a less structured basis with students. Even at these times, teachers will want to respond to student behaviors in a variety of ways. For example, teachers may respond to appropriate student behaviors by praising students, touching students (e.g., a pat on the back), or simply talking with them. When students are engaged in inappropriate behavior, teachers may ignore the behavior or may reprimand the students. (If this inappropriate behavior is one that has a specific intervention plan, teachers should employ those procedures. The next section discusses a means for evaluating this type of intervention.)

The form in Figure 9 provides one method of observing teachers during transition times to determine whether they are attending to adaptive behavior in an evenly distributed manner.

Supervisors, using a *partial interval recording system,* can observe

Teacher: _____ Date: _____
Supervisor: _____ Time of observation: _____
Lesson observed: _____

1. Observation purpose:

2. Summary of observation
   Discriminative stimulus correct: _____
   Use of task analysis correct: _____
   Number of prompts given: _____ Number correct: _____
      Percent prompts correct: _____
   Number of reinforcers given: _____ Number correct: _____
      Percent reinforcement correct: _____
   Number of error corrections used: _____ Number
      correct: _____ Percent error corrections correct: _____
   Percent total trials correct: _____
   Percent student independent correct responses: _____

3. Questions/comments:

4. Teacher's goals for next observation (completed by supervisor and teacher):

5. Date/time of next observation: _____

Figure 8. Post-observation summary.

teachers interacting with six different students. During each 1-minute interval, supervisors slash the letters representing the type of interactions observed. If the teacher interacts with students who are engaged in inappropriate behavior, the supervisor underlines the corresponding letter to indicate that the interaction occurred during an inappropriate behavior.

At the conclusion of the observation period, supervisors can summarize the data to provide feedback to teachers. Summaries can include the rates at which teachers interacted with students, as well as types of interaction. Supervisors and teachers might work together to set goals for interacting with students during future transition times and to specify errors that teachers would want to avoid.

Common Errors   Various errors concerning the manner in which teachers interact with students can occur during transition times. The first type of error occurs when interactions with students are not evenly distributed across students or across the transition period. For example, one particular student may be ignored for the entire time even though that student is engaging in appropriate behavior. A second error involves positive attention (e.g., praising or talking with students) while students engage in inappropriate behavior. By attending to students when these behaviors occur, the teacher may inadvertently reinforce them. When students are behaving appropriately, the teacher may make the opposite mistake and provide only instructions as compared to

Differential Reinforcement

Instructor: _____ Date: _____ Time: _____
Observer: _____ Reliability observer: _____

Clients' names

Minute 1	I C S^R R P G	I C S^R R P G	I C S^R R P G	I C S^R R P G	I C S^R R P G	I C S^R R P G
2	I C S^R R P G	I C S^R R P G	I C S^R R P G	I C S^R R P G	I C S^R R P G	I C S^R R P G
3	I C S^R R P G	I C S^R R P G	I C S^R R P G	I C S^R R P G	I C S^R R P G	I C S^R R P G
4	I C S^R R P G	I C S^R R P G	I C S^R R P G	I C S^R R P G	I C S^R R P G	I C S^R R P G
5	I C S^R R P G	I C S^R R P G	I C S^R R P G	I C S^R R P G	I C S^R R P G	I C S^R R P G
6	I C S^R R P G	I C S^R R P G	I C S^R R P G	I C S^R R P G	I C S^R R P G	I C S^R R P G
7	I C S^R R P G	I C S^R R P G	I C S^R R P G	I C S^R R P G	I C S^R R P G	I C S^R R P G
8	I C S^R R P G	I C S^R R P G	I C S^R R P G	I C S^R R P G	I C S^R R P G	I C S^R R P G
9	I C S^R R P G	I C S^R R P G	I C S^R R P G	I C S^R R P G	I C S^R R P G	I C S^R R P G
10	I C S^R R P G	I C S^R R P G	I C S^R R P G	I C S^R R P G	I C S^R R P G	I C S^R R P G
11	I C S^R R P G	I C S^R R P G	I C S^R R P G	I C S^R R P G	I C S^R R P G	I C S^R R P G
12	I C S^R R P G	I C S^R R P G	I C S^R R P G	I C S^R R P G	I C S^R R P G	I C S^R R P G
13	I C S^R R P G	I C S^R R P G	I C S^R R P G	I C S^R R P G	I C S^R R P G	I C S^R R P G
14	I C S^R R P G	I C S^R R P G	I C S^R R P G	I C S^R R P G	I C S^R R P G	I C S^R R P G
15	I C S^R R P G	I C S^R R P G	I C S^R R P G	I C S^R R P G	I C S^R R P G	I C S^R R P G

Differential Reinforcement Observation Code

Code	Meaning
I	Instruction
C	Conversation/comment (with a minus sign ("−") indicates criticism)
S^R	Praise (with "L" indicates labeled)
R	Reprimand (with "L" indicates labeled)
P	Physical
G	Gesture
Circle	Teacher error (e.g., C or S^R during undesirable behavior)
Underline	Response while engaging in undesirable behavior (e.g., I, R, or P)
Slash	Occurred during interval

Figure 9. Example of an observation form for general management of behavior.

general conversation or praise. By systematically observing transition times, supervisors can provide specific feedback to teachers regarding interactions. Additionally, error patterns can be identified, and goals for improving future interactions can be established.

Observation of Specific Management of Problem Behaviors Sometimes, through careful planning, specific contingencies have been designed for problem and alternative behaviors. For example, teachers may have planned to praise students for working on assigned tasks at a variable interval schedule of once every 2 minutes. A contingency for the problem behavior might also be planned, such as blocking attempts to hit peers, and ignoring a student for 30 seconds after an attempt to hit. Since such specific plans often require teachers to invest extra planning and effort, and may lead to more intrusive plans if unsuccessful, supervisors may want to assess the teachers' consistency in applying these defined contingencies. One of the methods for doing this is to calculate the frequency within intervals for the occurrence of the problem behavior and record the teachers' use of the appropriate contingency. Frequency within intervals can also be used to assess teachers' adherence to a schedule for praise statements or other differential reinforcement. Figure 10 shows an example of an assessment of a teacher's adherence to a specific management plan. The second half of the table shows a method for assessing both teaching and management behaviors concurrently. This concurrent observation can provide useful information for teachers who typically must apply contingencies while teaching.

Assessment of Teachers' Plans for Problem Behaviors Contingencies for problem behaviors, such as the ones shown in Figure 10, should be the result of careful planning to: a) define the behavior, b) consider the rationale for intervention, c) identify improvements in the students' general environment to decelerate the problem behavior, and d) develop educative interventions to encourage alternative adaptive behaviors. A sequence for planning for behavior problems by using an educative approach was presented in the previous chapter (Chapter 8). Given that such planning requires teachers to invest time and effort, and may lead to more intrusive interventions if success is not attained, supervisors may consider the review of this planning a high priority for supervision. Figure 11 presents a checklist to guide the review of this planning. The reader is referred to Chapter 8 to note the forms that teachers typically would have completed as evidence of this planning.

Applications to Community-Based Instruction

Most teachers of students with severe handicaps will implement some instruction outside the classroom setting. For example, money use and shopping skills might be taught at a grocery store or shopping mall to enhance generalization to similar environments. Observation of instruction and management of behavior will need to occur wherever a lesson is typically taught. In Chapter 6, ideas were given for making student assessment portable and manageable in community settings. Supervisors will also need to adapt data collection for community settings so that it does not intrude on instruction and does not draw negative public attention to the group. Sometimes, supervisors can position themselves so that instruction and management can be observed at a distance from shoppers or other people in the setting. While time-based data may not be as appropriate for these settings, it can be accomplished by using a Walkman-type cassette

---

Problem behavior: Attempting to hit

Definition of problem behavior: Hand extended or raised toward another person (*Exceptions:* hand extended as for handshake or to offer toy or other material)

Defined contingency: Block actual striking of another person by putting one's hands or arm between the raised hand and the other person, and, if necessary, assisting the other person to move. Provide no eye contact or verbalization to the student for 30 seconds after the attempt to hit. During this 30 seconds, give positive attention (e.g., smile and praise or conversation) to at least one other student who is sitting or working appropriately.

Alternative behaviors: 1. Appropriate appeal for attention from peers or teacher; 2. "other" behavior

Definition of alternative behaviors: 1. Raising the hand in the air, vocalizing while looking at a peer or teacher, tapping the teacher's arm, signing "help" while vocalizing; 2. absence of attempts to hit

Defined contingency: Use specific, labeled praise for the defined appropriate appeals for attention. Use specific, labeled praise for whatever adaptive behavior the student is exhibiting, and converse with the student after each 15 minutes without hitting. (Set a kitchen timer to cue use of the 15-minute fixed interval DRO.)

Scoring: / = hitting
           Ⓘ = Correct consequence for hitting
           A = Appropriate appeal for attention
           Ⓐ = Correct consequence for appeal
           P = Praise and conversation after 15 minutes of not hitting
           * = Errors

Optional scoring (instructional behaviors):   I = action verb statement to begin a task
           G = gesture prompt
           V = verbal prompt
           M = model prompt
           P = physical guidance
           R = reinforcement for correct response

(continued)

Figure 10.   Example of observation form for implementation of specific behavior management contingencies. (Form would be continued for 15–30 minutes of intervals.)

Scoring for management	Scoring management and instruction

Minute 1
Intervals (10-second intervals; record each occurrence within intervals)

1	⊘	
2		(No interaction—ignoring)
3		
4		
5		I G V
6		M P R

Minute 2

1	Ⓐ	
2		
3		I G V M
4		P R
5	* /	I G V
6		M P R

Minute 3

1	⊘	
2		(No interaction—ignoring)
3		
4		
5		I
6		G V M P

Minute 4

1		R
2	* A	
3		I G V M
4		P R
5		
6		I G V M R

Minute 5

1	Ⓐ	
2		
3		I G
4		V M R
5		
6		

Summary·   Number of hits: 3

Number of correct use of contingency for hitting: 2

Number of appropriate appeals: 3

Number of correct use of contingency for appeals: 2

Total errors/opportunities to use contingencies: 2/6

Figure 10.   *(continued)*

I. Documentation of rationale for formal consideration

_____ 1. Behavior has been defined in observable, measurable terms.
_____ 2. Student's medical examinations are up to date. Medical problems have been considered and discounted.
_____ 3. A written rationale is given for seriousness of behavior and need for intervention.
_____ 4. If planning has proceeded, 1–3 are completely documented.

II. Documentation of simple environmental changes tried

_____ 5. A log exists with type of change, date of change, and observed influence on student's behavior, if any.
_____ 6. If planning has proceeded to III, several simple changes have been tried, or evidence is stated that behavior is dangerous to the student or others.

III. Documentation of curricular changes

_____ 7. Observations have been conducted using either ABC, discrepancy, or functional analyses of behavior to identify alternative skills to be taught.
_____ 8. Lesson plan exists for instruction of alternative skills identified by the analyses and contains all of components listed on the Written Plan Evaluation Checklist.
_____ 9. Instruction has been implemented consistently for at least 2 weeks.
_____ 10. Graphs of acquisition of alternative skills show acceleration.
_____ 11. If planning has proceeded to IV, 7–10 have all been checked, or evidence is stated that behavior is dangerous to the student or others.

IV. Documentation of high rates of differential reinforcement

_____ 12. A DRI or DRO schedule has been defined. If DRI is used, the alternative behavior is defined.
_____ 13. The DRI or DRO schedule has been implemented as planned (teacher self-monitoring or supervisor observation).
_____ 14. If planning has proceeded to V, evidence is stated that the behavior is dangerous to the student or others, and high rates of differential reinforcement for other or alternative behavior have not decelerated it. Also, I–III have been retried and documented at regular intervals.

V. Documentation for the use of punishment procedures

_____ 15. A punishment procedure has been defined that uses the least intrusive procedures considered to be effective.
_____ 16. Written parental and administrative approval for the defined procedure is attached.
_____ 17. A differential reinforcement schedule has also been defined.
_____ 18. The punishment procedure has decelerated the problem behavior or has been discontinued.
_____ 19. I–IV have been retried and redocumented at regular intervals.

Figure 11. Checklist for evaluation of plans to manage problem behavior.

player and headphones with tapes containing cues to indicate intervals. Since this equipment has become popular with many joggers and teenagers, it may blend into the setting depending on each supervisor's appearance. (One supervisor known to the author has worn a warm-up suit during community observations of street crossing so that the use of a time interval cueing tape and data collection appears to be part of an exercise program.)

Appraisal of Teacher Implementation of Ongoing Evaluation

Another important planning activity is the periodic review of student progress needed to make decisions about instructional changes. To make these decisions, teachers must collect reliable data on students' behaviors and summarize this data with a graph.

Reliability of Data Collection The use of applied behavior analysis in teaching settings is typically carried out by one staff person who may or may not be assisted by an aide trained in its use. Thus, interobserver reliability checks are more difficult to attain than in research. By contrast, to never conduct interobserver checks leaves teachers with the dilemma of having data with uncertain reliability. One solution involves the use of supervisors who observe data on the student to check reliability, while at the same time evaluating teacher performance. If reliability is poor during evaluation observations, further observations may need to be scheduled. The teacher definitions for the target responses may also need to be reviewed to make sure that they are sufficiently explicit to obtain agreement across observers. In Figure 6, an example was given of a supervisor observation of task analytic instruction. In this case, the teacher recorded the highest level of prompt used for each step. Reliability was evaluated by comparing the last prompt recorded by supervisors with each prompt recorded by the teachers. Reliability can then be calculated by dividing agreements by agreements plus disagreements and multiplying by 100. Similar procedures can be developed for incorporating reliability checks in observations of other forms of instruction.

Reviewing Graphs In addition to checking reliability during the observation, supervisors may ask to examine the ongoing data for the programs observed. This examination serves two purposes in that it allows supervisors to evaluate both student progress and the construction of the graph. Data collected on student behavior should indicate improvement concurrent with, or subsequent to, teacher improvement. For example, in a study by Koegel et al. (1977), several students showed task improvement prior to teacher mastery of the targeted teaching behaviors. However, after the teachers mastered the skills, improvements in student behavior were more rapid and resulted in more correct responses. Similarly, supervisors and teachers may find that student behavior improves before teachers master the teaching techniques. However, student performance after teacher mastery should reflect greater teaching efficiency (i.e., student mastery with fewer teaching trials).

As stated earlier, reviewing student graphs permits supervisors to evaluate the construction of the graph. Figure 12 can be used to evaluate several graphs pertaining to one student, or for several students receiving instruction on the same program. If the graph is poorly constructed, it may not convey an accurate picture of the student's progress. If teachers do not include all the necessary information (e.g., labels on both axes) on the graph, or if the information is incomplete (e.g., a label reads number of steps vs. number of steps independently completed), it will be difficult to interpret the graph. Therefore, periodic reviews of teachers' graphs are important.

Review of Data-Based Instructional Decisions   In Chapter 4, a method was described for systematic evaluation of data patterns for making instructional decisions that was based on the research of Haring et al. (1979) and on a subsequent replication by Browder, Liberty, et al. (1986). Browder, Liberty, et al. (1986) found that teachers' evaluation of the data pattern and choice of instructional decisions disagreed with the supervisor's review prior to the implementation of self-monitoring. While self-monitoring is described in a subsequent section, it is notable that teachers often make inaccurate judgments about data patterns. This inaccuracy for data evaluation has been noted in other research with teachers (Liberty, 1972), graduate students (Wampold & Furlong, 1981), and experts (DeProspero & Cohen, 1979). By contrast, accuracy typically improves when a standard method for data evaluation is used (Bailey, 1984; White, 1972). Thus, the supervisor's role in encouraging instructional decisions based on accurate data evaluation will probably be to teach a standard procedure if teachers are unfamiliar with this (see Chapter 4), and to conduct reliability checks of the data evaluation and decisions. A form to summarize these reliability checks is shown in Figure 13.

Annual Evaluation of Progress

The evaluation procedures suggested throughout this chapter are intended to help teachers improve instruction and student management. However, none of these procedures per se demonstrate the overall success of the program in achieving this goal. To evaluate this important overall goal, supervisors may ask teachers to complete a periodic (e.g., quarterly or annual) evaluation of progress for each student in which a summary is given for the: (a) percent of IEP objectives mastered, (b) percent of IEP objectives for which some progress was evident for the year, and (c) percent of IEP objectives for which no progress was evident. Such a summary will be discouraging to teachers who, after periodic review of graphs, have not made instructional changes to improve progress. It will also be discouraging when many changes have been made, but progress has still not been evident. However, facing these difficult realities of minimal progress can help teachers and supervisors plan for overall changes for students. For example, students who show minimal progress may be excellent candidates for the comprehensive educational assessment to design a new

Instructor: _____ Supervisor: _____

Graphs

	Wash hands					
1. Label for student/skill	yes					
2. Vertical axis label	yes					
3. Horizontal axis label	yes					
4. Horizontal axis dates	yes					
5. Vertical dashed lines for changes	yes					
6. Changes labeled	no					
7. Dots connected	yes					
8. Current	yes					
9. Other	N/A					

Figure 12. Graph checklist.

curriculum chart. Such an assessment may lead to the identification of new objectives that are more attainable by students, and more relevant to daily use. When most of a class shows minimal progress, supervisors will want to help teachers look carefully at variables that may have influenced this result, and to identify variables that teachers can change. For example, in a class of students with physical deterioration due to life-threatening illnesses, the teacher may have minimal influence on progress. Instruction might be redesigned to maintain skills for as long as possible, or to teach new adaptive skills to cope with impending loss of physical functioning (e.g., teach self-ambulation in a wheelchair or use of nonverbal communication). By contrast, other teachers may note that minimal progress is probably due to minimal teaching because time has been invested in caregiving (e.g., feeding, toileting). This variable is one that teachers can probably change by teaching during caregiving routines and by making these routines more efficient.

SELF-MONITORING

Throughout this chapter, suggestions have been given for supervisor appraisal of teacher performance. However, many of these suggestions can, and probably should, be implemented by the teachers themselves. Additionally, teachers may perform best when they set their own standards for performance. For

Client: ___Nat_____   Staff: ___Ms. S._____

Period of review: _____10/22–11/10_____   Date: _____11/10_____

Behavior	Previous review		Current review	
	Trend/mean	Decision	Trend/mean	Decision
1. Wash hands.	Acceleration X̄ = 32%	Continue program.	Acceleration X̄ = 32%	Inadequate progress— improve prompts.
2. Pour from pitcher.	No progress X̄ = 0%	Simplify— use smaller pitcher.	Acceleration X̄ = 43%	Continue programs.
3. Play "Cross 4" with peer.	Acceleration X̄ = 23%	Continue program.	Acceleration X̄ = 54%	Continue program.
4. Clean up after snack.	Acceleration X̄ = 54%	Continue program.	Deceleration X̄ = 35%	Motivation problem— schedule play time after clean-up.
5. Put on coat.	Insufficient data X̄ = 23%	Continue program.	Acceleration X̄ = 47%	Continue program.

Figure 13. Example of a form to summarize data review. (The reader is referred to Chapter 4 for explanations of trends and decisions.)

example, Csapo (1981) compared teacher effectiveness under self-imposed and externally imposed, stringent and lenient standards (e.g., number of work units that students should master in a given time period). Teacher effectiveness was greatest and most lasting in the self-imposed stringent standard condition. Reinforcement for self-imposed standards was provided in the form of recognition at staff meetings for teachers who had set high standards. Other research has also supported self-management of teaching behavior that can include self-monitoring (self-recording and self-evaluation), goal-setting, or self-reinforcement (Kissel, Whitman, & Reid, 1983; Korabek, Reid, & Ivancic, 1981).

To self-manage improvement in data-based supervision, teachers might: (a) select the target lesson, (b) recommend a standard for themselves and students' behavior, (c) collect data on their own teaching (e.g., using Figure 5), and/or (d) self-praise in the post-conference. The form in Figure 5 would easily permit teachers to monitor their own teaching behaviors. Instead of simply recording the level of prompt at which students respond, the teacher can record each prompt provided to the student as well as reinforcement given and error correction provided. When instruction is completed, teachers can review the data to determine the percent of correct prompts, reinforcement, and error correction procedures. Supervisors could periodically review these data and reinforce teachers for selection of difficult lessons, setting high standards, collecting data, and accurate self-praise.

GROUND RULES FOR DATA-BASED SUPERVISION

Data-based supervision can be misused and become a threat to teachers rather than a helpful guide for improvement. One of the first ground rules for data-based supervision that should be established is how these data will influence job evaluations that are considered in promotions or job maintenance. It would be unfair to schedule one observation to evaluate a teacher's performance since the data obtained might not represent typical performance. Supervisors in the Lehigh University programs have found it useful to set criteria for teacher performance (i.e., those stated in Table 2), and a timeline for mastery of these criteria each year (e.g., over 2–3 months for new teachers). New teachers, and teachers in new classes, receive the most frequent observations to give them the opportunity to meet the criteria with frequent feedback during the timeline. Returning teachers receive less frequent maintenance observations. Additional observations are scheduled if teachers do not demonstrate maintenance. Teachers are encouraged to self-monitor and to share data so that they are better prepared for observations, and so that supervisors and teachers can compare observations to the teachers' self-monitoring of typical daily performance. Thus, job evaluation is based on meeting a criteria by a specified deadline. Observations to help teachers meet these criteria are never averaged or summarized on their performance evaluation. Rather, the performance evaluation states which criteria have been mastered or partially mastered by the specified deadline. Thus, teachers may perform poorly on some observations and still achieve the criteria by the deadline and receive an excellent evaluation.

A second ground rule that must be established is that these data, like any assessment, are subject to due process considerations. That is, teachers always have the right to review all data collected and notes written about their performance. Supervisors should not share these data or comments with anyone unless the individual teacher's written permission has been obtained. Thus, for example, public posting of data would be a violation of confidentiality unless written teacher permission is provided. Such public posting is also a highly intrusive method for documenting behavior change in comparison, for example, to self-evaluation.

A third ground rule is that teachers have the same right to reliable and valid measurement as do students. Supervisors should also check reliability periodically, for example, by comparing data collected to the teachers' self-monitoring during the same observation. The supervisors should also be prepared to give the rationale or references to relevant research to support the teaching competencies expected. In the end, student progress is the ultimate criteria for the validity of any teacher activity assessed.

Finally, teachers, as professionals, should have considerable authority over the standards set for their classrooms and their own performance. As mentioned, teachers' self-management should be a primary activity in program improvement. Supervisors should support this activity through data-based supervision. Supervisors' criteria for quality should be well-known to teachers, and (ideally) derived from teacher and supervisor consultation. Supervisors should also solicit feedback from teachers to ascertain the helpfulness of the data-based supervision and for ideas for improvement.

SUMMARY

Data-based supervision can document the effectiveness of programs for students with severe handicaps. This supervision can be most useful if provided along with consultation to help the teachers remediate deficiencies observed. Teachers should be encouraged to self-manage their improvement by setting standards, and self-monitoring their own performance. Through an annual evaluation of the students' progress on IEP objectives, teachers and supervisors can note the impact of the program on this primary goal for high quality service provision.

APPENDIX A

CURRICULUM CHARTS FOR CASE STUDIES

In the charts to follow, a brief description is given of the student's current skills and deficits. Environments identified through the ecological inventory process are noted. For each student, a list of skills follows the student description. These skills will be the focus of instruction for 3–5 years. Priorities for the first year's plan are noted with asterisks. These charts are based on comprehensive assessments conducted of real students by their teachers. Names and details have been changed to protect confidentiality. Further information on the comprehensive assessments can be found throughout the book.

Student's name: <u>Nat</u>   Current age: <u>6</u>
Plan is for years: <u>1985–1990</u>   Teacher: <u>Ms. S.</u>

Brief student description: <u>Nat has received several classifications including</u>
<u>severe mental retardation, autism, and severe emotional disturbance. Nat at-</u>
<u>tended a preschool program where he mastered basic self-care (feeds himself,</u>
<u>schedule trained for toileting) and acquired a vocabulary of 10 manual signs. Nat</u>
<u>uses his signs to label objects in the environment (e.g., point to toy car and sign</u>
<u>"car"). Nat has frequent severe tantrums and resists guidance during instruction.</u>
<u>Nat's parents and siblings are eager for him to learn daily living and social skills.</u>
<u>Nat's family lives in the suburban community of a medium-size city. Nat at-</u>
<u>tends a "life skills" special education program.</u>

Environments used in planning: <u>Nat's home, current school setting, middle</u>
<u>school setting, convenience store, shopping mall, fast food restaurants, varied</u>
<u>streets, mainstream classroom during recess</u>

I. Skills for the home

A.   Personal maintenance
Eliminate toilet accidents.*
Wash hands.*
Use restroom alone.
Dress alone (simplified clothing).*
Dress alone (zippers, snaps).
Eat with spoon without spilling.
Drink without spilling.
Eat with a fork.

B.   Housekeeping and food preparation
Pour from a pitcher or carton.
Prepare simple snacks.*
Clean up after snack.
Open food packages.
Prepare sandwiches.
Pick up toys.*
Put laundry in hamper.
Dust furniture.
Wipe tables.

C.   Recreation/socialization
Play "Cross 4" with siblings or school peer.*
Play "Trouble."
Play board games with counting moves (generalized).
Play matching card games and board games (generalized).
Display a matchbox car collection to peers, family.
Feed family's dog.

D. Community preparation
    Put coat on alone.*
    Gather belongings for school.
    Communicate destination by pointing to picture.

II. Skills for the community

A. Vocational skills
    Store belongings upon arrival.*
    Prepare simple foods.
    Work without teacher guidance or verbal instructions for 30 minutes
        (first year, 10 minutes*).
    Follow picture instructions.
    Wipe tables.
    Perform tabletop assembly and bagging tasks (simulation of high school
        and adult program jobs).

B. Community recreation
    Take leisure walks with friends or family.*
    Attend spectator events with family.

C. Other community skills
    Use a wallet.*
    Communicate choice for purchase of snack.*
    Purchase snack without help.
    Accompany adult by walking close by.*
    Stop at curbs while walking with adult in community.*
    Order meal at fast food restaurant.
    Purchase one item in grocery store or clothing store.

III. Related skills

A. Communication
    Greet familiar people.*
    Communicate choice of display by pointing.*
    Use existing signs as social replies.*
    Ask "What is it?" with sign and pointing.
    Communicate "yes" and "no" with headshakes.
    Converse with family and friends about daily routine with signs and
        picture wallet.
    Expand picture and sign vocabulary each year.*
    Show identification card upon request.

B. Motor skills
    Throw a ball.*
    Run to base or end of relay line.
    Catch a ball.

Play kickball with nonhandicapped peers.
Play basketball (lowered basket) with nonhandicapped peers.

C. Academic

Perform action shown on picture (vocational assignment).
Select food versus nonfood packages during food preparation.
Discriminate quarters from other coins while using wallet.
Discriminate dollars from coins while using wallet.

D. Social and interfering behavior

Look at peer when name is called.*
Initiate and respond to social interactions during recess.
Problem: running away in public; *Alternative:* Carry items, make choices, and walk with adults.*
Problem: tantrums; *Alternative:* Signal "help" and "I'll do it alone" with signs and gestures; accept assistance.*

Student's name: Dennis   Current age: 8
Plan is for years: 1985–1988   Teacher: Ms. K.

Brief student description: Dennis has been classified as profoundly mentally retarded with severe spastic quadriplegia. He has few observable, voluntary motoric responses. These few responses include lifting his head and moving one arm in a horizontal plane. Dennis must be properly positioned in his wheelchair or on other adaptive equipment to make these responses. To date, Dennis has made minimal progress in his school program. All personal care is provided for him. Dennis requires a mechanical soft diet due to oral muscular problems. He wears diapers. He has no communication system. Dennis's parents are discouraged with his lack of progress to date, but are dedicated to keeping him at home. Dennis's family lives in a rural area that is about 20 miles from a medium-size city.

Environments used in planning: Dennis's home, respite care facility, city and state park, city indoor stadium, current school, middle school, shopping mall, family restaurant, family's church

I. Skills for the home

A. Personal maintenance
  Communicate need to be changed by pressing buzzer and touching side when asked "What's wrong?".
  Signal readiness to be dressed or fed by holding head up.*
  Communicate food choice by lifting the head when asked "Do you want ____?" and not lifting the head for nonpreferred items.*
  Communicate clothing choice as above by lifting head.
  Communicate hunger and thirst by pressing buzzer and lifting head for "yes" when asked "Are you (hungry)?".
  Communicate pain by pressing buzzer repeatedly.
  Decrease time required to be fed.
  Eat a greater variety of food types, textures, and temperatures.

B. Housekeeping and food preparation
  Operate blender by using adaptive switch.*
  Wipe tray after meals.*
  Dust furniture using same motion as tray wiping.
  Release dirty clothes into laundry hamper.

C. Recreation/socialization
  Operate tape recorder using adaptive switch.*
  Select tape choice by lifting head for "yes" when asked "Do you want?".
  Operate page turner with family photo album and other books.
  Operate page turner to initiate or respond to family conversation.

D. Community preparation
  Lift head to signal readiness to leave.*

II. Skills for the community

A. Vocational skills

No vocational skills were identified at this time. Expand recreation for increased experiences in the community and potential recreational placement as an adult. Continue to explore technological adaptations for existing jobs.

B. Community recreation

Hold head up while being pushed during family walks in community or park.*

Lift head and look up at destination upon arrival.*

Communicate "yes" by lifting head when asked about preferences in outdoor recreation (e.g., sit in shade, go in water).

Communicate choice about attending spectator events.

Play tape recorder for peers in mainstream setting.

C. Other community skills

Decrease time to be fed in community settings.* (first year, small snack only*).

Hold head up while being pushed in shopping mall.*

Indicate choice during shopping.

Release item into cart during shopping.

III. Related skills

A. Communication

Greet familiar people by lifting head and smiling.*

Communicate "yes" by lifting head, "no" by lowering head.*

Push buzzer on chair or beside mat with hand to signal need for assistance.

Converse with peers and family by operating page turner for picture album.

Expand questions used for yes/no communication yearly.*

B. Motor skills

Remove food from spoon and swallow during eating (improve fluency).*

Increase time with head erect.*

Increase range of motion in arm in context of daily activities.*

Increase the distance he can be pushed in chair before he tires.*

(improvement targeted for each of these areas annually)

C. Academics

Not applicable

D. Social skills and interfering behavior

(See social responses listed for communication.)

Increase generalization across people for each social response.

Student's name: Al   Current age: 18
Plan is for years: 1985–June 1989 (graduates)   Teacher: Mr. A.

Brief student description: Al has been classified as having multiple handicaps including severe behavior disorders, moderate mental retardation, and brain injury. Al was recommended for the "life skills" special education program because of his socially intolerable behaviors (hitting, destroying materials, profanity), and his poor academic progress. In Al's 3 years in the life skills program, he acquired new social skills and stopped engaging in his problem behaviors. He also learned to apply his academic skills to daily living situations. For example, Al can read simple recipes, write a grocery list, and perform computation with a calculator. Al's parents have been extremely pleased with his progress in the life skills program. They are eager to help the teacher secure a job for Al upon graduation. Al also will be applying for a placement in a group home that provides transitional training for supervised apartment living.

Environments used for planning: Al's home, group home for adults, bowling alley (vocational placement), city bus routes, street routes, shopping mall with grocery store, medical facility, YMCA

I. Skills for the home

A. Personal maintenance
  Shave.*
  Maintain neat appearance throughout the day.*

B. Housekeeping and food preparation
  Do all laundry (clothes, sheets, etc).*
  Operate dishwasher.
  Prepare balanced meals (increase meal repertoire annually).*
  Store food safely.*
  Respond correctly to simulated emergencies for injuries, fire, or break in.*

C. Recreation/socialization
  (Not a priority; has a repertoire of skills that he uses at home during his leisure time)

D. Community preparation
  Use telephone to call for bus information.*
  Use telephone to call to make plans with friends.
  Plan purchases within budget.
  Keep an appointment calendar.

II. Skills for the community

A. Vocational skills (highest priority area)
  Annually increase duration of work time without interaction or prompts to continue.*

Clean restrooms (generalization).*
Prepare short-order meals.*
Operate an industrial dishwasher.*
Operate a soda fountain.*
Clean lunch counter and food preparation area.*
Manage time using a checklist and watch.*
Replicate above skills in bowling alley or similar facility in second and third year job placement time; fade teacher supervision across these 2 years.

B. Community recreation
Increase fitness through use of YMCA facility.*
Interact appropriately with others at the YMCA.*

C. Other community
Purchase groceries or other items from list alone.*
Use city bus across varied and changing routes.
Demonstrate skill to go to medical appointment alone.

III. Related skills

A. Communication
Use personal pronoun "I."
Use social links in conversation.
Respond with more information when asked for clarification. (Teach these skills incidentally in context of other activities.)

B. Motor skills
Improve fitness (see community recreation).

C. Academics
Maintain use of calculator in shopping, budgeting.*
Read times, words, pictures to follow work schedule.*
Read and respond to signs found in employment setting.

D. Social skills and interfering behavior
Shop or travel alone.*
Refuse invitations to accompany people who do not know a code word.
Refuse to stop working when given directions by people other than the designated boss.
Ignore unwanted attention by moving away and continuing to work or perform activity.
Problem: inappropriate social comments: *Alternative:* no comments are initiated to strangers; respond to appropriate requests from strangers with social amenities; initiate discussion about daily activities or give compliments to familiar people.*

Student's name: Ann   Current age: 32
Plan is for years: 1985–1990   Teacher: Ms. P.

Brief student description: Ann has only lived in the community for a little over
1 year. Ann was placed in an institution as an infant. She left to enter a group
home as a result of deinstitutionalization litigation at the age of 31. Ann has been
classified as profoundly mentally retarded. She walks alone but has always been
escorted. Thus, she currently does not walk across a room without assistance.
Ann feeds herself with her fingers with considerable spilling and oversized bites.
If unsupervised, she will choke while feeding herself because she does not judge
mouthsize portions. Ann is partially schedule trained for toileting but has several accidents per week. Ann speaks occasionally, but the content is similar to
delayed echolalia and not relevant to the context. She also shouts profanity
when sick or distressed. She has no other communication. Ann does smile and
laugh appropriately when other adults are laughing. Ann lives in a home with
two other adult women from her previous placement. The home has 24-hour
supervision and instruction in home skills. Ann's assessment was developed
primarily for her adult education placement. This placement provides Ann the
opportunity to work for pay and receive daily living instruction in varied community settings. The placement is designed for adults like Ann who have had
minimal education and have recently left an institution.

Environments used for planning: Group home where Ann lives, continuing
education and work center, mailroom of a business, senior citizen recreational
center (future), indoor city stadium, shopping center near home, fast food restaurant, family restaurant, convenience store, bus station

I. Skills for the home

A.   Personal maintenance
> Eliminate toilet accidents through schedule training.* (Generalize con-
> tinence across changes in daily settings.)
> Push pants down/pull pants up in bathroom.*
> Use towel when washing hands (discard paper towel in public).*
> Use restroom without help (5-year goal).
> Communicate need to use restroom (5-year goal).
> Feed self finger foods without stuffing mouth.*
> Feed self with spoon without spilling.
> Feed self with fork.
> Drink from a glass without spilling.*
> Brush teeth.

B.   Housekeeping and food preparation
> Discard trash after lunch at work.*
> Carry dishes to sink at home, lunchbox to shelf at work.
> Wipe table after meals.

Push in chairs after cleaning.
Open containers (lunch containers, food packages).

C. Recreation/socialization (taught during breaks between work sessions)
Play electric self-playing piano.*
Operate volume control on radio that is on.*
Operate radio alone.
Operate cassette tape player.
Turn pages in photo album.
Select and use leisure materials without prompts.

D. Community preparation
Put on coat.
Get lunch from kitchen (or lunchbox from shelf).*
Carry belongings to van.
Pack tote bag with change of clothes.

II. Skills for the community

A. Vocational skills (based on paid jobs at center, and routines observed in business mailroom)
Put label on mailings.*
Operate electric stapler.
Seal envelopes with sponge.*
Put letter in envelope.
Prepare mailing with inserts.
Put paper in self-feeding copier.*
Staple paper using electric stapler.
Use photocopier without help.
Put supplies on shelves.

B. Community recreation
Walk several blocks with escort.
Drink soda from can.*
Use vending machine.*
Walk up/down steps alone.*
Attend adult spectator events (e.g., music program).

C. Other community
Stop at curb and wait for escort's signal to cross.*
Walk without being physically guided for 3–4 blocks (goal for next 5 years; increase distance each year).
Take wallet from pocket.
Use wallet alone.
Select choice of snack purchase by pointing.*
Walk with shopping cart.
Grasp/release item into shopping cart.
Order food in restaurant by using pictures.

III.   Related skills

A.   Communication

Point to make choice from a display.*

Nod "yes" and "no" for "Do you want" when no display is present.

Converse by turning to page in photo album that companion discusses.

Communicate hunger, thirst, need to toilet, or pain by using picture wallet.

Initiate communication by touching companion's arm.

Imitate social comments verbally (e.g., "Hello," "How are you"?).

Show identification card upon request.

B.   Motor skills

Use thumb in opposition to fingers to grasp glass, soda can; carry objects in activities listed for home, community.

Increase speed of ambulation (annually).*

Walk to nearby destination (e.g., restroom) without prompts (first year, walk across with instructor in sight).

Increase strength by carrying work supplies, tote bag.

Open doors without help (increase types each year).

C.   Academics

Not relevant for Ann

D.   Social skills and interfering behavior

Initiate social interaction by sitting near person, walking to person during break.

Respond to social comment with smile and eye contact.

Share picture photo album with new acquaintances.

Problem: loud cursing and delayed echolalia in public settings; *Alternative:*   communicate desire to leave by pointing to door.*

Student's name: <u>John</u>   Current age: <u>53</u>
Plan is for years: <u>1985–1990</u>   Teacher: <u>Ms. M.</u>

Brief student description: John left the institution where he spent most of his life about 3 years prior to this assessment. Since John left the institution, he lost his sight and most of his hearing ability. At one time, John was classified as moderately mentally retarded. However, as a young man, John rode his bicycle to leave the institution to visit his relatives in a nearby town. He also received subscriptions to magazines and newspapers in the institution. John has not yet acquired the skills to cope with his sensory losses. Instead, he has become sedentary with resultant deterioration in overall fitness, and has developed behaviors that create disruptions in his home life and community integration (e.g., screaming and grabbing people). When John first attended the adult education program that provides job training with pay and instruction in community skills, he had toileting accidents, ate with considerable mess and spilling, and spent much of his day wandering around the center. At the time of this assessment, John sits and works for brief periods (less than 10 minutes) and rarely has toileting accidents. He often asks to begin the next work session. He is learning to use a cane and to rely on a sighted guide for orientation and mobility. Although this curriculum was designed for John's adult education program, it was developed in consultation with the staff of the group home where he resides.

Environments used for planning: John's group home, John's sister's home where he visits, continuing education and work center, business mail room, shopping mall, city streets, city bus, restaurant, convenience store

I.   Skills for the home

A.   Personal maintenance
      Pour from a thermos (lunch at work).*
      Adjust pants in restroom only.*

B.   Housekeeping and food preparation
      Wipe the table.*
      Sweep the floor.
      Clean windows.
      Make coffee.

C.   Recreation/socialization (Teach during work breaks)
      Operate a tape recorder.*
      Select own tapes.*
      Insert new batteries in tape recorder.

D.   Community preparation
      State his daily schedule.*
      Keep an appointment calendar.
      Use a telephone with amplification to call brother.

II.   Skills for the community

A.   Vocational skills (Based on paid jobs in the center, and routine observed in business mailroom)

Complete one insert and label job at half rate of nonhandicapped worker.*

Complete multiple insert job.*

Fold letter and card style.

Increase rate of multiple insert job with folding to half rate of nonhandicapped worker.

Operate self-feeding photocopier alone.

Complete, collate, and staple multiple page photocopy job.

Work without standing or screaming until break, about 90 minutes (first year's goal is 30 minutes*).

B.   Community recreation

Plan and participate in senior citizen bus tour.

(See communication, social, and motor skills needed.)

C.   Other community skills

Walk to familiar room in center or home by trailing wall.*

Walk with escort using cane to negotiate curbs.*

Take city bus with escort.

Take long bus tour with escort.

Use wallet.*

Select quarters from coins.*

Select dollars.

Organize wallet by type of money.

Count dollars to make purchase.

State order in restaurant or at convenience store.*

III.   Related skills

A.   Communication

Respond with factual answer when asked about schedule.*

Respond to most social comments or questions directed to him (generalization to new acquaintances).*

Ask for supplies when needed during work sessions.

Ask questions for clarification about his schedule or activities.

State identification (name, address, phone number).

B.   Motor skills

Walk four city blocks without stopping to rest.*

Increase speed of walking with sighted guide.

C.   Academics

Write signature on checks or forms using guide.

Apply counting skills to job assignments.

D. Social skills and interfering behaviors
   Use social amenities (please, thank you).
   Initiate topics appropriate to adult conversation.
   Problem: attempts to kiss and hug all women when they say good-
     bye; *Alternative:*   express parting greeting with handshake and po-
     lite comment.*
   Problem: When unsure of schedule, wanders, screams, and grabs
     strangers; *Alternative:*   time management skills, appropriate wait-
     ing, and asking questions about the schedule when uncertain.*

EXAMPLE OF A WRITTEN REPORT FOR A COMPREHENSIVE EDUCATIONAL ASSESSMENT

EDUCATIONAL EVALUATION

Student: Dennis Smith
Age: 8   DOB: 6-3-79
Placement: Elementary SPMR
School: Lehigh Elementary

Date of report: October 12
Initial or reevaluation: Reevaluation
Evaluator: Ms. Dana Kay
Position: Teacher

BACKGROUND INFORMATION

Brief Student Description

Dennis Smith has received the medical diagnosis of severe spastic quadriplegia, and the educational classification of profound mental retardation with an accompanying severe physical handicap. Dennis has a few observable, voluntary motoric responses. These responses include lifting his head and moving one arm in a horizontal plane. Dennis must be positioned properly in a wheelchair or on other adaptive equipment to make these responses.

Educational History

Dennis was first evaluated for educational services by United Cerebral Palsy in 1980. Dennis and his mother participated in an infant stimulation program at United Cerebral Palsy one day per week from January 1980 to May 1982. According to Mrs. Smith, this program included physical therapy and parent training in infant stimulation. Mrs. Smith shared a written evaluation from United Cerebral Palsy dated February 4, 1980 that summarized the use of the Koontz Developmental Assessment (Koontz, 1974). The summary identified no existing skills on the scale, and stated that Dennis's level was "below 1 month."

On August 1, 1982, Dennis was evaluated for the school district's preschool program. This evaluation utilized the *Denver Developmental Screening Test* (Frankenburg, Dodds, & Fandal, 1968–70). Again, the evaluation concluded that Dennis's developmental level was "below 1 month." Dennis's preschool IEP included objectives in visual tracking, head control, swallowing food, swallowing liquid, and "sensory stimulation." These objectives remained the same from 1982 until 1984.

In September 1984, Dennis was placed in the elementary class for students with severe and profound mental retardation. On September 15, 1984, his teacher completed a school–district designed developmental checklist. On this checklist, the teacher noted that Dennis could swallow liquids and mechanical soft solids (e.g., foods prepared with a blender). He had begun to lift his head for a few seconds at a time, and occasionally made eye contact and smiled. Dennis's IEP for 1984–1985 and 1985–1986 contained objectives in visual tracking, head control, removing food from a spoon with his lips, drinking liquids with minimal spilling, and "sensory stimulation." On the 1985–1986 IEP, Dennis's mother wrote, "While I approve this IEP because I know of no other alternatives for Dennis, I am discouraged that his IEP has been virtually the same since he entered the preschool program in 1982."

The current evaluation was conducted in response to Mrs. Smith's note on the 1985–1986 IEP to identify new objectives for Dennis's IEP for 1986–1987. Also, Dennis's educational program until 1985 had been based on infant development. This evaluation was conducted to develop a chronologically age–appropriate life skills curriculum for Dennis.

Prior Educational Evaluations

The only educational evaluations conducted for Dennis up to this report were the developmental assessments mentioned earlier. Dennis's previous teachers did not conduct direct ongoing assessment, but rather, kept anecdotal notes on Dennis. These notes were not available in Dennis's records. Mrs. Smith shared copies of several of these reports that typically summarized the teaching activities in which Dennis had participated. Mrs. Smith could not recollect any written reports of progress except the speech therapist's evaluations of Dennis's improved eating skills in the reevaluation in September 1985.

Other Evaluations

This report is one component of a multidisciplinary evaluation of Dennis that includes medical, physical therapy, occupational therapy, speech therapy, and educational evaluations. The family physician's report noted the need for Dennis to improve his overall health and stamina. Dennis currently tires easily and frequently is ill with viruses and other infections. The physical therapist recommended new equipment to accommodate Dennis's growth since his current equipment was purchased. Specifically, a large-size wedge and wheelchair were recommended. The physical therapist also noted that Dennis's improved head control should be encouraged. The occupational therapist noted that Dennis had some range of motion in one arm that might be useable to operate adaptive switches if it became stronger and more consistent. The speech therapist targeted improved eating skills in removing food from the spoon and swallowing. The speech therapist concluded that speech development was improbable for Dennis and that a "yes/no" communication system should be developed.

CURRENT ASSESSMENT

Identification of Skills for Assessment

Adaptive Behavior Screening An adaptive behavior assessment was used as a general screening of Dennis's current skills. The *Comprehensive Test of Adaptive Behavior* (Adams, 1984) was completed by using the *Parent Survey* form and observations of Dennis in the classroom. At the time of this assessment, Dennis had no self-care, daily living, or recognizable communicative responses.

Family Contact An ecological inventory was conducted through a teacher-made survey that was sent to the parents on September 2, 1986. This inventory revealed that Dennis shows some preference for bright lights and sweets, and dislike for applesauce and being cold. The parents would like for Dennis's progress in eating to be maintained in his ongoing curriculum plan. They would like to see "new goals" and "skills that will make him a more active member of the family" added to his plan. The mother noted that she provides most of Dennis's care and would be interested in implementing some daily instruction with Dennis. This survey was also used to identify the environments for further inventories. The parents identified these environments as ones that the family uses or would like to use: a respite care facility, city and state parks, an indoor stadium, a shopping mall, a family restaurant, and the family's church.

Ecological Inventories Ecological inventories were conducted for the identified environments through observations and interviews with significant people in each environment listed by the parents, and in the student's current and future school environments. In each inventory, activities of other young elementary-age children were noted to identify possible skills to adapt for Dennis. From these various inventories, several general skills were noted: peer interaction, communication of preferences to parents and others in the environments, general conversation with family members and peers, making small purchases of toys or snacks, eating, and watching events or looking for a destination.

Priorities for Further Assessment From these inventories, it was concluded that Dennis would need to learn to use his few motoric responses in ways that would make him an active participant in various routines. For the next few years, the goal of partial participation in a variety of home and community activities was viewed as most important and feasible. Communication of preference was targeted as the highest priority because it would provide the quickest way for Dennis to become active in his daily routines. The parents' priority of maintenance of eating skills was also noted for further assessment and planning.

Direct Assessment

To address the priorities, assesment was planned and conducted over the period of 2 weeks in the classroom or the community environment noted. The results of this assessment follow.

Home Observation The adaptive behavior assessment provided minimal direction for planning home skills for Dennis because he had no skills listed on the survey. An observation was made of Dennis's mother performing Dennis's caregiving routine to identify responses that might be targeted for Dennis's participation. Feeding, diaper changing, and dressing were observed. From this observation, it was concluded that Dennis might learn to communicate preferences for food or clothes, and might communicate the need to be changed. It also was apparent that Dennis's eating skills would need to become more fluent in order for the family to take him to a restaurant since it required over an hour to feed him.

Assessment of Head Control A teacher-made assessment was also used for head control. This response was considered a possible one for use in a yes/no communication system, and also was important for Dennis to observe events in his environments. The teacher presented repeated trials distributed across activities in which some object involved in the activity was shown to Dennis. Using a stopwatch, the number of seconds that Dennis held his head up was timed.

Communication Assessment A checklist was used to note any idiosyncratic responses that Dennis used to communicate, and the function of these responses over a 2-week period (see checklist in Figure 3, Chapter 7). Although Dennis typically sat passively and made no responses, five responses were observed over the 2-week period that could be considered communicative. On the first occasion, Dennis cried when his diaper was soiled and the teacher was preoccupied with another student. On the next occasion, Dennis looked at the teacher and smiled when she said "Good morning, Dennis." During one day's lunch, Dennis was given spinach. He grimaced and spit it out. The fourth event occurred when his mother visited the class. When she left, Dennis cried and hit his arm against the side of the chair. In the fifth event observed, the teacher was conducting assessment to identify leisure skills. Dennis smiled and laughed when the teacher played a tape with upbeat music. A second checklist was used in consultation with the speech, occupational, and physical therapists to identify a response that might be used for yes/no. These professionals concurred that lifting his head for "yes" would be the simplest to train since he could already lift his head. This response would also be portable across settings and activities.

Home Leisure A teacher-made observation was used to identify both Dennis's preferences for leisure materials and skills to use them. Task analytic assessment of pressing a flipper switch to activate a toy bus was used. Dennis made some effort to depress the switch but could not do so alone. This switch could be used to adapt many battery activated toys for Dennis. Preference was observed by noting whether or not Dennis made any response of pleasure in repeated-trial presentations of items (e.g., smile, laugh, watching as the teacher activated the material). Dennis showed the strongest preference for upbeat music. He showed no interest in electronic games, and some interest for colorful pictures. Dennis could not operate a switch-activated page turner when assessed in task analytic assessment on this skill.

Community-Based Observation Dennis was taken to a shopping mall to observe his skills in that environment. A teacher-made checklist was used to summarize skills that Dennis might acquire for community environments. It was observed that Dennis rarely lifted his head to see the environment. He did not look at a peer who talked with him during the outing. He also fell asleep after the first 10 minutes in the mall, and slept for most of the rest of the day (about 2 hours). A phone call to Mrs. Smith indicated that Dennis frequently tired during outings, and slept for several hours after being taken somewhere.

Assessment of Use of Arm and Hand in Daily Living Activities Task analytic assessment was used to assess Dennis's use of his horizontal arm movement and grasp for daily activities. He was assessed in wiping his tray, and releasing clothes into a hamper. Dennis made slight voluntary movements in each of these assessments. For example, he moved his arm slightly to the right when a sponge was placed in his hand on his tray. He slightly uncurled his fingers when clothes were placed in his hand and his hand was placed on the edge of the hamper. These movements could be targeted for training across activities (e.g., dusting, releasing objects in a shopping cart).

Assessment of Eating Skills Repeated-trial assessment was used to assess removing food from a spoon, and drinking from a glass when fed. The first 10 bites or sips were assessed for each new food or liquid. Dennis consistently removed food for some foods (pudding, potatoes, peaches), but only did so for from two to six trials for other foods (meat, green beans, beets). He drank from a cup consistently. Dennis's lunches were also timed for 2 weeks. Dennis's feeding time ranged from 30 to 55 minutes depending on the amount of food. Although not timed, Dennis seemed to eat meat and vegetables more slowly than sweets and fruits.

SUMMARY AND RECOMMENDATIONS

This assessment revealed that Dennis has virtually no skills to be active in his daily routines. His communication is limited to smiling, laughter, grimaces, and crying. He does occasionally indicate preferences with these forms. Dennis's ability to lift his head and move his right arm provide responses that can be developed for partial participation in many daily living routines. Dennis's poor stamina and lack of communication are hindrances to his participation in community activities with his family. Both might be improved through gradually increasing time and instruction in community settings. The priorities for Dennis's curriculum for the next 3 years are communication and active participation in a variety of home and community activities that the family enjoys. (The reader is referred to Dennis's curriculum chart in Appendix A for the specific skills proposed.)

STANDARD FORMS
FOR GRAPHS

STANDARD SLASH-NUMBER
DATA COLLECTION/GRAPH FORM

Behavior: _____ Name: _____ Mastery: _____

	100																				
		20	20	20	20	20	20	20	20	20	20	20	20	20	20	20	20	20	20	20	20
	90	19	19	19	19	19	19	19	19	19	19	19	19	19	19	19	19	19	19	19	19
		18	18	18	18	18	18	18	18	18	18	18	18	18	18	18	18	18	18	18	18
	80	17	17	17	17	17	17	17	17	17	17	17	17	17	17	17	17	17	17	17	17
		16	16	16	16	16	16	16	16	16	16	16	16	16	16	16	16	16	16	16	16
	70	15	15	15	15	15	15	15	15	15	15	15	15	15	15	15	15	15	15	15	15
		14	14	14	14	14	14	14	14	14	14	14	14	14	14	14	14	14	14	14	14
	60	13	13	13	13	13	13	13	13	13	13	13	13	13	13	13	13	13	13	13	13
		12	12	12	12	12	12	12	12	12	12	12	12	12	12	12	12	12	12	12	12
	50	11	11	11	11	11	11	11	11	11	11	11	11	11	11	11	11	11	11	11	11
		10	10	10	10	10	10	10	10	10	10	10	10	10	10	10	10	10	10	10	10
		9	9	9	9	9	9	9	9	9	9	9	9	9	9	9	9	9	9	9	9
	40	8	8	8	8	8	8	8	8	8	8	8	8	8	8	8	8	8	8	8	8
		7	7	7	7	7	7	7	7	7	7	7	7	7	7	7	7	7	7	7	7
	30	6	6	6	6	6	6	6	6	6	6	6	6	6	6	6	6	6	6	6	6
		5	5	5	5	5	5	5	5	5	5	5	5	5	5	5	5	5	5	5	5
	20	4	4	4	4	4	4	4	4	4	4	4	4	4	4	4	4	4	4	4	4
		3	3	3	3	3	3	3	3	3	3	3	3	3	3	3	3	3	3	3	3
	10	2	2	2	2	2	2	2	2	2	2	2	2	2	2	2	2	2	2	2	2
		1	1	1	1	1	1	1	1	1	1	1	1	1	1	1	1	1	1	1	1
**********	0 %	0	0	0	0	0	0	0	0	0	0	0	0	0	0	0	0	0	0	0	0

Dates: _____

		Reviews	
Date	Trend/mean		Decision

_____

_____

_____

STANDARD FILL-IN
DATA COLLECTION/GRAPH FORM

Behavior: _____ Name: _____ Mastery: _____

```
100
 90
 80
 70
 60
 50
 40
 30
 20
 10
  0
  %
```

Dates: _____

Date	Trend/mean	Decision

STANDARD EQUAL
INTERVAL GRAPH

Behavior: _____ Student: _____ Mastery: _____

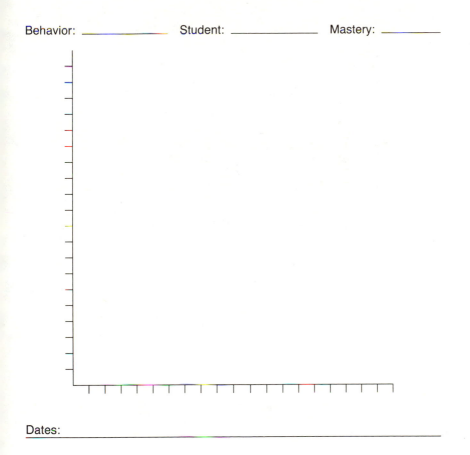

Dates:

PERCENTAGE TABLE

Number Total

Number correct	20	19	18	17	16	15	14	13	12	11	10	9	8
20	100												
19	95	100											
18	90	95	100										
17	85	89	94	100									
16	80	84	89	94	100								
15	75	79	83	88	94	100							
14	70	74	78	82	88	93	100						
13	65	68	72	76	81	87	93	100					
12	60	63	67	71	75	80	86	92	100				
11	55	58	61	65	69	73	79	85	92	100			
10	50	53	56	59	63	67	71	77	83	91	100		
9	45	47	50	53	56	60	64	69	75	82	90	100	
8	40	42	44	47	50	53	57	62	67	73	80	89	100
7	35	37	39	41	44	47	50	54	58	64	70	78	88
6	30	32	33	35	38	40	43	46	50	55	60	67	75
5	25	26	28	29	31	33	36	38	42	45	50	56	63
4	20	21	22	24	25	27	29	31	33	36	40	44	50
3	15	16	17	18	19	20	21	23	25	27	30	33	38
2	10	11	11	12	13	13	14	15	17	18	20	22	25
1	5	5	6	6	6	7	7	7	8	9	10	11	13
0	0	0	0	0	0	0	0	0	0	0	0	0	0

REFERENCES

Adams, G. L. (1984). *Comprehensive Test of Adaptive Behavior*. Columbus, OH: Charles E. Merrill.

Adubato, A., Adams, M. K., & Budd, S. (1981). Teaching a parent to train a spouse in child management techniques. *Journal of Applied Behavior Analysis, 14*, 193–205.

Angney, A., & Hanley, E. M. (1979). A parent-implemented shaping procedure to develop independent walking of a Down's syndrome child: A case study. *Education and Treatment of Children, 2*, 311–315.

Armstrong v. Kline, 476 F. Supp. 583 (E.D. Pa. 1979).

Arwood, E. L. (1981). *Pragmatism*. Rockville, MD: Aspen Systems.

Ayres, A. J. (1981). *Sensory integration and the child*. Los Angeles: Western Psychological Services.

Bailey, D. B. (1984). Effects on lines of progress and semi-logarithmic charts on ratings of charted data. *Journal of Applied Behavior Analysis, 17*, 359–365.

Battle v. Commonwealth, 79-2158, 79-2188-90, 79-2568-70 (3rd Cir., July 18, 1980).

Becker, J. V., Turner, S. M., & Sajwaj, T. E. (1978). Multiple behavioral effects of the use of lemon juice with a ruminating toddler-age child. *Behavior Modification, 2*, 267–278.

Beckman-Bell, P. (1981). Child-related stress in families of handicapped children. *Topics in Early Childhood Special Education, 1*, 45–53.

Beckman-Brindley, S., & Snell, M. E. (1985). *Family perspectives on parent participation in educational and behavioral programs*. Unpublished manuscript, University of Virginia, Charlottesville.

Bellamy, G. T. (1985). Severe disability in adulthood. *Newsletter of the Association for Persons with Severe Handicaps, 11*, 1, 6.

Bellamy, G. T., Horner, R. H., & Inman, D. P. (1979). *Vocational habilitation of severely retarded adults*. Baltimore: University Park Press.

Bellamy, G. T., Rhodes, L. E., Wilcox, B., Albin, J. M., Mank, D. M., Boles, S. M., Horner, R. H., Collins, M., & Turner, J. (1984). Quality and equality in employment services for adults with severe disabilities. *Journal of The Association for Persons with Severe Handicaps, 9*, 270–277.

Bigge, J. L. (1982). *Teaching individuals with physical and multiple disabilities* (2nd ed.). Columbis, OH: Charles E. Merrill.

Bijou, S. W., & Baer, D. M. (1961). *Child development: Vol. II. Universal states of infancy*. New York: Appleton-Century-Crofts.

Blankenship, C. S. (1985). Using curriculum-based assessment data to make instructional decisions. *Exceptional Children, 52*(3), 233–238.

Blau, A., Lahey, M., & Oleksiuk-Velez, A. (1984). Planning goals for intervention: Can a language test serve as an alternative to a language sample? *Journal of Childhood Communication Disorders, 7*, 27–37.

Bleck, E. E., & Nagel, D. A. (Eds.). (1975). *Physically handicapped children: A medical atlas for teachers*. New York: Grune & Stratton.

Bloom, L. (1970). *Language development: Form and function in emerging grammars*. Cambridge: MIT Press.

Brehony, K. A., Benson, B. A., Solomon, L. T., & Luscomb, R. L. (1980). Parents as behavior modifiers: Intervention for three problem behaviors in a severely retarded child. *Journal of Clinical Child Psychology, 36,* 213–216.

Browder, D. (1986). *Decision rules handbook.* Unpublished manuscript, Lehigh University, Bethlehem, PA.

Browder, D., Hines, C., McCarthy, L. J., & Fees, J. (1984). A treatment package for increasing sight word recognition for use in daily living skills. *Education and Training of the Mentally Retarded, 19,* 191–200.

Browder, D., & Lentz, F. E. (1985). Extended school year services: From litigation to assessment and evaluation. *School Psychology Review, 14,* 188–195.

Browder, D., Lentz, F. E., Knoster, T., & Wilansky, C. (1984). *A record-based evaluation of extended school year eligibility.* Unpublished manuscript, Lehigh University, Bethlehem, PA.

Browder, D., Liberty, K., Heller, M., & D'Huyvetters, K. (1986). Self-management by teachers: Improving instructional decision-making. *Professional School Psychology, 1,* 165–175.

Browder, D., Mace, F. C., D'Huyvetters, K., & Ambrogio, B. (1984). *An evaluation of a data-based supervision approach.* Unpublished manuscript, Lehigh University, Bethlehem, PA.

Browder, D., & Martin, D. (1986). A new curriculum for Tommy. *Teaching Exceptional Children, 18,* 261–265.

Browder, D. M., Morris, W. W., & Snell, M. E. (1981). Using time delay to teach manual signs to a severely retarded student. *Education and Training of the Mentally Retarded, 4,* 252–257.

Browder, D., Shapiro, E., & Ambrogio, B. (1986). Movement training: When self delivered reinforcement is not enough. *International Journal of Rehabilitation Research, 4.*

Browder, D., & Snell, M. E. (1987). Functional academics. In M. E. Snell (Ed.), *Systematic instruction of students with moderate and severe handicaps.* Columbus, OH: Charles E. Merrill.

Browder, D., & Snell, M. E. (in press). Assessment of individuals with severe handicaps. In E. S. Shapiro & T. R. Kratochwill (Eds.), *Behavioral assessment in schools: Approaches to classification and intervention.* New York: Guilford Press.

Browder, D. M., & Stewart, K. L. (1982). Curriculum development for the severely handicapped student. *Journal of Special Education Technology, 5*(3), 43–52.

Brown, D. K., & Mace, F. C. (1985). *An integrated system for assessment and teaching in a community living group home.* Unpublished manuscript.

Brown, F. A., Evans, I. M., & Weed, K. A. (1985). *A component model of functional life routines* (Tech. Rep. No. 6). Binghamton, NY: University Center at Binghamton.

Brown, K. M., Willis, B. S., & Reid, D. H. (1981). Differential effects of supervisor verbal feedback and feedback plus approval on institutional staff performance. *Journal of Organizational Behavior Management, 3,* 57–68.

Brown, L., Branston, M. B., Hamre-Nietupski, S., Pumpian, I., Certo, N., & Gruenewald, L. (1979). A strategy for developing age appropriate and functional curricular content for severely handicapped adolescents and young adults. *Journal of Special Educaton, 13,* 81–90.

Brown, L., Branston-McLean, M. B., Baumgart, D., Vincent, L., Falvey, M., & Schroeder, J. (1979). Using the characteristics of current and subsequent least restrictive environments as factors in the development of curricular content for severely handicapped students. *AAESPH Review, 4,* 407–424.

Brown, L., Nietupski, J., & Hamre-Nietupski, S. (1976). Criterion of ultimate functioning. In M. A. Thomas (Ed.), *Hey, don't forget about me!* (pp. 2–15). Reston, VA: Council for Exceptional Children.

Brown, L., Shiraga, B., York, J., Kessler, K., Strohm, B., Rogan, P., Sweet, M., Zanella, K., VanDeventer, P., & Loomis, R. (1984). Integrated work opportunities for adults with severe handicaps: The extended training option. *Journal of The Association for Persons with Severe Handicaps, 9,* 262–269.

Brown, R., Fraser, C., & Bellugi, U. (1964). Explorations in grammar evaluation. In U. Bellugi & R. Brown (Eds.), The acquisition of language. *Monographs of the Society for Research in Child Development, 92*(29), 79–92.

Budd, K. S., Green, D. R., & Baer, D. M. (1976). An analysis of multiple misplaced parental social contingencies. *Journal of Applied Behavior Analysis, 9,* 459–470.

Bunker, L. K., & Moon, S. (1983). Motor skills. In M. E. Snell (Ed.), *Systematic instruction of the moderately and severely handicapped* (pp. 203–226). Columbus OH: Charles E. Merrill.

Campbell, P. (1983). Basic considerations in programming for students with movement difficulties. In M. E. Snell (Ed.), *Systematic instruction of the moderately and severely handicapped* (pp. 168–202). Columbus, OH: Charles E. Merrill.

Carrow-Woolfolk, E., & Lynch, J. I. (1982). Use of naturalistic observation. *An integrative approach to language disorders in children* (pp. 247–249). New York: Grune & Stratton.

Cartledge, G., & Milburn, J. F. (Eds.). (1980). *Teaching social skills to children.* Elmsford, NY: Pergamon.

Certo, N. (1983). Characteristics of educational services. In M. E. Snell (Ed.), *Systematic instruction of the moderately and severely handicapped* (pp. 2–15). Columbus: Charles E. Merrill.

Certo, N., Haring, N., & York, R. (Eds.). (1984). *Public school integration of severely handicapped students: Rational issues and progressive alternatives.* Baltimore: Paul H. Brookes Publishing Co.

Cole, M. L., & Cole, J. T. (1981). *Effective intervention with the language impaired child.* Rockville, MD: Aspen Systems.

Cone, J. D. (1984). *The Pyramid Scales: Criterion-referenced measures of adaptive behavior in severely handicapped persons.* Austin, TX: PRO-ED.

Cossairt, A., Hall, R. V., & Hopkins, B. L. (1973). The effects of experimenter's instructions, feedback, and praise on teacher praise and student attending behavior. *Journal of Applied Behavior Analysis, 6,* 89–100.

Craighead, W. E., Mercatoris, M., & Bellack, B. (1974). A brief report on mentally retarded residents as behavioral observers. *Journal of Applied Behavior Analysis, 7,* 333–340.

Crist, K., Walls, R. T., & Haught, P. (1984). Degree of specificity in task analysis. *American Journal of Mental Deficiency, 89,* 67–74.

Cronin, K. A., & Cuvo, A. J. (1979). Teaching mending skills to retarded adolescents. *Journal of Applied Behavior Analysis, 12,* 401–406.

Csapo, M. (1981). Evaluation of the teaching effectiveness of special education teachers-in-training. *Teacher Education and Special Education, 4,* 21–30.

Cuvo, A. J. (1978). Validating task analysis of community living skills. *Vocational Evaluation and Work Adjustment Bulletin, 11*(3), 13–21.

Cuvo, A. J., Jacobi, E., & Sipko, R. (1981). Teaching laundry skills to mentally retarded students. *Education and Training of the Mentally Retarded, 11,* 54–64.

Cuvo, A. J., Leaf, R. B., & Borakove, L. S. (1978). Teaching janitorial skills to the mentally retarded. Acquisition, generalization and maintenance. *Journal of Applied Behavior Analysis, 11,* 345–355.

Deno, S. L. (1985). Curriculum-based measurement: The emerging alternative. *Exceptional Children, 52*(3), 219–232.

Deno, S. L., & Mirkin, P. K. (1977). *Data-based program modification: A manual.* Reston: VA: Council for Exceptional Children.

DeProspero, A., & Cohen, S. (1979). Inconsistent visual analysis of intrasubject data. *Journal of Applied Behavior Analysis, 12,* 573–579.

Donnellan, A. M. (1984). The criterion of the least dangerous assumption. *Behavioral Disorders: Journal of the Council for Children With Behavioral Disorders, 9*(2), 141–150.

Dorry, G. W., & Zeaman, D. (1973). The use of a fading technique in paired-associate teaching of a reading vocabulary with retardates. *Mental Retardation, 11*(6), 3–6.

Duncan, D., Sbardellati, E., Maheady, L., & Sainato, D. (1981). Nondiscriminatory assessment of severely physically handicapped individuals. *Journal of The Association of the Severely Handicapped, 6*(2), 17–22.

Dunst, C. J. (1980). *A clinical and educational manual for use with the Uzgiris and Hunt Scales of Infant Psychological Development.* Baltimore: University Park Press.

Durand, V. M. (1982). Analysis and intervention of self-injurious behavior. *Journal of The Association for the Severely Handicapped, 7*(4), 44–53.

Evans, I. M., & Meyer, L. H. (1985). *An educative approach to behavior problems: A practical decision model for interventions with severely handicapped learners.* Baltimore: Paul H. Brookes Publishing Co.

Falvey, M. A. (1986). *Community-based curriculum: Instructional strategies for students with severe handicaps.* Baltimore: Paul H. Brookes Publishing Co.

Falvey, M., Brown, L., Lyon, S., Baumgart, D., & Schroeder, J. (1980). Strategies for using cues and correction procedures. In W. Sailor, B. Wilcox, & L. Brown (Eds.), *Methods of instruction for severely handicapped students* (pp. 109–133). Baltimore: Paul H. Brookes Publishing Co.

Fialkowski v. Shapp, 405 F. Supp. 946 (E.D. Pa. 1975).

Fixsen, D. L., Phillips, E. L., & Wolf, M. N. (1972). Achievement place: The reliability of self reporting and peer reporting and their effects on behavior. *Journal of Applied Behavior Analysis, 5,* 19–30.

Forehand, R., Wells, K. C., & Griest, D. L. (1980). An examination of the social validity of a parent training program. *Behavior Therapy, 11,* 488–502.

Frankenburg, W. K., Dodds, J. B., & Fandal, A. W. (1968–70). *Denver Developmental Screening Test.* Denver: Ladoca Project and Publishing Foundation, Inc.

Fraser, B. A., & Hensinger, R. N. (1983). *Managing physical handicaps: A practical guide for parents, care providers, and educators.* Baltimore: Paul H. Brookes Publishing Co.

Freagon, S., Wheeler, J., Hill, L., Brankin, G., Costello, D., & Peters, W. H. (1983). A domestic training environment for students who are severely handicapped. *Journal of The Association for Persons with Severe Handicaps, 8,* 49–61.

Fredericks, H. D., Anderson, R., & Baldwin, V. (1979). The identification of competency indicators of teachers of the severely handicapped. *AAESPH Review, 4,* 81–95.

Gaylord-Ross, R. J. (1979). Mental retardation research, ecological validity, and the delivery of longitudinal education programs. *Journal of Special Education, 13,* 69–80.

Gaylord-Ross, R. (1980). A decision model for the treatment of aberrant behavior in applied settings. In W. Sailor, B. Wilcox, & L. Brown (Eds.), *Methods of instruction for severely handicapped students* (pp. 135–158). Baltimore: Paul H. Brookes Publishing Co.

Gaylord-Ross, R., Haring, T. G., Brien, C., & Pitts-Conway, V. (1984). The training and generalization of social interaction skills with autistic youth. *Journal of Applied Behavior Analysis, 17,* 229–247.

Gaylord-Ross, R., & Holvoet, J. (1985). *Strategies for educating students with severe handicaps.* Boston: Little, Brown.

Geiger, W. L., & Justen, J. E. (1983). Definitions of *severely handicapped* and requirements for teacher certification: A survey of state departments of education. *Journal of The Association for the Severely Handicapped, 8*(1), 25–29.

Georgia Association of Retarded Citizens v. McDaniel. Civ. A. No. C-78-1950A. (N.D. Georgia, 1979).

Greene, B. F., Willis, B. S., Levy, R., & Bailey, J. S. (1978). Measuring client gains from staff-implemented programs. *Journal of Applied Behavior Analysis, 11,* 395–412.

Greenspan, S., & Shoultz, B. (1981). Why mentally retarded adults lose their jobs: Social competence as a factor in work adjustment. *Applied Research in Mental Retardation, 2,* 23–38.

Guess, D., Horner, D., Utley, B., Holvoet, J., Maxon, D., Tucker, D., & Warren, S. (1978). A functional curriculum sequencing model for teaching the severely handicapped. *AAESPH Review, 8*(3), 202–215.

Halderman v. Pennhurst State School and Hospital, 446 F. Supp. 1295 (E.D. Pa. 1977).

Hammill, D. D., & Larsen, S. C. (1974). The effectiveness of psycholinguistic training. *Exceptional Children, 40,* 5–12.

Handleman, J., Powers, M., & Harris, S. (1981). *The teaching of labels to autistic children.* Paper presented to the American Association of Behavior Therapy, Toronto.

Hanley, E. M., Perelman, P. F., & Homan, C. I. (1979). Parental management of a child's self-stimulation behavior through the use of timeout of DRO. *Education and Treatment of Children, 2,* 305–310.

Haring, N., Liberty, K., & White, O. (1979). *Handbook of experimental procedures.* Seattle: University of Washington, Instructional Hierarchies Research Project.

Haring, N., Liberty, K., & White, O. (1980). Rules for data-based strategy decisions in instructional programs: Current research and instructional implications. In W. Sailor, B. Wilcox, & L. Brown (Eds.), *Methods of instruction for severely handicapped learners* (pp. 159–192). Baltimore: Paul H. Brookes Publishing Co.

Haring, N., Liberty, K., & White, O. (1981). *An investigation of phases of learning and facilitating instructional events for the severely/profoundly handicapped.* Final project report. Seattle: University of Washington.

Henry, J. C. (1977). *The effect of parent assessment and parent training on preschool mentally retarded children on Piaget tasks of object permanence and imitation.* Unpublished doctoral dissertation, Temple University, Philadelphia.

Hersen, M., & Barlow, D. (1976). *Single-case experimental designs: Strategies for studying behavior change.* Elmsford, NY: Pergamon.

Hill, J. W., Hill, M., Wehman, P., Banks, P. D., Pendleton, P., & Britt, C. (in press). Demographic analyses related to successful job retention for competitively employed persons who are mentally retarded. *American Journal of Mental Deficiency.*

Holvoet, J., Guess, D., Mulligan, M., & Brown, F. (1980). The individualized curriculum sequencing model. (II): A teaching strategy for severely handicapped students. *Journal of The Association for the Severely Handicapped, 5,* 325–336.

Holvoet, J., O'Neil, C., Chazdon, L., Carr, D., & Warner, J. (1983). Hey, do we really have to take data? *Journal of The Association for the Severely Handicapped, 5,* 56–70.

Horner, R. H., Sprague, J., & Wilcox, B. (1982). General case programming for community activities. In B. Wilcox & G. T. Bellamy, *Design of high school programs for severely handicapped students* (pp. 61–98). Baltimore: Paul H. Brookes Publishing Co.

Hutchison, J. M., Jarman, P. H., & Bailey, J. S. (1980). Public posting with a habilitation team: Effects on attendance and performance. *Behavior Modification, 4,* 57–70.

Inge, K. J., & Snell, M. E. (1985). Teaching positioning and handling techniques to public school personnel through inservice training. *Journal of The Association for Persons With Severe Handicaps, 10,* 105–110.

Irons, D., Irons, T., & Maddux, C. D. (1984). A survey of perceived competence among psychologists who evaluate students with severe handicaps. *Journal of The Association for the Severely Handicapped, 9*(1), 55–60.

Ives, C. C., Harris, S. L., & Wolchek, S. A. (1978). Food refusal in an autistic type child treated by a multi-component forced feeding procedure. *Journal of Behavior Therapy and Experimental Psychiatry, 9,* 61–64.

Iwata, B. A., Dorsey, M. F., Slifer, K. J., Bauman, K. E., & Richman, G. S. (1982). Toward a functional analysis of self injury. *Analysis and Intervention in Developmental Disabilities, 3,* 3–20.

Johnson, B. F., & Cuvo, A. J. (1981). Teaching mentally retarded adults to cook. *Behavior Modification, 5,* 187–202.

Johnson, M. R., Whitman, T. L., & Barloon-Noble, R. (1978). A home-based program for a pre-school behaviorally disturbed child with parents as therapists. *Journal of Behavior Therapy and Experimental Psychiatry, 9,* 65–70.

Kahn, J. V. (1978). Acceleration of object permanence with severely and profoundly retarded children. *AAESPH Review, 3,* 15–22.

Kayser, J. E., Billingsley, F. F., & Neel, R. S. (1986). A comparison of in-context and traditional instructional approaches: Total task, single trial versus backward chaining, multiple trials. *Journal of The Association for Persons with Severe Handicaps, 11,* 28–38.

Kazdin, A. E. (1977). Assessing the clinical or applied importance of behavior change through social validation. *Behavior Modification, 1,* 472–452.

Kazdin, A. E. (1980). *Behavior modification in applied settings* (2nd ed.). Homewood, IL: Dorsey Press.

Kazdin, A. E. (1982). *Single-case research design.* New York: Oxford University Press.

Keogh, W. J., & Reichle, J. (1985). Communication intervention for the "difficult-to-teach" severely handicapped. In S. F. Warren & A. K. Rogers-Warren (Eds.) *Teaching functional language: Generalization and maintenance of language skill.* (pp. 157–196). Baltimore: University Park Press.

Kirk, S., McCarthy, J., & Kirk, W. (1968). *Illinois Test of Psycholinguistic Abilities* Urbana: University of Illinois Press.

Kissel, R. C., Whitman, T. L., & Reid, D. H. (1983). An institutional staff training and self-management program for developing multiple self care skills in severely profoundly retarded individuals. *Journal of Applied Behavior Analysis, 16* 395–415.

Koegel, R. L., Glahn, T. J., & Nieminen, G. S. (1978). Generalization of parent training results. *Journal of Applied Behavior Analysis, 11,* 95–109.

Koegel, R., Rincover, A., & Egel, A. (1982). *Educating and understanding autisti children.* San Diego: College Hill Press.

Koegel, R., Russo, D. C., & Rincover, A. (1977). Assessing and training teachers in the generalized use of behavior modification with autistic children. *Journal of Applied Behavior Analysis, 10,* 197–205.

Koontz, C. W. (1974). *Koontz Child Developmental Programs: Training activities for the first 48 months*. Los Angeles: Western Psychological Services.

Korabek, C. A., Reid, D. H., & Ivancic, M. T. (1981). Improving food intake of profoundly handicapped children through effective supervision of institutional staff. *Applied Research in Mental Retardation, 2,* 68–88.

Lee, L. (1974). *Developmental sentence analyses*. Evanston, IL: Northwestern University Press.

Lentz, F. E. (1982). *An empirical examination of the utility of partial interval and momentary time sampling as measurements of behavior*. Unpublished doctoral dissertation, University of Tennessee, Knoxville.

Liberty, K. A. (1972). *Data decision rules*. Unpublished manuscript, University of Oregon, Regional Resource Center, Eugene.

Liberty, K. A. (1985). Enhancing instruction for maintenance, generalization, and adaptation. In K. C. Lakin & R. H. Bruininks (Eds.), *Strategies for achieving community integration of developmentally disabled citizens* (pp. 29–71). Baltimore: Paul H. Brookes Publishing Co.

Lindsley, O. R. (1964). Direct measurement and prosthesis of retarded behavior. *Journal of Education, 147,* 60–82.

Lloyd v. Regional Transportation Authority, 548 F. 2d 1277, 1280-84 (F. cir 1977).

Lovaas, O. I., Koegel, R., Simmons, J. Q., & Long, J. (1973). Some generalization and followup measures on autistic children in behavior therapy. *Journal of Applied Behavior Analysis, 6,* 131–166.

Lucas, E. A. (1981). *Pragmaticism*. Rockville, MD: Aspen Systems.

MacDonald, J. (1981, January). *ECO taxonomy checklist*. Paper presented at the national conference of the Association for the Severely Handicapped, New York.

MacDonald, J. D. (1985). Communication in autistic persons: Characteristics and intervention. In S. F. Warren & A. K. Rogers-Warren (Eds.), *Teaching functional langauge: Generalization and maintenance of language skills* (pp. 89–122). Baltimore: University Park Press.

MacDonald, J. D., Gillette, Y., Bickley, M., Rodriguez, C. (1984). *ECO conversation routines: Models for making everyday activities into language teaching conversations*. Columbus: Ohio State University.

Mahoney v. Administrative School District No. 1. 601 P 2nd (Or. Ct. Appls, 1979).

Markel, G. (1982). Doctoral training in supervision: Meeting an unrecognized but important need. *Teacher Education and Special Education, 5,* 43–50.

Matson, J. L. (1981). Assessment and treatment of clinical fears of mentally retarded children. *Journal of Applied Behavior Analysis, 14,* 287–294.

Matson, J. L., DiLorenzo, T. M., & Esveldt-Dawson, H. (1981). Independence training as a method of enhancing self help skills acquisition of the mentally retarded. *Behavior Research and Therapy, 19,* 399–405.

McClannahan, L. E., Krantz, P. J., & McGee, G. G. (1982). Parents as therapists for autistic children: A model for effective parent training. *Analysis and Intervention in Developmental Disabilities, 2,* 223–252.

McClennen, S. E., Hoekstra, R. R., & Bryan, J. E. (1980). *Social skills for severely retarded adults: An inventory and training program*. Champaign, IL: Research Press.

McGregor, G., Janssen, C. M., Larsen, L. A., & Tillery, W. L. (1986). Philadelphia's urban model project: A system-wide effort to integrate students with severe handicaps. *Journal of The Association for Persons with Severe Handicaps, 11,* 61–67.

McLean, J. E., & Snyder-McLean, L. K. (1978). *A transactional approach to early language training*. Columbus: Charles E. Merrill.

McLean, J. E., Snyder-McLean, L. K., Sack, S. H., & Decker, D. K. (1982). *A *transactional approach to early language: A mediated program*. Columbus: Charles E. Merrill.

Meyer, L., Reichle, J., McQuarter, R., Cole, D., Vandercook, T., Evans, I., Neel, R., & Kishi, G. (1985). *Assessment of social competence (ASC): A scale of social competence functions*. Minneapolis: University of Minnesota Consortium Institute for the Education of Severely Handicapped Learners.

Miller, J. (1980). *Assessing language production in children*. Baltimore: University Park Press.

Mithaug, D. E., & Hagmeier, L. D. (1978). The development of procedures to assess prevocational task preference in retarded adults. *AAESPH Review, 3*, 94–115.

Moon, S., Goodall, P., Barcus, M., & Brooke, V. (Eds.). (1985). *The supported work model of competitive employment for citizens with severe handicaps: A guide for job trainers*. Richmond: Virginia Commonwealth University, Rehabilitation Research and Training Center.

Mulligan, M., Lacy, L., & Guess, D. (1982). Effects of massed, distributed, and spaced trial sequencing on severely handicapped students' performance. *Journal of The Association for the Severely Handicapped, 7*, 48–61.

Muma, J. R. (1978). *Language handbook: Concepts, assessment, intervention*. Englewood Cliffs, NJ: Prentice-Hall.

Mundel, M. E. (1978). *Time and motion study: Improving productivity*. Englewood Cliffs, NJ: Prentice-Hall.

Nordquist, V. M., & Wahler, R. G. (1973). Naturalistic treatment of an autistic child. *Journal of Applied Behavior Analysis, 6*, 79–87.

Nutter, D., & Reid, D. H. (1978). Teaching retarded women a clothing selection skill using community norms. *Journal of Applied Behavior Analysis, 11*, 475–487.

Page, T. J., Iwata, B. A., & Reid, D. H. (1982). Pyramidal training: A large scale application with institutional staff. *Journal of Applied Behavior Analysis, 15*, 335–351.

Pennsylvania Association for Retarded Citizens v. Commonwealth of Pennsylvania, 343 F. Supp. 279 (E.D. Pa. 1972).

PL 93-380. (1974). The Family Educational Rights and Privacy Act. 20 U.S.C. §1232 g.

PL 94-142. (August 23, 1977). Education of the Handicapped Act of 1975. *Federal Register, 42*, 163.

Powell, J., Martindale, B., Kulp, S., Martindale, A., & Bauman, R. (1977). Taking a closer look: Time sampling and measurement error. *Journal of Applied Behavior Analysis, 10*, 325–332.

Powers, M. D., & Handleman, J. S. (1984). *Behavioral assessment of severe developmental disabilities*. Rockville, MD: Aspen Systems.

Realon, R. E., Lewallen, J. D., & Wheeler, A. J. (1983). Verbal feedback vs. verbal feedback plus praise: The effects on direct care staff's training behaviors. *Mental Retardation, 21*, 209–212.

Renzaglia, A. M., & Bates, P. (1983). Socially appropriate behavior. In M. E. Snell (Ed.), *Systematic instruction of the moderately and severely handicapped* (pp. 314–356). Columbus, OH: Charles E. Merrill.

Renzaglia, A., Cullen, M. B., & Ruth, B. (1985, December). *The use of industrial methods to identify needed vocational task adaptations for individuals with severe physical handicaps*. Paper presented at 12th annual TASH Conference, Boston.

Repp, A. (1983). *Teaching the mentally retarded*. Englewood Cliffs, NJ: Prentice-Hall.

Repp, A. C., & Deitz, D. E. D. (1979). Improving administrative-related staff behaviors at a state institution. *Mental Retardation, 17*, 185–192.

Risley, R., & Cuvo, A. J. (1980). Training mentally retarded adults to make emergency telephone calls. *Behavior Modification, 4*, 513–525.

Romanczyk, R. G., Kent, R. M., Diament, C., & O'Leary, D. O. (1973). Measuring the reliability of observational data: A reactive process. *Journal of Applied Behavior Analysis, 6,* 175–184.

Rusch, F. (1983). Competitive employment training. In M. E. Snell (Ed.), *Systematic instruction of the moderately and severely handicapped* (pp. 503–520). Columbus, OH: Charles E. Merrill.

Sailor, W., & Guess, D. (1983). *Severely handicapped students: An instructional design.* Boston: Houghton Mifflin.

Salvia, J., & Ysseldyke, J. E. (1981). *Assessment in special and remedial education* (2nd ed.). Boston: Houghton Mifflin.

Salzberg, C. L., & Villani, T. V. (1983). Speech training by parents of Down syndrome toddlers: Generalization across settings and instructional contexts. *American Journal of Mental Deficiency, 87,* 403–413.

Sanders, R. M. (1978). *How to plot data.* Lawrence, KS: H & H Enterprises.

Sandler, A., & Coren, A. (1981). Integrated instruction at home and school: Parents' perspective. *Education and Training of the Mentally Retarded, 16,* 183–187.

Schutz, R. P., & Rusch, F. R. (1982). Competitive employment: Toward employment integration for mentally retarded persons. In K. P. Lynch, W. E. Kiernan, & J. A. Stark (Eds.), *Prevocational and vocational education for special needs youth: A blueprint for the 1980s* (pp. 133–159). Baltimore: Paul H. Brookes Publishing Co.

Shapiro, E. S., & Lentz, F. E., Jr. (1986). Behavioral assessment of academic behavior. In T. R. Kratochwill (Ed.), *Advances in School Psychology, 5,* 87–140.

Shevin, M., & Klein, N. K. (1984). The importance of choice-making skills for students with severe disabilities. *Journal of The Association of the Severely Handicapped, 9*(3), 159–166.

Shoemaker, J., & Reid, D. H. (1980). Decreasing chronic absenteeism among institutional staff: Effects of a low-cost attendance program. *Journal of Organizational Behavior Management, 2,* 317–328.

Simeonsson, R. J., Huntington, G. S., & Parse, S. E. (1980). Assessment of children with severe handicaps: Multiple problems—multivariate goals. *Journal of The Association for the Severely Handicapped, 5*(1), 55–72.

Snell, M. E. (Ed.). (1983). *Systematic instruction of the moderately and severely handicapped.* Columbus, OH: Charles E. Merrill.

Snell, M. E. (Ed.). (1987). *Systematic instruction of persons with severe handicaps* (3rd ed.). Columbus, OH: Charles E. Merrill.

Snell, M., & Beckman-Brindley, S. (1984). Family involvement in intervention with children having severe handicaps. *Journal of The Association for the Severely Handicapped, 9,* 213–230.

Snell, M. E., & Browder, D. (1986). Community-referenced instruction: Research and issues. *Journal of The Association for Persons with Severe Handicaps, 11,* 1–11.

Snell, M. E., & Gast, D. L. (1981). Applying delay procedures to the instruction of the severely handicapped. *Journal of The Association of the Severely Handicapped, 5*(4), 3–14.

Snell, M. E., & Grigg, N. C. (1987). Instructional assessment. In M. E. Snell (Ed.), *Systematic instruction of people with severe handicaps.* Columbus, OH: Charles E. Merrill.

Spears, D. L., Rusch, F. R., York, R., & Lilly, M. S. (1981). Training independent arrival behaviors to a severely mentally retarded child. *Journal of The Association for the Severely Handicapped, 6*(2), 40–45.

Stokes, T. F., & Baer, D. M. (1977). An implicit technology of generalization. *Journal of Applied Behavior Analysis, 10,* 349–367.

Stowitschek, J., Stowitschek, C. E., Hendrickson, J. M., & Day, R. M. (1984). *Direct teaching tactics for exceptional children: A practice and supervision guide.* Rockville, MD: Aspen Systems.

Striefel, S., Wetherby, B., & Karlan, G. (1976). Establishing generalized verb-noun instruction-following skills in retarded children. *Journal of Experimental Child Psychology, 22,* 247–260.

Sulzer-Azaroff, B., & Mayer, G. R. (1977). *Applying behavior-analysis procedures for children and youth.* New York: Holt, Rinehart & Winston.

Thvedt, J. E., Zane, T., & Walls, R. T. (1984). Stimulus functions in response chaining. *American Journal of Mental Deficiency, 88,* 661–667.

Tucker, D. J., & Berry, G. W. (1980). Teaching severely multi-handicapped students to put on their own hearing aids.

Tucker, J. A. (1985). Curriculum-based assessment: An introduction. *Exceptional Children, 52*(3), 199–204.

Uzgiris, I. C., & Hunt, J. M. (1978). *Assessment in infancy: Ordinal scales of psychological development.* Urbana: University of Illinois Press.

van den Pol, R. A., Iwata, B. A., Ivancic, M. T., Page, T. J., Neef, N. A., & Whitely, F. D. (1981). Teaching the handicapped to eat in public places: Acquisition, generalization, and maintenance of restaurant skills. *Journal of Applied Behavior Analysis, 14,* 61–69.

Voeltz, L. M., & Evans, I. M. (1983). Educational validity: Procedures to evaluate outcomes in programs for severely handicapped learners. *Journal of The Association for the Severely Handicapped, 8,* 3–15.

Voeltz, L. M., McQuarter, R. J., & Kishi, G. S. (in press). Assessing and teaching social interaction skills. In W. Stainback & S. Stainback (Eds.), *Integration of severely handicapped students with their nonhandicapped peers: A handbook for teachers.* Reston, VA: The Council for Exceptional Children.

Voeltz, L. M., Wuerch, B. B., & Bockhaut, C. H. (1982). Social validation of leisure activities training with severely handicapped youth. *Journal of The Association for the Severely Handicapped, 7,* 3–13.

Wahler, R. G., & Fox, J. J. (1980). Solitary toy play and time out: A family treatment package for children with aggressive and oppositional behavior. *Journal of Applied Behavior Analysis, 13,* 23–40.

Wampold, B. E., & Furlong, N. J. (1981). The heuristics of visual inference. *Behavioral Assessment, 3,* 79–82.

Warren, S. F. (1985). Clinical strategies for the measurement of language generalization. In S. F. Warren & A. K. Rogers-Warren (Eds.), *Teaching functional language: Generalization and maintenance of language skills* (pp. 197–224). Baltimore: University Park Press.

Warren, S. F., & Rogers-Warren, A. K. (1985). *Teaching functional language: An introduction.* In S. F. Warren & A. K. Rogers-Warren (Eds.), *Teaching functional language: Generalization and maintenance of language skills* (pp. 3–23). Baltimore: University Park Press.

Waryas, C. L., & Stremel-Campbell, K. (1978). Grammatical training for the language-delayed child: A new perspective. In R. L. Schiefelbusch (Ed.), *Language intervention strategies* (pp. 145–192). Baltimore: University Park Press.

Wehman, P., Renzaglia, A., & Bates, P. (1985). *Functional living skills for moderately and severely handicapped individuals.* Austin, TX: PRO-ED.

Wetzel, R. J., & Hoschouer, R. L. (1984). *Residential teaching communities: Program development and staff training for developmentally disabled persons.* Glenview, IL: Scott, Foresman.

White, O. R. (1972). *A manual for the calculation and use of the median slope—A technique of progress estimation and prediction in a single case.* Eugene: University of Oregon, Regional Resource Center.

White, O. R. (1980). Adaptive performance objectives: Form versus function. In W. Sailor, B. Wilcox, & L. Brown (Eds.), *Methods of instruction for severely handicapped students* (pp. 47–69). Baltimore: Paul H. Brookes Publishing Co.

White, O. R. (1981). *Making daily classroom decisions.* Paper presented to American Educational Research Association, Los Angeles, CA.

White, O., & Haring, N. (1980). *Exceptional teaching.* Columbus, OH: Charles E. Merrill.

Whitman, T. L., Hurley, J. D., Johnson, M. R., & Christian, J. G. (1978). Direct and generalized reduction of inappropriate behavior in a severely retarded child through a parent-administered behavior modification program. *AAESPH Review, 3,* 67–77.

Whyte, R. A., Van Houten, R., & Hunter, W. (1983). The effects of public posting on teachers' performance of supervision duties. *Education and Treatment of Children, 6,* 21–28.

Wilcox, B., & Bellamy, G. T. (1982). *Design of high school programs for severely handicapped students.* Baltimore: Paul H. Brookes Publishing Co.

Wolf, M. M. (1978). Social validity: The case for subjective measurement, or how applied behavior analysis is finding its heart. *Journal of Applied Behavior Analysis, 11,* 203–214.

Wolfensberger, W. (1972). *The principle of normalization in human services.* Toronto: National Institute of Mental Retardation.

Wuerch, B. B., & Voeltz, L. M. (1982). *Longitudinal leisure skills for severely handicapped learners: The Ho'onanea curriculum component.* Baltimore: Paul H. Brookes Publishing Co.

Zlutnick, S., Mayville, W. J., & Moffat, S. (1975). Modification of seizure disorders: The interruption of behavioral chains. *Journal of Applied Behavior Analysis, 8,* 1–12.

INDEX